# Dear Parents

# Dear Parents

*Communicating the Christian &
Classical Vision to Families*

BY TOM GARFIELD

Published by Logos Press
P.O. Box 8729, Moscow, Idaho 83843
800.488.2034 | www.logospressonline.com

Tom Garfield, *Dear Parents: Communicating the Christian & Classical Vision to Families*
Copyright ©2004, 2020 by Tom Garfield. First published as *The Return of Dear Parents* (2004)
Quotations marked NASB are from the New American Standard Bible®, copyright © 1960, 1962, 1963, 1968, 1971, 1972, 1973, 1975, 1977, 1995 by the Lockman Foundation. Used by permission.

Cover design by James Engerbretson.
Interior layout by Samuel Dickison.

Printed in the United States of America.

All rights reserved. No part of this publication may be reproduced, stored in a retrieval system, or transmitted in any form by any means, electronic, mechanical, photocopy, recording, or otherwise, without prior permission of the author, except as provided by USA copyright law.

*Library of Congress Cataloging-in-Publication Data*

Garfield, Tom, author.
Dear parents : communicating the Christian and classical vision to
   families / Tom Garfield.
Moscow, Idaho : Logos Press, [2020]
LCCN 2020022783 | ISBN 9781952410505 (paperback)
LCSH: Logos School (Moscow, Idaho) | Christian
   education—Philosophy. | Classical education. | Home and school.
Classification: LCC BV1464 .G37 2020 | DDC 268/.432—dc23
LC record available at https://lccn.loc.gov/2020022783

*To Julie, my sweet, circumspect wife, thank you for the gentle urging to finally get this put together.*

# Contents

INTRODUCTION ..................................................................... i

CHAPTER ONE
Father Knows Best: Family Issues ......................................... 1

CHAPTER TWO
What Are Little Boys and Girls Made Of? ........................... 29

CHAPTER THREE
"One Fish, Two Fish"—Classical Instruction & Curriculum ............ 47

CHAPTER FOUR
Bad Moon Arising—Modern Trends in Education ............... 85

CHAPTER FIVE
Even a Child is Known by His Deeds ................................. 119

CHAPTER SIX
It's Not Just a Job ................................................................ 135

CHAPTER SEVEN
The Junk Drawer ................................................................ 161

CHAPTER EIGHT
Fruit of the Labor ............................................................... 175

CHAPTER NINE
Personal Thoughts .............................................................. 199

# Introduction

As of this writing, Logos School has been serving families from many towns around and including Moscow, Idaho, for almost forty years. Logos School opened its doors in September of 1981. It represented the concerted efforts and convictions of primarily three individuals: Doug Wilson, Shirley Quist, and Larry Lucas. Their goal was to provide high-quality Christian education for children. These three people were Logos School's founding board of directors. I was hired in January of 1981 to be Logos School's administrator.

Logos (which means "word" in Greek) began with eighteen students in rented facilities at the Paradise Hills Church of God. Primarily through word-of-mouth the school grew quickly. Parents say they are highly pleased with the dedicated, loving staff members, the smaller class sizes, and the consistently high level of academic and spiritual encouragement their children receive. As the school expanded in size and scope, bus service and a preschool were added (bus service was later dropped). At all levels, the math, reading, science and other disciplines are continuously and systematically reviewed and upgraded to qualitatively increase the learning of the students. For example, in 1993, with the assistance of a qualified school parent, the entire elementary science program was redesigned and a new Logos Elementary Science guide for teachers was written and published.

The school moved to 110 Baker, a former roller rink, in November of 1987, after extensive prayer, fundraising, and remodeling. Subsequent improvements have included the addition of a two portable classrooms, carpeting, an outstanding library, and finally, in 1999, a field house. The school's annual auctions continue to provide much-needed funding for capital improvements to the facility, as well as discretionary money for the teachers to use in their classrooms.

In 1990, Doug Wilson, the key founding board member for Logos, wrote a book titled *Recovering the Lost Tools of Learning*. The book recalled how, over its ten year history at that time, Logos School had attempted to follow the classical, trivium model, as described by Dorothy Sayers in her 1940's article, *The Lost Tools of Learning*, published in the National Review. Doug's book, published on a nationwide scale through Crossway Publishing, produced so much interest in the classical approach that several Logos staff members helped form the Association of Classical and Christian Schools (A.C.C.S.) to practically assist people in forming their own classical schools. This organization continues to offer conferences and practical assistance to forming and growing A.C.C.S. school members in every region of the United States. Logos is a charter member of A.C.C.S. and annually sells many of its administrative and curriculum materials to these schools and other people around the United States.

As the administrator for Logos since day one, I have been privileged (and challenged) to see the school go through the many changes mentioned above. Because of the uniqueness of the kind of education we offer, not only have hundreds of children been blessed with a good academic foundation, even I of the thick skull have learned a few things. Our Lord Himself said that a student doesn't rise above his teacher. That makes me all the more thankful that we have obviously hired very intelligent people to teach these little ones over the years. But I, too, have been forced to try to learn a plethora of new tricks, since I have taught classes of some sort every year it has been no easy feat to stay ahead of these kids. After all, as I often tell my high school classes, in my defense, they need to remember I am a victim of a government-designed education.

Another aspect to my work here has been to construct a monthly newsletter. In the early years, this mostly looked like a school version of those Christmas form letters we all get in spades each winter. Yawn. As time went on, however, I got increasingly excited by all the new things I saw the kids and the school learning through applying the classical philosophy. I also got increasingly excited, but in the opposite polarity, by all the things I saw our culture and government foisting on families, in the name of education. So, rather than use my newsletter column to describe the latest spelling bee or attendance policy, I found that it was a real good vehicle for me to vent my excitement about all sorts of things. Surprisingly, this change in content didn't altogether wipe out our list of subscribers. In fact, I have heard downright positive and encouraging remarks made about a number of my columns. These remarks even came from people other than my mother!

This small volume, then, is a compilation of those columns that addressed a part of the broad spectrum of ideas and events that have come through Logos at some time or other. As you will see, some touch on ideas or events that were, or could have been, very unsettling to us. Most, though, address the joy of the work we do day after day because it truly is an honor to minister to families in God's Name and for His glory. These columns are drawn from the unique times and people at Logos, especially the unique people and their experiences. I have learned much from the many staff members, parents, and especially the children. It is to them that I am indebted, for they have made my life rich indeed!

This then is submitted to you, the reader, in the hope that if you work in Christian education you can benefit in some way from what we've learned here at Logos, as evidenced in these columns. And, if you are not working in Christian education directly, but have a good acquaintance with it, then I hope you can just enjoy these ramblings, while ensconced in your favorite chair, sipping your favorite beverage, and being pleasantly diverted for a brief time. Blessings on you and yours!

# 1

## FATHER KNOWS BEST: FAMILY ISSUES

*Logos School has, from day one, committed itself to assisting, not replacing families in educating their children. This commitment has caused us, at times, to make decisions, policies, and day-to-day practices that treat our families differently from the way our culture treats families. We really do believe that, despite some appearances these days, God really did know what He was doing when He designed the "nuclear" family structure to be the building block of every lasting society. And within that structure, every member has a God designed role. Unlike the National Public Radio t-shirt that proclaims, "A family is a circle of friends who love you!", God proclaims in His Word that a family is comprised of a father, a mother, and children, all of whom have very serious responsibilities that God set forth.*

*We do have families at Logos that for a variety of reasons, some from sin and some from God's acts, do not have every role present or functioning as God designed. Nevertheless, as we teach and love all the children and respect each parent's authority, we do not redefine the biblical family based on exceptions. The following columns address some of the ramifications to the way we view families.*

\* \* \*

DEAR PARENTS

## THE (OFTEN IGNORED) PREREQUISITE TO A GOOD EDUCATION

> Slowly and weightily, Pa said, "Miss Wilder, we want you to know that the school board stands with you to keep order in this school." He looked sternly over the whole room. "All you scholars must obey Miss Wilder, behave yourselves, and learn your lessons. We want a good school, and we are going to have it." When Pa spoke like that, he meant what he said, and it would happen.
> ~*Little Town On the Prairie*, by Laura Ingalls Wilder

> And, fathers, do not provoke your children to anger; but bring them up in the discipline and instruction of the Lord.
> ~Ephesians 6:4 (NASB)

The above verse from Ephesians is often used by Christian educators, and rightly so, to demonstrate God's view of the *kind* of instruction children are supposed to receive, that is, a completely God-centered one. What isn't pointed out often enough from this verse is *to whom* the imperative is given, that is, the *father*. I know it isn't pointed out enough because so many fathers, even in our church-saturated culture, have ignored the application of this clear teaching. To be fair, many fathers do consider this verse, but believe they are obeying it adequately by regularly taking their families to church. The application is far more encompassing.

Not long ago I had a conference with a mom who was agonizing over whether or not to have her child repeat a grade. She was asking my advice on what factors she should consider in making this tough decision. Instead of spending much time on answering her immediate questions, I told her as diplomatically as possible that this decision which was weighing on her so heavily was not hers to make; it was her *husband's*. At first I was concerned that I may have offended her, but instead I had the joy of almost visibly seeing a burden fall from her shoulders. She was still understandably concerned for her child, but obviously had more peace knowing that indeed it *was* her husband's decision, and, being the good father he is, he would gladly assume that decision. (By the way, he did assume it, and decided to have his daughter repeat. It was a very wise decision and she did very well in adapting to her new class.)

Unfortunately, that type of father is all too rare in the Christian community, not to mention our general American culture. It hasn't always been so, as evidenced by the brief excerpt above from the *Little House* series. Fathers were not always the emasculated, "sensitive," fearfully non-assertive wimps our current cultural wind would have them be. I don't know if Mrs. Laura Wilder (eventual sister-in-law to the teacher in the book) was a Christian, but her father was certainly recognized as *the* authority for his children's education. American history shows us that he was not unique or unusual in his assuming of that role in that era, circa late nineteenth century.

## Fathers were not always the fearfully emasculated, "sensitive," fearfully non-assertive wimps our current cultural wind would have them be.

God designed mothers to be the nurturers to their children, and as such, they naturally take a very active part in their children's education. Moms feel the 'nest-leaving' far more deeply than do the dads. When the first little one starts kindergarten, it's often mom who sheds the tears and diligently scrutinizes every aspect of the school's instruction over those first critical years. As I've mentioned to many people, I would rather meet with a concerned dad vs. a concerned mom any day; I readily admit that I fear facing what I call the "Mother Bear Syndrome," based on the proverb. You know, the one about meeting a mother bear deprived of her cubs (Prov. 17:12). It's not a pretty picture. Nevertheless, having designed mothers that way, God still insists that dads take the lead in the education of their children.

How is this to be done? First, it means recognizing that it *is* the God-ordained role of a father to take the *responsibility* for his children's welfare and education. This will likely mean some type of delegation of tasks, but the responsibility cannot be averted. The father is the *Elder*, the *Superintendent*, and the *Chief Justice* in the home, all the while being a true gentleman. Just like the captain of a ship, who, though not at the helm when the ship runs aground, will still be the one held responsible, dads must be ready to acknowledge that any failure in the home is their responsibility.

Dad should be at every formal parent-teacher conference. He needs to know what his kids are studying and how well they're doing. (With four kids in school,

I know how hard it is just to look at all their papers each night, but Julie lays them out for me, and it happens.) All problems in school, academic and disciplinary, should receive top priority by Dad. And a "Well done!" from Dad should be frequent and meaningful. All our current school board members are fathers of children in Logos School. This is not a requirement, nor are women excluded by policy; this is just the way it is, and I am very grateful!

A word about fatherless homes: I am very pleased to see that in the Christian community surrounding Logos School, many single moms are actively supported and encouraged by families with fathers fulfilling their biblical roles. As a school, we seek to do the same for single moms seeking to raise godly children. The scriptural mandate of caring for widows and the fatherless is very appropriate to these situations.

A vast number of problems we currently see in both the government schools and Christian schools could be dispelled if just the Christian fathers re-assumed their God-given privileges and responsibilities toward their precious sons and daughters. Pray for and encourage those fathers you know who are doing their most important jobs well.

\* \* \*

*It may be an anachronistic practice in our society, (though based on the numbers of families I know who use it often, I don't think it's that outmoded) but regardless of its lack of trendiness, spanking is still alive and well-placed at Logos School. Once in a rare while I have applying families balk at the idea, but even then, frequently their concern is that we do not supersede their authority to spank. God forbid! Usually I am able to reassure those families that we fully intend to support their authority in the school: That's why we spank in the first place; in loco parentis.*

AN HONORABLE TRADITION:
SPANKING IN A CHRISTIAN CONTEXT

In one of the best children's stories I've enjoyed reading to my own children, Frances, a young badger, has been having a hard time staying in bed and going to sleep. Things in her darkened room concern her and she goes to discuss them with her parents ... several times. Her parents calmly and wisely address her concerns and send her back to bed. Finally Frances goes to her father in his bed and, after waking him with her concern about the wind moving the curtains, her father replies:

> "If the wind does not blow the curtains, he will be out of a job. If I do not go to the office, I will be out of a job. And if you do not go sleep now, do you know what will happen to you?"
> "I will be out of a job?" said Frances. "No," said Father.
> "I will get a spanking?" said Frances. "Right!" said Father.
> "Good night!" said Frances, and she went back to her room. Frances closed the window and got into bed."
> ~From *Bedtime for Frances*, by Russell Hoban

That book was published in 1960, back before the enlightened age in which we live that has come to see spanking as a Neanderthal means of discipline, if not actual child abuse. During my graduate work years ago, I found myself one evening as the sole defender, among many school administrators, of this ancient practice. The others argued heatedly that "violence begets violence," as though that little phrase could write off centuries-old, successful child-rearing practices. When I pointed out that the most secure and well-loved students I knew came from homes that included spanking as a normal punishment, one administrator told me straight-faced, "Well, if children are secure, they can stand a certain amount of problems in their homes." Arrrggghhh! Yes, and if children are born educated, they can put up with the nonsense in the public schools, right? What logic!

Historically in our culture, Christians and non-Christians alike used to be steeped in the biblical traditions and principles of raising children. "Spare the rod and spoil the child" was one verse (albeit paraphrased) every parent knew (Prov. 13:24) and frequently practiced. And, strangely enough, kids were better behaved as a result. I do not have the space or time to go into why this very healthy practice has become virtually a crime. The saddest aspect of its decline is that even many Christian parents have meekly accepted the world's way of "disciplining" children and have abandoned the clear biblical imperatives. I don't know how many times, during a conference with parents of a rowdy student, I have heard the comment, "We tried spanking him, but it didn't seem to make any difference." "Tried?" Do we "try" feeding our kids to see if they grow? If we don't notice a significant change overnight do we stop the feeding "experiment?"

Logos School believes that God knows more about raising children than our current culture does, or ever will. Therefore, I have had the honor of reinforcing, through the use of a wooden paddle (actually, a variety of sizes) in my office, the good discipline begun in many homes. Here are some characteristics of a good spanking:

It is never done in anger! Love and calm determination should exude from the parent/adult.

The actual strokes should be limited (I use three) and each one should sting. (It really is all in the wrist.)

Limited crying is acceptable; wailing or screaming tantrums are not.

A quiet hug and prayer of restoration and forgiveness should immediately follow. (Since the child may not be a Christian he should not be pressured to pray vocally, but the adult should always pray for the child.)

A clear, verbal expression of love for the child should be made. Then any directions for other apologies and restitutions should be given.

# A good spanking is like a good spring thunderstorm; after the noise, darkness, and wet, the sun comes out; warm, blue sky fills the heavens; and the world is a better place for having experienced the storm.

I have not included every aspect leading up to the spanking for the sake of space. One of the best indicators of a really good and proper spanking is that five minutes later, complete, restored fellowship is evident between the spanker and the spankee. I have experienced this countless times, when I encounter a student in the hallway who was recently in my office. The air is clear, all is forgiven, and we may hug again, or just say 'Hi' warmly. Fellowship is restored, as it should be.

God knows what He is doing. He honors those who honor Him and His Word. We take that seriously here at Logos. We also take seriously the application of His Word about training children through spanking and other forms of love, delegated to us for a time, by our school parents. It works...well.

\* \* \*

"READ ANY GOOD BOOKS LATELY?"

> Once there were four children whose names were Peter, Susan, Edmund, and Lucy. This story is about something that happened to them when they were sent away from London during the war because of air raids. They were sent to the house of an old Professor who lived in the heart of the country.
> ~From *The Lion, the Witch, and the Wardrobe* by C. S. Lewis

Consider the marvelous power of the written word. Here I am, typing thoughts into a computer and not saying a word aloud. After some editing, printing, and mailing, this is now in your hands and your mind is hearing my thoughts! Downright scary, in some ways, isn't it? But such is the magic of reading. Further, given a well thought-out collection of words, *any* reader can be mentally transported to any place on earth, or even space, meet and get to know famous people from any period of history, and, after some quiet time in a comfortable chair, get up and walk away better educated. Books are our best and only time-machines.

Photographs and pictures may be worth a thousand words at times, but they are hardly worth one word unless the viewer already understands a fair bit of what he is seeing. Consider all that it takes for a typical movie (moving pictures) to try to convey the same message or story contained in a neatly bound book. The movie-making consumes millions of dollars and thousands of hours in production, it requires the acting ability (assuming there is some) of numerous people, and then it requires usually about two hours of viewing to say its short message. Its format never encourages the viewer to stop it, pause, and quietly ponder its message as it may relate to other great thoughts or stories, and then start it up again. When was the last time you, or someone you know, said of a movie, "Gee, that was just as great as the book!"? Lest I be unfair, it is true that movies are largely meant for consumption in a social setting and not the private, mind-to-mind, intimate setting that great books require.

Whenever parents come to check out the educational program at Logos, I want to ensure they clearly understand that reading is a very high priority here. In the early years, kindergarten and first grade, using phonics and little stories, the students learn to read. From about second grade on, the emphasis switches to reading to learn. The ability to read and increase in reading proficiency are the keys to promotion from grade to grade. We don't use basals or primers for a number of reasons, the main one being they're lethally boring. The elementary literature lists we have accumulated for each grade over the years contain many titles that should be old friends to adults. From the *Francis* series (a personal favorite), *Frog and Toad*, *The Little House*, Dr. Seuss stories, *The Oxcart Man*, and *Make Way for Ducklings* among the early grades' titles to the Narnia series (the best children's books in the world), *Stuart Little*, *The Borrowers*, *The Lord of the Ring* series, and *The Adventures of Tom Sawyer* among the upper elementary grades, each year's reading is a feast for the minds of these students. We also integrate wonderful historical biographies and novels into our required reading, helping the students visualize and empathize with the great people and works in history.

## Children who come to us from homes where books and reading aloud have been part of the fabric of the home since birth do far better than children from homes where the TV or videos have been the primary mental nutrition.

At the secondary level, reading continues to play a tremendously important role. You will find many of the great works of Western literature on the reading lists from seventh through twelfth grade. From the *Iliad* and the *Odyssey*, to *Pride and Prejudice*, from *Moby Dick* to *Penrod* and Dickens, the students are stretched in their mental landscapes. These great works help them form a worldview that reinforces biblical definitions of morality, consequences of sin, nobility, honor, self-sacrifice, and the sheer sweat, feasting, and profound satisfaction of living in a world God has created for us to enjoy.

Children who come to us from homes where books and reading aloud have been part of the fabric of the home since birth do far better than children from homes where the TV or videos have been the primary mental nutrition. That's a fact. Further, because children imitate and value what is important to their parents, those of us who are trying to train our children in a way far different from what we received must read and read a lot. (Dad & Mom thank you for the example you were to your kids!) Reading takes far more work than viewing, but it is very worth the effort. For Christian homes and schools, reading timeless children's classics and powerful works of history and literature are not optional activities—not if the parents are serious about equipping their children in every way to face a God-hating culture.

So defy the popular culture, bless your children, and help yourself and the teachers here and at similar schools by just picking up a valuable book and sitting down to read. (Don't forget to read aloud to your kids: they love it.) Thank God for this marvelous gift!

\* \* \*

*Admitting students can often seem like an uncommon form of gambling. No matter what the family is like, no matter how nice the student may seem, you just don't know what you're getting. Of course, that is true from the family's viewpoint, too. We might do a lousy job of training their child, no matter what nice things they've heard about the school. But then, they don't have to make that kind of decision very often we have to make it many times every year. Do we admit this student or not? And what are the parents really expecting from us?*

"TO BE OR NOT TO BE"... THAT IS THE DILEMMA!

RING! "Good afternoon, Logos School..."

"Hello. I'm wondering who I could talk to about getting our son enrolled in your high school. You see, he's really a good boy, but due to being strongly influenced by a bad group of friends, well, he has done some things. Can you help us out?"

That introduction, virtually verbatim, we have heard far too many times over the years. I say too many times for a couple of reasons. One is that sadly far too many students "hit the wall," i.e. finally really do something bad enough for even the government schools to notice and find themselves in that position. Another reason is that many people in our community think of a Christian school as a reform school for students who can't "make it" in the public schools.

I think the reasoning for that last assumption goes something along the lines of the following:

See, historically churches have accepted anyone, especially the downtrodden and the outcasts and we are a "Christian" institution, so we should also accept these troubled students. Also, the reasoning continues, not only should we accept them, but since we are a "religious" school and since we have tougher discipline and academic standards, somehow just being *here* will straighten these students out. However, very often, as with a reform school, the time here has been practically considered a "sentence" to be filled before the student returns to take his rightful place in society (i.e. back to the public school).

**Imagine our naive shock when time and time again we saw that not only were we *not* seeing these students repent and achieve; they were actually having the effect of dragging other students down with them!**

Early in our history as a Christian school, we were faced with this dilemma: Do we accept these problem students and count on our love and program to turn them around, or do we cold-heartedly reject them and be labeled as a school for only the "best and the brightest?" In our educational infancy and naivete, we chose the former, since it was "obvious" that these students *needed* the kind of education and atmosphere we could offer.

Imagine our naive shock when time and time again we saw that not only were we *not* seeing these students repent and achieve; they were actually having the effect of dragging other students down with them! We did not, at least in practice, believe the scriptures that teach "bad company corrupts good morals." The reason it took us literally years to realize this ageless truth is due, I believe, to our thinking that when scripture says that good should and will triumph over evil, we acted as though Logos School was *the* agent for that "good," instead of the Lord and the students' parents. As much as we love and pray for students, only God alone, through Jesus Christ can truly make men new. So ... *what* then is our role?

A very wise, grandfatherly man who had known our Lord and worked in the ministry for many years visited our school several years after we began operating. He came to one of my staff meetings and in the space of five minutes encapsulated this whole dilemma which I thought was unique to us and unsolvable. Without even my broaching the subject, essentially he said we needed to decide whether we were: A. A school for rebellious and troubled (discipline-wise) students, or B. A school whose primary goal is to help parents who want to train their children biblically. The structure of every aspect of the school would be different, based on the choice we made. He came right out and said, "You cannot do both!"

I trust it is obvious which path we chose. However, the dilemma has not disappeared. Yes, we know what our limits and goals as a Christian school are, but that does not make it any easier to tell a weeping parent that we cannot accept her child. Few of these belatedly desperate parents can understand why we must think of the obligation we have to the many other families whose children would come in contact with this student. It looks and sounds like unabashed elitism and possibly even a lack of compassion. We *do* accept students, who, with their parents, understand and want the kind of education offered here. We will accept these students, even with problems. Key questions we ask include: How much are the parents and student willing to work with the school to make changes; is Logos expected to "do it all"? Are the parents and students looking for a new direction or just a 'fix-it-quick-so-we-can-get-back-to-the-routine diversion? And most important: Can Logos meet this student's needs?

There are many ramifications to the choice we have made. However, ignoring our Lord's command for compassion is not one of them. We have (and will again, if it seems wise) accepted pregnant young women who would have otherwise possibly aborted their child in order to stay in a school. Those were unique situations, but there may be other unique students in the future. We have committed to do certain things for our families here and by God's grace and wisdom through your prayers we will continue to do so.

\* \* \*

## SANTA CLAUS & HARRY POTTER ARE NOT THE BAD GUYS

No doubt the pastor thought he was taking a stand for righteousness. He hadn't been allowed a full-fledged book burning, so he had to settle for renting a conference room at a Ramada Inn. There, with great zeal in front of a number of his parishioners, he literally sliced and diced some Harry Potter books. The release of the second Harry Potter movie and its huge following had inspired this pastor to make his stand. Somewhat reminiscent of Carrie Nation taking an axe to a saloon back in the good ol' temperance movement days. Whack, whack! That will show the devil we mean business!

And we Christians wonder why our culture has a hard time taking anything we say or do seriously. If that kind of action is supposed to be salt and light, the world need have no fear of experiencing sharp tastes or having to squint their eyes when we're around.

When I read the article about this misguided and misguiding brother, I couldn't help but wonder, "Where do the folks in that church send their kids to school?" Certainly that's partly due to the fact that I live, breathe, and eat Logos, but it's still a legitimate question. If such zeal is generated from the potential influence of a book series and a movie (ok, a long movie), how much more zeal must those folks have for how their children are educated five days a week, nine months a year, for thirteen years, or so! Is their zeal for righteousness exhibited consistently and proportionately in the kind of schooling their children receive? I don't know and my cynical nature leads me to think while their children are banned from J.K. Rowling, they are dipped to the eyeballs in John Dewey, all in the name of being salt and light.

> ... we Christians, especially in Christian schools, frequently vilify Santa Claus, as though he were the Saddam Hussein of celebrating Christmas.

We Christians frequently have a profound similarity to those Pharisees whom Jesus accused of "straining at gnats and swallowing camels." We major on the minors and minor on the majors. Such is the imbalance that comes when we lose sight of grace and try to do religious works that have the appearance of godliness.

At this time of year another form of this foamy thinking manifests itself. Much in the same way the secularists abhor the talk, sight, or sound of Christ particularly at Christmas time, we Christians, especially in Christian schools, frequently vilify Santa Claus, as though he were the Saddam Hussein of celebrating Christmas. Sadly, many Christian high school grads don't know the biblical reasons why Karl Marx's ideas were so evil or how to logically refute the claims of Darwinism, but they sure know that Santa is anathema. And that often goes for almost anything else that has to do with fantasy and the realm of imagination. Both the secularists and these brothers share a similarity to Scrooge and the Grinch when it comes to truly celebrating our Lord's advent.

Jesus Christ, in words and actions, showed us who the real "bad guys" are: they aren't the prostitutes, tax collectors, fantasy writers, or mythical figures. They aren't even the political tyrants (Jesus certainly knew what the emperor was up to). No, He took off the gloves when it came to thumping the religious hypocrites, the priests (pastors) who were misusing their role as God-appointed shepherds of His people. He gave what-for to the lawyers and teachers who were lying to and cheating the people who trusted their counsel. Who are those people today? I mentioned a few above; you can probably fill in the blanks otherwise.

As we reflect (which Christmas should always cause us to do) on the incredible fact of Immanuel, may more Christians see our culture, their children, and their churches, the way Christ would have us see. May we know where the battle for righteousness really takes place and be more effective warriors *there*, not somewhere else. May we identify the real "bad guys" who would seduce us, lie to us, and rob us of our legacy, our children, and their faith.

Have a blessed and uplifting Christmas celebration, read lots of great books, sing great songs, eat a lot of great food, and worship our great God!

* * *

*"You can't please everyone all the time." How true, how true. Yet, in my heart of hearts, how I would love to be able to do just that. I think I get that desire genetically from my mom she hates to disappoint anyone, too. But it seems that the best I can hope for at Logos,*

*sometimes, is to try, as Paul said, "to be at peace with all men." Actually that part's not so hard; it's often the women who are the hardest to please. Yet for all we do, there are inevitable occasions when a family is not satisfied with the education we offer, or the way we discipline, or the kinds of books we use, or my face. After years of watching a number of disgruntled parents leave us for what, from my biased perspective, seemed like trivial reasons, and put their kids in the government schools, I just had to write the following column...*

## STRAINING GNATS AND SWALLOWING CAMELS

> "You blind guides, who strain out a gnat and swallow a camel."
> ~Jesus Christ, Matthew 23:24 (NASB)

Since I am going to apply a principle from the above verse in a way some may find objectionable, I desire to convince you from the start that I really did read and understand the context. Jesus uses this jibe smack dab in the middle of soundly and emphatically denouncing some of the Pharisees' and Jewish teachers' practices and beliefs. Put simply, our Lord was not in favor of "majoring on the minors", when it comes to seeking a right standing before the Almighty God. Tithing from every food item was fine and even appropriate, but not at the expense of neglecting true, spiritual worship. These "blind guides" had missed the big picture!

In using the proverb of gnats and camels, Jesus was vividly illustrating the foolishness of convoluted priorities. We all recognize extreme forms of priorities out of whack: a bumper sticker I recently saw stated, "My wife, maybe my dog, but never my gun!" (I wondered if he still had his wife.) Even allowing a hard-core interpretation of the second amendment, most Christians would agree that the marriage covenant pulls rank even on the United States Constitution. The guy in the pickup (of course!) obviously had his priorities thoroughly confused.

**In using the proverb of gnats and camels, Jesus was vividly illustrating the foolishness of convoluted priorities.**

Unfortunately, confused priorities also make themselves apparent in Christian education. For example, too many Christian schools take great pains to ensure their dress codes are keeping every bizarre fashion trend at bay by the application of nit-picking policies, and yet they frequently allow "Christian" teachers to gossip, teach from a humanistic worldview, and discipline in an unbiblical manner. I will never forget a so-called Christian school I visited that was a disaster almost from top to bottom. This was brought home to me in spades when the administrator told me that when she heard I was coming to look at their school, she was tempted to "put more God-words in the hallways." Mercy! Talk about missing the big picture.

Parents also do their share of gnat-straining and camel-gulping. From my experience, it has been a consistent pattern that Christian parents will hold Christian schools and staffs to a very severe accountability in every aspect of the school's program. This is right and good, though sometimes a bit uncomfortable. It's not always enjoyable to be under a microscope. Nevertheless, parents have that authority and their scrutiny keeps us on our toes. Yet, parents I would have considered hard-nosed about their childrens' education, based on their concerns while at Logos, suddenly become docile if their children transfer to the public sector. Even when faced with what I would consider flagrant undermining of their rights as parents, these same people seem to quietly acquiesce to the powers-that-be and too often their children suffer for it.

Christian schools, yes even Logos, have real "gnats": problems that may frustrate parents in their desires for their children. These problems may even have camel-like proportions at times. So, if these cannot be eliminated in a constructive manner, whatever their size, the parents are totally justified in removing their children from that Christian school. Nowhere does the Bible endorse or encourage us to pretend gnats don't bother us. However, it doesn't follow that these parents should then take up camel-chugging by transferring their children to a totally unbiblical, God-hating school environment. Homeschooling would be at least a biblically consistent step, even if it would be difficult practically.

I pray I haven't offended you with my application of our Lord's principle. I also pray that more and more parents will not compromise the biblical standards God has placed before them for the education of their children. (And feel free to point out our gnats!)

* * *

DEAR PARENTS

*Loving and working with children, for days, months, sometimes years at a time, means getting to know them well. You learn about the things they love and hate, especially when they are allowed to share their prayer requests in an assembly. I stopped inwardly laughing long ago at sincere prayers being offered for sick kittens and goldfish. My Father doesn't laugh at my dearest cares, though smaller than a kitten in the great scheme of things. You also learn to love and appreciate the parents of the kids you love. That's why, when you work in Christian education, your heart can and should be vulnerable...*

### DEATH AND LIFE AT LOGOS

> Then Aslan stopped, and the children looked into the stream. And there...lay King Caspian, dead. And all three stood and wept. Even the Lion wept: great Lion-tears, each tear more precious than the Earth would be if it was a single, solid diamond. And Jill noticed that Eustace looked neither like a child crying, nor like a boy crying and wanting to hide it, but like a grown-up crying. At least, that is the nearest she could get to it...
>
> ~From *The Silver Chair*, by C.S. Lewis

Working with *families* is a worthwhile, heart-warming, but also, sometimes risky, and heart-rending business. But this is what we do at Logos School. We would not choose, as though we could, to deal just with the students; every child here comes from a family. So we realize that for each student at his or her desk, there are numerous other people who take a special interest in that child. This is a weighty realization when we take the time to reflect on it.

In light of this fact, death or a severe personal crisis that affects even just one person here tends to affect many here at Logos, much like as it would in a family.

## The world has nothing except platitudes and even lies to offer students when a death strikes close to home.

Recently, a death directly affected not just one student here, but six; all from the same family. Their father was killed when a tree from an old snag fell on him while he and his two oldest sons were snowmobiling. The oldest son held his dad until it was over. The father was also a highly-respected and well-liked doctor in the community. Hence, his passing has left a huge hole. He and his wife put their two oldest sons in Logos last year. Being much like their dad and mom, warm and congenial, the boys were immediately and widely accepted by the other students, making many friends in the junior high and senior high classes. This year, the four younger children joined us and they too quickly became part of the fabric of Logos.

After a tragic death, as this was, people are often tempted to paint a somewhat embellished, rose-colored picture of the person and those close to him. That is not what I am doing, nor is it necessary; this is a family that truly and openly *loves*; each member cares deeply for the others. At the special secondary assembly held during the week after the accident, the junior and senior high students were asked by the speaker how many had heard the boys praise their parents. All the boys' classmates and many other students raised their hands. That said it all. A time for prayer was included in the assembly. What a profound, deeply felt joy I received as I saw and heard these secondary students pray earnestly for this family! Then a number of promise-filled hymns were sung, emphasizing God's providence and sustaining grace. Yes, tears abounded, but like the quote above, these students shed "grown-up" tears in love and empathy for their friends.

Death is part of life and when you work with children you work with *every* aspect of life. The world has nothing except platitudes and even lies to offer students when a death strikes close to home. Even "trained" counselors are sore comfort to the needy. I truly pity and ache for students in public schools when a tragedy strikes close to their homes. So often all that is offered these confused, hurting kids is the chance to "visit counselors who are available." Where are the parents? Especially those who know the real Answer to grief. Only in Christ is there any cause for hope and peace. Through Christ we, along with families, have the honor of daily teaching children about abundant life in a world made by a loving God. And, when necessary, we are privileged to offer real *hope* in facing death, because of that same loving God.

\* \* \*

*As we learned, rather quickly in our history, we couldn't do it all for our students. In fact, there was very little we could do, even educationally, for students who came from shipwrecked families. It was almost like God actually ordained parents to set up their children for success or failure, even before they come to school. That is, obviously He directs all parents to train their children up in the Lord from birth; the sad fact is that when parents disobey those directions from Scripture, unless God's grace intervenes otherwise, there isn't much even a Christian school and teacher can do to significantly heal hurting children.*

## LIMITS OF LOGOS

One of this century's movie superheroes, Clint Eastwood, made the following memorable remark in one of his films: "A man's got to know his limitations." Please bear with me. I know it's a little strange to quote Clint Eastwood in a Christian school, but it seemed appropriate to what I'd like to share with you.

You hear regularly about the many positive, biblical aspects of our program. All those things are true, and we are grateful for the grace granted to us to accomplish them. However to be accurate, we should tell you some of the things we, as a school, cannot do, i.e. our limitations.

## There are sinners here; unrepentant ones, too.

No matter how we may try, Logos School is unable to do the following things:
1. We cannot totally makeup for the parents' failure in fulfilling the role mentioned above. Many times I've told tearful mothers that we cannot accept their rowdy junior high students. We've learned the hard way that it is more likely that a rebellious teenager will have a negative effect on students at Logos, than Logos will have a positive effect on the student.
2. We cannot be the first place children hear about the gospel, discipline, sex, drugs, hard work, safety, or even basic hygiene and nutrition. The nation's public schools have received an agenda, willingly or unwillingly, of tasks that have historically and biblically been a part of a parent's job description. Logos is unwilling to accept that agenda.
3. We cannot keep sin at bay by closing the school doors. There are sinners here; unrepentant ones too. Through God's truly amazing grace, these

sinners are under the tutelage of former unregenerate sinners. By the application to that same grace and through sometimes years of diligent prayers, the sinners here often become new creatures too!

4. We cannot operate independent of financial gifts, above tuition payments. Just like all soldiers in God's spiritual army, the staff members at Logos are real people who must eat and pay bills. Our school facility houses eternal beings, yet relies on very earthly items like electricity, gas, regular cleaning, and repairs. God has chosen to communicate His marvelous, universal gospel through decaying, physical individuals and materials.

5. We cannot keep its vision pure and dynamic in years to come without continuous prayer support for the board, staff, and families. We see daily the effect of your prayers! If the prayer support ceases, our limitations will far exceed those I've listed here.

Thank you for keeping our limits in bounds!

\* \* \*

### OVERCOME EVIL WITH GOOD

> "Yes," said Queen Lucy. "In our world too, a Stable once had Something inside it that was bigger than our whole world." It was the first time she had spoken, and from the thrill in her voice Tirian now knew why. She was drinking everything in more deeply than the others. She had been too happy to speak.
>
> ~*The Last Battle* by C.S. Lewis

**A gift we can give our children that will not only last a lifetime, but will help them overcome evil with good, is the gift of loving what is truly beautiful.**

When Paul the Apostle said, "Do not be overcome by evil, but overcome evil with good" (Rom. 12:21, NASB), he was saying more than just counter evil acts with good works or words. We are not just to counter, as in blow-for-blow, in order to stay on our feet. With Christ's authority, which is total as He said in Matthew 28, we are to overcome, that is, win the victory. That means overcoming with good all that evil tries to claim as its own. What has evil claimed and what must be reclaimed? How about Christmas, or more broadly, broadly, the beauty of Christmas?

Far too many Christians spend a good portion of the Christmas season Grinching about the way the pagans have "commercialized" and "secularized" this wonderful holiday. They have come to resent almost every aspect of the cultural Christmas trappings: they hate the fake, perfectly conical Christmas trees that spring up in almost every store practically the day after Labor Day, they hate the insipid, humanistic holiday ditties booming from every speaker in the mall. If they had the power, they would take a blowtorch to Frosty. But their greatest hatred is saved for that Satan in red satin, that Beelzebub in a beard, the Evil Elf Santa Claus! All the fuss and bother of shopping, sending cards, making special meals, and on and on, robs them of any real joy. When confronted or convicted about this lack of joy, they often respond by blaming their stressful schedule on the world's way of celebrating. How is that overcoming evil with good? Frankly, it sometimes seems that many non-Christians enjoy and have more fun at Christmas than many Christians!

Christmas brings a time of reflection for many people, even amongst the bustle and extra activities. It should be a time to reflect on what we are giving our children. By that I don't just mean what presents we buy them, though those decisions, too, should not be driven by cultural pressures. Rather, I mean our reflection should, at least once in a while, dwell on what lifelong, intangible gifts we are giving our children. Virtually every tangible item we buy for them will, as our Lord said, rust or decay, or even be stolen; probably most may be just outgrown.

A gift we can give our children that will not only last a lifetime, but will help them overcome evil with good, is the gift of loving what is truly beautiful. No other time of the year provides us with so many opportunities to expose our children to beauty than Christmas. Rather than moan about "Jingle Bell Rock," why not overcome by filling our homes and our children's minds with the rich lyrics and sounds of Handel's "Messiah?" Or reading great stories together like *The Christmas*

*Carol*, or C.S. Lewis's *Narnia* series (a must for any child or adult)?

But Christmas should not be the only time we actively encourage our children to relish beauty with their hearts and minds. If from their earliest years children are not trained day in and day out, as Deuteronomy commands, to cling to what is beautiful and good, then trying to start that training when they are fourteen will be very difficult. Wouldn't it be wonderful to have our children not just reject the world's plastic, false beauty, but *overcome* by having the habit of seeking out, recognizing, and cherishing what is truly beautiful? My wife, Julie, has been blessed with the wonderful gift of pointing out beauty in the creation every time we take a walk or drive somewhere with the family. If I were to try to paint all the outdoor scenes she loves and wants me to paint, I would have a new day job (and starve our family in the process).

Giving our children that gift will take years of thoughtful work by parents (and Christian teachers), but there will be Christmas each year to give us a boost. And before too long, we may see our grandchildren bring us an old, well-worn book, climb into our laps and ask us to read them the "great story you read to mama at Christmas-time!"

\* \* \*

HOMEGROWN MORALITY

This was going to be great! I could hardly wait. I had made sure I was safely situated, well beyond the range of the shrapnel. The flames were starting to rise above the top of the barrel... any second now...

For context, as a young, healthy preteen, I was given the task of gathering all combustible trash in our home and burning it in the fifty-gallon drum my dad had placed behind our woodpile. Our home in Ann Arbor, Michigan, was built outside the city limits, in a lovely wooded area. That meant, among other things, that we had no city services, hence my task. Since I was a semi-normal boy, I was obligated to grumble about any assigned task. However, I secretly loved this job. Being a closet pyromaniac, I had added a nifty twist to the mundane burning of boxes and bags. While ostensibly garnering all the trash in the house, I covertly sought out empty or almost empty aerosol cans (this was pre-ozone "hole" days). I had been tipped to their unique possibilities for excitement by the warning label "Combustible contents: Do not place near heat source explosion may result." YES!

So, buried deep within almost every pile of trash I set a match to, there was a little time bomb. And, as I anticipated with beating heart, this fire should produce the same spectacular results I had achieved every other time. I could see it in my mind's eye already the wonderful sound, WHOOOMP!, and then the flames leaping a dozen feet in the air. Sometimes the aerosol can itself flew as high as the lowest trees. That was a neat bonus.

Any moment now ... just then out of the corner of my eye I saw my father emerge from the back door with another bag of trash in his hand. He was walking toward the FIRE BARREL! Moral quandary time: Do I warn my father, indicting myself instantly on the federal crime of being an idiot about fire, or do I keep quiet and allow my father to be blown up, just to protect my reputation? Seconds mattered... "Dad! Wait! Don't put that in just yet!"

He stopped and came back toward me. "Why not, Tom?" "Well, I don't thin..."

WHOOOOMP! Whoooshhh! Zinnnnnnnng! It was the best yet, I thought even while simultaneously realizing it was the last time I would be able to witness such a marvelous spectacle.

Throughout the land these days is the cry for moral, and possibly even religious training to become part of the government schools' curriculum. Recently, I was invited by the local district's superintendent to be present at a meeting of public school and religious leaders, to discuss that very issue. There was the predictable hand-wringing talk about the degenerate state of our youth. It was as hopeless as it was sincere. Their answer? "We need more programs!" We have come almost full circle from the early sixties when we (in the form of the U.S. Supreme Court) capped a century of humanistic rebellion by openly removing Bibles and prayer from the government schools. Now seeing that, gee whiz, kids really do need some specific moral guidance vs. morally "neutral" education, we wonder if there might be another open door to the ark. We're getting really wet out here.

Christian schools were more than happy to take up the fallen banner of morality and try to run with it to the high ground. "We can make kids good, because we've got God on our side!" So, why is it that, even among Christian schools, we are talking in too many conferences, seminars, and new curriculum materials about the increasing problem of teen pregnancies, theft, swearing, drug-use, etc. among these "good" Christian school students? The responses to these growing problems tend to fall into two categories: either the Christian school lowers its standards of behavior and does its best to tolerate and assimilate these kids instead of expelling them; or they call for more "biblical" education about these problems. The former is a cave-in, and the latter is a baptized version of the government school "answer."

I grew up with the "Just Say Yes To Drugs!" generation of the sixties and seventies. The schools didn't even try to teach us about the nasty effects of drugs on our brains. We knew anyway, and that was exactly why many of my friends used them. But even though friends literally thrust joints (marijuana) at me with the strong advice to just try them, I said no. It certainly wasn't my knowledge of the bad effects of the drugs or even some particular Bible verse I recalled that kept me from indulging. It was the plain and simple fact that if I took drugs, I would deeply hurt my parents and destroy their trust in me. That knowledge was stronger than any program or pastor's admonition.

## Sadly, many Christian schools and all government schools continue to disregard God's primary agency for instilling morals in children— the parents.

I have written, in various contexts, on the unequaled, profound influence the home has on children. The home's effectiveness and character is showcased by the moral decisions the children make, particularly when they are absent from their parents like they are at school. Sadly, many Christian schools and all government schools continue to disregard God's primary agency for instilling morals in children the parents. The good news is that more and more parents are getting tired of being left out of the equation and are starting schools where their God-given authority is recognized and included practically in all the school's policies and programs. Even there, however, each family and set of parents affects the child's moral decisions far more than the school. That's as it should be. Otherwise, we might as well start programs to teach pyromaniac kids about the bad effects of

DEAR PARENTS

blowing up their fathers.

\* \* \*

Possibly the most unsung portion of our society, even in the Christian subset, is that element which is over sixty years old. Grandparents offer families, not to mention Christian schools (yet), a rich dimension that no one else can give. They are the family historians, wisdom-givers, and often, spiritual patriarchs. And they are pretty neat baby-sitters, too, but that is hardly their most important function. Blessed indeed, because God says so, is the family (and school) that has and recognizes those wonderful people whom our Father has endowed with long life and accompanying perspective.

POLISHING CROWNS

With a title like the one above you might expect to read a column on the reward of believers. Rather, the crowns I'm referring to are living ones.

"Grandchildren are the crown of old men..." (Proverbs 17:6, NASB).

Traditionally, all crowns have had at least two things in common. They are extremely valuable articles, and they are used to adorn royal or noble personages. Solomon as the wisest and one of the greatest kings certainly knew about crowns and their implication. Therefore, his comparison of grandchildren to crowns takes on a special significance.

## Grandparents see the tremendous importance of time and love spent for children.

Few social cliches are as well known as the proud grandparent thrusting photos of his grandchildren upon friends and strangers alike. Grandparents very often have a special relationship with their children's children that even the immediate parents can't understand. Why is this? From my admitted "youthful" view, I'd like to offer a hypothesis.

Grandparents, having lived through the trials and blessings of raising to adulthood at least one child, have a view of the value of childhood that sometimes eludes parents. Grandma knows that the spills from the high-chair won't go on forever, so she stays calm and even kisses the messy face. Grandpa knows that there will come a time when the little person on his lap will sit in the driver's seat. Grandparents see the tremendous importance of time and love spent for children.

Since this seems to be almost universally true, how much greater and deeper is the vision of Christian grandparents for their grandchildren? Perhaps that is why at almost every school assembly I see at least one or two grandparents. Many of them know the value of a godly heritage. They see their living crowns being polished and refined by the daily application of God's love. They can see into the future in a way we can't because they have seen almost a complete past.

One of my favorite bits of wisdom is the idea that "every time an older person dies, a library burns down." Grandparents frequently love to tell stories from their past, and children normally love to listen to stories—a match made in heaven! But this aspect goes far beyond even the cozy storytelling while on grandpa's lap. This is a precious learning time for these little ones as they get a glimpse into the past, and come to understand the world did not begin with their own birth, a misconception that is pandemic today. The children also come to see their grandparents as people who, wonder of wonders, were young once, too.

It is, therefore, tantamount to an appalling waste of resources, to say the least, for a Christian school not to honor and involve grandparents in every possible aspect of the school. They can offer much, they ask little, and God commands that we see them as He does. May we all see the preciousness of these crowns and the valuable wisdom of the crown wearers.

\* \* \*

## THE OTHER END OF THE PHONE CALL

> When I was a child, I used to speak as a child, think as a child, reason as a child; when I became a man, I did away with childish things.
> ~1 Corinthians 13:11 (NASB)

"Well, do you think he may need some special testing or something? I've heard that the university can do that for free. The doctor says he's fine, but our older son seemed to catch on so much quicker than he does. What do you think we should do?" The furrowed brow of the mother bespoke many hours of concern for her son's progress in school.

In numerous situations like this over the years, I have always wished I had something really profound to suggest. But, from what we have seen in almost all those other situations, I had to lay down my best card: "Frankly, Helen, I think he just needs time to mature. Little boys especially sometimes need more time to grow up." And that's about as good as it gets.

The problem is we are all rather competitive creatures from the starting gun. We grow up comparing ourselves with ourselves (something Scripture warns against). It is often the bread-and-butter of adolescence. Then when we become parents, if we honestly admit it, our children's progress frequently becomes a matter of honor and pride for us. Christian parents are no less tempted to fall prey to this appeal to pride than are non-Christians. The difference should be in how the temptation is handled. As with most things, it is a matter of balance, best considered in the light of Scripture.

# Even though we don't know all that is happening, we would be foolish to deny that there is indeed more going on than we can see.

There is nothing wrong with a doctor noting a child's physical growth, as compared to the "average" for the child's age and weight. This can help detect a medical problem in the offing. A child's academic or educational capability is not so easily tracked. It is not just a matter of chronological age, or gender, or genetics, although those things certainly have a profound affect. Educating a child is much like feeding one. It requires not only spooning in the tasty stuff: it requires certain reciprocal skills from the child. We don't feed a one-year-old hefty, juicy bites of a two-inch thick, New York steak for the simple reason that he is unable to adequately chew it in his tiny mouth. It certainly is "tasty stuff" and worth eating (it's sounding really good to me right now!), but the child can't "take it in." But given time and growth, that steak will become a very well-liked and easily processed item by the same child.

It isn't only parents who agonize over the enigma of children's maturity. Teachers wrestle with the same mystery every year. In discussions with these teachers, I often refer to their quandary as trying to figure out what's being said on the other end of a phone call. As teachers, we can see and understand a limited amount of what is happening with every student. The "other side," the aspect of their maturing, we cannot "hear" very well, much less significantly affect the process. But, just as with a phone call, we need to acknowledge that we are not "hearing" the whole conversation. Even though we don't know all that is happening, we would be foolish to deny that there is indeed more going on than we can see. Classical teachers especially should be sensitive to what level of maturity their students exhibit. There is a significant difference, for instance, between a child with the maturity of the "pert" (logical) stage, and one who is ready to be considered at the "poetic" (rhetoric) stage. For the teacher, then, it can mean the difference between successful, appropriate classical teaching (giving them food they can digest), and trying to cram in knowledge for its own sake (stuffing their mouths, and risking their choking on it).

Ultimately, as always, the Word of God guides us toward alleviating our puzzlement. Paul, while in a discussion of the mystery of God's redemptive love, reveals a bit of God's view of childhood. Children speak, think (observe), and reason in a way that is distinctly different from a mature adult. Children enjoy "childish things." Note that Paul doesn't call them silly or worthless things, just childish. The classical method of teaching allows children to be children, teaches to their strengths, all the while watching for and patiently waiting for the maturity that will come.

Don't hang up the phone just because you can't hear the other end; listen better to what you can hear and wait quietly for the conversation to be completed.

# 2

## WHAT ARE LITTLE BOYS & GIRLS MADE OF?

*Like many an older, maiden aunt, our current culture shrilly insists on telling us how to raise our children; all the while being profoundly ignorant of what children are really like. This is especially true of those "maiden aunts" prolific among the educationists. As I have said to quite a few up and coming teachers, most colleges of education don't correctly teach teachers how to love, discipline, effectively teach or understand children; other than that the colleges aren't too bad. Scripture, on the other hand (the upper hand), has much to say about children. At Logos we're still learning about how best to love, discipline, teach and understand children. But the effort is worth the trials.*

\* \* \*

DESPITE MODERN EDUCATION'S BEST EFFORTS BOYS AND GIRLS ARE STILL DIFFERENT! (PART I)

"What are little girls made of?
Sugar and spice and everything nice, That's what little girls are made of."
"What are little boys made of?
Frogs and snails and puppy dogs' tails, That's what little boys are made of."

Now that little ditty is not likely to be found in any self-respecting (read: politically correct) children's literature of the enlightened 90's. Heavens! Not only is it patronizing and chauvinistic, it flies right in the face of the "truth" we as a culture are being so carefully taught: girls and boys are only anatomically different. Underneath their skins and in their brains they are equal and the same, by George (or Georgina). Not to mention the lack of sensitivity this heretical poem shows toward our animal friends.

## This "sameness doctrine" is especially evident in the expectations placed on children entering school.

Please pardon my sarcasm, but I read and hear so much tripe in this vein that my tolerance has worn as thin as the argument presented by the educationists.

God, in His limitless wisdom, has created boys and girls to be different since Time began. Countless cultures and centuries have confirmed this fact; it is only in the latter part of the twentieth century, here in a remote corner of the globe, that parents are being sold the ridiculous notion that their sons and daughters are exactly alike. It would be humorous except for the fact that droves of parents are buying it and becoming frustrated, even abusive, when their children insist on displaying behaviors once considered "typical" for boys or girls. One professor I know was profoundly frustrated, when, after all his efforts to raise his daughter to be androgynous ("not displaying traditional characteristics of either sex"), she found great delight in playing with dolls and wearing dresses! What a failure.

This "sameness doctrine" is especially evident in the expectations placed on children entering school. Little girls in kindergarten are frequently encouraged to play with traditionally male-type toys (trucks, cars, bugs), while little boys in the class are encouraged to check out the toy stoves and dolls. There are school supply catalogs galore, stuffed with these offerings for the schools of today. Perhaps in the near future we'll finally get a best-seller entitled "Why Johnny Can't Be a Man."

And it continues on through the remainder of their educational career. It may become less overt, but actually far more detrimental. If Johnny can't read as soon as Sally, then, of course, it means he is probably learning disabled and needs a specialist. It certainly wouldn't have anything to do with his maturing slower than she did. Jane is having trouble with math and doesn't seem to have any interest in science. Send in the specialists. Jane's problem is obviously that she needs to understand she is subconsciously conforming to archaic notions of what have been male domains. It couldn't be that she just isn't that interested in the subjects.

Yes, there are students with real problems who need extra help. But have you ever stopped to wonder why, with all our culture's other advances, it is in this generation we have the lowest proportion of readers and the largest special education bureaucracy in educational history? Could it have something to do with how the children are taught, and not a problem with the children themselves?

Then in the latter years of high school, students, especially the girls, are virtually compelled to outline their lifetime careers. Sally is urged to become a lawyer, a neurosurgeon, or at least a CEO of a Fortune Five Hundred company. Johnny should sensitively consider studying nursing, clothing design, or at least being a stay-at-home dad, so his wife can adequately fulfill her career options. I am exaggerating a bit for emphasis, but, frankly, that's not too far off the mark. If you don't believe me, check out the local high school and see how much time is given to girls interested in becoming full-time wives and mothers, or boys who want to be the primary breadwinner (what an ancient term) for his family, so that his wife doesn't "have" to work.

This "doctrine" of gender egalitarianism is thankfully not the trend among the vast majority of Logos families. It is a joy to be among young women who are not offended, but rather flattered by being referred to as "ladies." Many of the dads here insist that their sons treat their mothers, sisters, and by extension, other females, with proper respect. In recent years, we have actively encouraged this respect for the God-given differences between the genders by instituting "Protocol Nights" for the high school years. The students are given several hours of real etiquette training, and then go out as a group to a formal dinner and evening of high-class entertainment. Dating or pairing-up is not part of the program; all the boys are to be gentlemen to all the girls, and the girls are to act as ladies, not girlfriends. And believe it or not, it has been a huge, popular success!

\* \* \*

DEAR PARENTS

## DIFFERENCES BETWEEN BOYS AND GIRLS, II

"That's right. (said Edmund) Cross it and strike up hill, and we'll be at the Stone Table (Aslan's How, I mean) by eight or nine o'clock. I hope King Caspian will give us a good breakfast!"

"I hope you're right," said Susan. "I can't remember all that at all."

"That's the worst of girls," said Edmund to Peter and the Dwarf. "They never can carry a map in their heads."

"That's because our heads have something inside them," said Lucy.

~From *Prince Caspian* by C.S. Lewis)

Up-front and openly I freely admit I will be using sweeping generalities in this column. However, if C.S. Lewis can do it without apology, so can I. For openers, the above quote came to mind recently when I was reading a communique from the National Geographic Society regarding their annual Geography Bee. It seems they were wringing their collective hands over the indisputable fact that, year after year, 90+% of the winners in the bee are boys! Surprise, surprise, now they are planning on doing a study to determine why this is happening. I guess these young men haven't heard of Affirmative Action and egalitarianism in every sphere of human endeavor. (Last year's winner at Logos was a girl, by the way.)

Historically, and in almost every culture, only boys received a formal education. Then, in the western cultures within the last couple of centuries, all-girl schools began to pop up. Separate schools were the norm for quite some time. Relatively speaking, 'coed' schools are a new invention. Why were schools so long "gender specific"? (Sorry, the 90's are affecting me.) The simplest and most obvious answer is that, until recent history, people recognized the fact that girls and boys act, learn, and even think differently. Here are some examples:

Ladies first. Appearances are very important to the girls. How something looks is critical. Every detail should be just right. This naturally combines with a propensity to neatness and orderliness. Girls often have views of people and the world that would be considered Romantic, in the classic sense that is, honor, virtue, nobility are real and important. Relationships, how individuals are feeling about each other receives a lot of thought and attention. These feelings are often based on their intuitions and assumptions; sometimes they're even right. Girls like to communicate ... a lot! This is done orally and in writing. Expressing their thoughts and feelings comes as naturally as breathing.

It should be no surprise then to discover that girls consistently do very well in the communication subjects: reading, writing (both composition and handwriting —neat!), spelling, and speech. They also excel in drama, art, and music.

They tend to get far better grades and have better behavior in school than boys do. Why? Modern schools are structured around feminine interests: neatness and organization are stressed, most work in class is written or visual, there are neat rows of desks and chairs, as well as cute, colorful wall decorations; and positive feelings, for their own sake, have become almost a liturgy.

Now the gentlemen: Appearances have little value to the boys; substantive accomplishments carry the day. One-up-manship is part of every male-dominated conversation. "Oh yeah? Well, I pulled out four of my teeth at one time!" Achievements matter. Boys would much rather win something than just get a high mark. Competition is their bread and butter. Having their pride hurt is worse than physical pain. Boys love collections of things; it doesn't matter how valuable the things are, they just want lots of them. Boys are sensory-oriented from infancy to old age, I think. Touch, taste, smell, adjust, grab, tear-apart, fiddle-with, and generally manipulate are their bywords. "How does this thing work?" Analyzing and probing are common practices.

With these characteristics, boys tend to do well in the tangibles: science, geography, PE, history; and the puzzles: math and logic. However, they lag behind girls in earned grades due partly to their slower physical and social maturation, but also to the fact that most schools use few, if any, tangible teaching and grading methods. Competition is often a naughty word.

A couple of typical examples: (both precious to me) Kajsa, my eight year-old, loves to labor at composing a typed letter expressing her affection for her teacher. Seth, my eleven year-old, would rather show his teacher a cardboard marble maze he designed and built with a friend.

Since we can't, for cultural and financial reasons, go back to the days of separate schools for boys and girls, we, as parents and teachers, need to recognize and teach to both genders' strengths. We need to allow and plan for their God-given differences and help them learn to assist each other, instead of mock. Ultimately this cooperation leads to another God-given human structure, marriage. Let's study our children, relax, and let them be who they are, as we train them in ways they best understand.

BOY MEETS GIRL

They were obviously a bit impatient, shuffling and yet tense, eager to depart the classroom in one explosive rush. But the teacher insisted they wait, even if it was a bit longer than usual. The last few girls were still gathering their personal items and heading out the door. Then, as the last young lady passed into the hallway, the teacher reminded the boys to "walk, not run" on their way to the lunchroom. They obeyed, but their steps were jerky, like a Ferrari having to drive 25 mph on an open stretch of highway. A good and necessary practice of self-control, with some outside encouragement, of course.

As most of our Logos parents know by now, for several years we have been highlighting the need for upgrading the cultural aspects of our school. One significant form this has taken is in the area of etiquette. Put in biblical language, this is practicing love in the details. "Details" in this case means the small opportunities we have every day to show consideration for others. Even more specifically, we are encouraging the children to make distinctions in how they show consideration for the opposite gender. The Bible is clear about these distinctions so we believe we should be also, regardless of our culture's never-say-die crusade to eliminate them.

## Are we just trying to hark back to the lost age of chivalry in some pathetic, anachronistic manner?

So, for instance, in every grade, the boys are required to allow the girls to leave the classroom first. In the lunchroom, as they file in, the boys are to stand until the girls are seated. Young men are to hold doors for young women and ladies. (This has had the side-effect of young men frequently holding doors even for older male teachers.) During secondary assemblies, the young men are to watch for ladies standing in the back and assist in getting a chair for them. What are the girls and young ladies supposed to do for their part? How do they show consideration for their male peers? By treating the boys' deference to them with respect, not scorn or mockery. A thankful attitude is pretty much all that's required.

Are we just trying to hark back to the lost age of chivalry in some pathetic, anachronistic manner? After all, our mascot is a knight. Aren't we kicking against the current social goads, or even worse, not preparing the kids for the "real world" out there, where the sexes are really the same?

No, to all the above. For one thing, the age of chivalry was hardly one we'd like to emulate: it was largely adulterous and generally without a biblical foundation. As for the "real world," by whose definition? God made us male and female and until He rewires us, that's what we are.

Our goal in this, as with ever other aspect of the education we provide, is to seek to prepare the students to think biblically about all they will face before and after graduation. That includes the rather critical, life-changing aspect of being married. To be clear: we are not going into the realm of marital counseling, child-rearing, or even providing home management courses, per se. But a young man doesn't turn into a gentleman, knowing how to show consideration for a young lady, by merely turning eighteen, or twenty-one, for that matter. He becomes what he has been practicing to be since he was old enough to observe the model of older men. If he has never seen a gentleman in action or been required to act like one at five, twelve and fifteen, he simply won't burst into one later, at the point when it matters to him. That is, when he meets a young lady to whom he does want to show special consideration. The ugly caterpillar won't become the impressive butterfly just by wishing.

To up the ante, God designed most people for the state of marriage. As Paul tells us, He grants a few folks a special gift of singleness. This means that the vast majority of those sweet little faces coming to kindergarten each morning are heading for either a God-honoring marriage or possibly a series of heart-rending, self-centered relationships. That sounds kind of harsh, put that way, but the facts and figures of the "real world" bear this out.

The only question that we face as a Christian school then is, in regard to those facts of life, what kind of behavior will we model and enforce for our students? Will we tacitly adopt the world's view and pretend that how boys and girls treat each other at school is of no consequence to marriage later on? Or will we, under the limited, delegated authority of our parents, seek to model and require the kind of countless, small considerations husbands should demonstrate to their wives and wives to their husbands? Which approach is really denying the reality to come in the lives of these students? Which approach encourages the biblical mandate that young men are to treat young women "as sisters, in all purity and respect?"

There is a lot to how boys and girls are to interact, wherever they are or how old they are. Suffice it to say here, in all matters of the mind and heart of a student, the Scripture and its principles are neither inappropriate or outdated. Pray for our wisdom in how we promote those principles at Logos.

\* \* \*

*The topic below, as with many of my columns, initially got its impetus from my being fed up to my hairline (and that's getting higher all the time) with hearing about this or that self-esteem enhancing programs/materials. Frustration can be a great motivator at times. But before I just spout, I need to think through why I have a knee-jerk reaction against the topic at hand. Sometimes that thinking process diffuses my frustration by making me realize that it just isn't worth the battle. Other times, thought actually produces clarity of convictions, and then I can type my little fingers off.*

CONFIDENCE VS. SELF-ESTEEM

> Confidence: A feeling of assurance or certainty
> Self-esteem: Pride in oneself
> ~Definitions from *American Heritage Dictionary*

It's probably because I am "educator" that I'm considered fair game for tasteless poster companies and other originators of visual drivel. Hardly a week goes by without the mail to Logos including a multicolored, ocular-assaulting order form for sets of posters and accompanying materials designed to "build students' self-esteem!" You've seen them. My favorite is the one with the sad-faced little boy and the message, "I am special, cuz God don't make no garbage!" (No, but the poster company sure does! Including the use of double negatives.) There are countless programs, materials, and even computer software available to assist teachers in pumping up their student's self-esteem. It has gotten to the point that to not have a "self-esteem" program in a school/class is bordering on child abuse.

## They had gained confidence in their abilities by accomplishment, not accolades.

Think about it. If you have had the occasion to hear educators talk about their students, how many more times is the term "self-esteem" used, versus the number of times you hear about developing "confidence?" Are these just synonyms for the same condition? Not according to traditional definitions of these terms. As noted above, one term relies on "pride in oneself," and the other relies on "assurance" or "certainty" especially in regard to one's abilities.

When I was teaching each of my four children to learn to ride a two-wheeler (and concurrently jogging more miles than our president ever has or will), I gasped out countless praises as to their personal attributes. Somehow all those praises didn't seem to make them feel good about themselves, much less assist them in actually riding the bike. It was only when they had mastered staying upright and mobile for lengthy periods that they exuded a positive outlook on bike-riding. They had gained confidence in their abilities by accomplishment, not accolades. Sure, my praises helped them more than criticisms would have, but it was their success in attaining their goal, through much effort, that produced a lasting confidence.

Over the years at Logos, we have seen innumerable similar situations. Our teachers try not to be short on dispensing praise, but we have seen that the kind of praise students respond to best is praise for their work. We have also observed the very real truth that "success breeds success." Students frequently prefer a task that includes the possibility of failure, if there is a chance for real success, vs. an "everyone wins" type of program. It seems only the very young enjoy a "Participant Ribbon," the meaningless, you-were-there "award." Very often just giving students a second chance to succeed after a failure is far more confidence-building to them than praising them for what they know was a poor job. Most self-esteem efforts and promotion materials I have seen focus on intangible, cotton candy feelings in an effort to make the students "feel good about themselves." Consistently in the numerous international testing comparisons from math to geography, students in the United States have been at or near the lowest rank for years. But, in one testing program they scored higher than any other students in the world; U.S. students ranked the highest in "feeling good" about themselves. Yippee.

The Bible nowhere commands, or even encourages us to feel good about ourselves; it does repeatedly command and encourage us to work ... hard, well, often, and with a good attitude, "as unto the Lord." Only this kind of work brings confidence and well-deserved praise. Ultimately, our goal as parents and Christian teachers is for the students to find their confidence in the Lord and seek His "Well done!" Children who live with these standards don't need artificial pumping up and their confidence will last a lifetime; "self-esteem" feelings are as temporary as a poster.

\* \* \*

*The pandemic abdication of parental authority, coupled with at least the last two generations of kids actively rebelling against that authority has produced predictable, albeit, disastrous results for kids. We now call maturity "outdated" and "old", and we worship and cater to youth, as though kids have an innate wisdom from birth. Again, we have to see what God says, and stick to that.*

## THE PARADOX OF MATURITY

> Even in this world, of course, it is the stupidest children who are most childish, and the stupidest grownups who are most grown-up.
> ~C.S. Lewis, *The Silver Chair*

Rather than start with supporting philosophical arguments, let me state right up front and as emphatically as I can, our culture lies, and lies constantly, to us about children! From the educationists at most universities, to our vast media network, from day unto day, they pour forth outrageous lies upon our heads. The saddest part of this is, as Lenin predicted and practiced, "If you tell the big lie long enough, and loud enough, the people will believe it." Not only have many non-Christian families bought and passed on the lies; so have great numbers of Christian families and churches.

Simply put, our culture, especially through our educational establishments, tells us that children can and should handle adult issues as soon as possible, and with the same mouth, they rail against the prerequisites needed by children to mature properly. They prescribe a precise, politically (if not medically) correct AIDS curriculum for first graders, but will recoil in horror should those same first graders practice gender-specific and "childish" activities, such as boys playing with Legos or guns and girls playing with American Girl dolls or (gasp) tea sets. In the name of education and sophistication, countless children are literally being robbed of their childhood. They have our warped adult culture thrust on them at earlier and earlier ages, then we turn around and wonder why so many young people are growing up without a sense of morality and community, not to mention without a sense of wonder and interest in the world around them.

The Bible states in no uncertain terms that children are profoundly different in thoughts, actions, appearance, abilities, interests, and emotions than adults (Proverbs, 1 Cor. 13, etc.). They are not small adults, trapped in tiny bodies, fully capable of correctly handling topics from nuclear catastrophes to drug abuse. Yet even many Christian families seem to believe our culture's lies and act as though it is inevitable that their children must throw off childhood far sooner than the parents did.

# They are not small adults, trapped in tiny bodies, fully capable of correctly handling topics from nuclear catastrophes to drug abuse.

For example, in a recent issue of a very popular Christian family magazine, a feature article was titled, "Are You Ready For Your Teens To Date?" Yes, I did read it and, surprise, surprise, not one mention was made of parents possibly choosing to not have their children date. Apparently dating is yet one more cultural thing that happens to all kids; parents beware! It may come as a shock to the culturally, up-to-date authors of the above article that more and more Christian families, with real-live teenagers, are choosing the archaic method of *courtship* (i.e. marriage-directed relations vs. the dating game), for their progeny.

With younger children, timeless, marvelous children's books and reading as a family have been subordinated to videos, Sesame Street, and Nintendo. I would submit that since children are made to imitate ideas and behavior they see, as

Christians, we will be held accountable for the models we place before them.

One of the most gratifying aspects I've enjoyed while working with families at Logos is seeing so many secure children from parent-run, not culture-run, homes. These children seem to have a number of things in common: they are not burdened with adult problems and issues, and therefore, enjoy being children, doing things like imaginative playing, reading, coloring, birthday party games, dressing up, and playing ball games. They also seem to have a maturing sense of the necessity of doing lots of work at home, doing it well, and respecting authority. Oh yes, they also seem to enjoy school! The latter traits are evident in the many secure teens I know, too. Sometimes, at the kindergarten or first grade levels it is necessary to propose to parents that they consider holding their son or daughter back a year before starting or continuing our program. The majority of families I've talked with understand the need and benefit of allowing their child time to be just that, a child who needs to grow up. We've never had a problem with giving a child "too much" time to grow.

There is no fire to get to, no need to rush through childhood. Let's invest in the brief years so that they will be truly mature. Our culture will and cannot give us the blueprint our children need, only the Scriptures and godly examples can do that.

\* \* \*

## DARTH VADER HAD NO CAPITAL

The multi-planetary, highly tolerant creatures were no problem. The incredible technology, combined with good ol' sword play, was easy to buy. But there is no way in this world or even on the Death Star, that Darth Vadar could do what he did. You remember, at the end of the Trilogy, *Return of the Jedi,* the nasty Emperor (who bore a startling resemblance to the Wicked Witch of the West) was slowly but surely roasting Luke Skywalker with blue death rays. Bolt after bolt hit Luke, shorting him out and sounding like the biggest bug-zapper in the world. Luke cried out to his father (Darth), who was standing by watching the barbecue. Then, just when Luke was almost flambe, Darth grabbed the Emperor from behind and tossed him and his blue rays into a nearby open shaft that went down about a mile. Foom! The end of the Emperor, but also the end of Darth, who had been hit with those deadly rays.

Later, in Darth's death scene, he gasps out that Luke has "saved" him by seeing the good that remained in his dear old dad. This salvation is confirmed at the very end of the movie by the fact that Darth (now Anakin Skywalker again) appears in a hazy blue form along with two other dead good guys. It seems that Darth's one good act of killing the Emperor overcame all his bad acts, including wiping out an entire planet of people in the first movie.

The problem with the above is not the lack of balance in good vs. evil acts; after all, biblical grace doesn't measure our works; it looks only to Christ's work on the cross for our salvation. No, the problem is that Darth had no capital from which to draw the moral strength necessary to kill the Emperor. In the two previous movies it was obvious that Darth was completely sold out to the "dark side," so much so that he had no problem trying to kill Luke in the first and second movies. A very wise man said that one cannot die well if one has not lived well. The idea that someone who has lived for himself his entire life will, at the last critical moment, sacrifice himself for others, makes for some interesting stories and movies but is not in line with our Adamic nature. Generations since Adam have confirmed this millions of times over. The thief on the cross didn't do anything noble at the last; grace reached out to him in his final moments on Earth.

## The thief on the cross didn't do anything noble at the last; grace reached out to him in his final moments on Earth.

Capital, the accumulation of a valuable commodity, is necessary for any worthwhile endeavor. In sports, an athlete that has not put in thousands of practice shots is unlikely to make the game-winning free throw in the basketball game. The actor who relies only on rehearsals to practice his part is likely to forget his lines or be wooden come opening night. Certainly God-given talents give children an edge in some situations but, unless they invest in and accumulate the necessary capital, others who have done their homework, so to speak, will pass the gifted ones up. There is a lot of wisdom in the fable of the tortoise and the hare, in this regard.

Students in a classical, Christian educational environment have great opportunities to gain and store up various forms of capital of the most valuable kinds. They are receiving, if it is passed on well, ageless wisdom from the Scriptures, and from the Western historical heritage. Their moral training, begun in the godly home and enhanced through this type of schooling, will build up a capital that, by God's grace, will be drawn on in their adult years. Conversely, today's post-modern families pander to, and yet morally starve children. Then at the magic age of eighteen, parents and society expect these fat, sluggish caterpillar children to emerge as well-equipped, strong citizen butterflies. And we all continue to be surprised to see moral invertebrate adults in every position of authority.

It should come as no surprise, just a profound, welcome blessing, to see students who have built up this kind of capital graduate from high school "full of grace and truth." And that is just the beginning for them and the works they will complete for the Kingdom. The important thing to remember is, with any kind of real capital, it takes years and years to accumulate a usable amount. All those years of imitation (grammar), precise inquiry (logic), and practice in research and presentations (rhetoric) stockpile the capital that will be drawn upon when they leave us and their families. That truth, by the way, also illustrates the folly of using our precious little ones as "salt and light" in the secular realm. They haven't the scriptural, knowledgeable, or moral capital yet to face and rightly handle all that they will encounter.

We don't live in a "galaxy, far, far away"; we are here on planet Earth, and as God designed us, we all need years of His tender mercies to have the capital to make large and small correct decisions. May God grant us and our children those mercies.

\* \* \*

## TRIPPING THOSE WHO TRUST...

OK, I admit it ... when Kathryn, my youngest, looks at me in that way of hers, I would just about grant any request she might make. What is it about kids, especially little ones, that often, unless we have hearts of stone, makes us eager to drop whatever we're doing and assist them? I won't keep you guessing, it is their trust in us that makes us want to move heaven and earth to see our children get what they need, or even want. Think about the times you don't want to grant their requests. I know from my experience as a parent and a teacher that when a child is *demanding*, instead of asking with trust, I'm not as quick to leap into action.

## We are here to foster and nourish the God-given trust children have in the Father, in their parents, and in their teachers.

Our Father knew exactly what He was doing when He bestowed every child with a vast quantity of built-in trust of adults. That's partly why it is natural for children to easily and readily accept the Father, through His loving Son. Jesus Himself points to this young trust as an example of how adults should approach the Father. "Truly I say to you, unless you are converted and become like children," He said, while gently holding a child in His arms, "you shall not enter the kingdom of heaven" (Matt. 18:13). He went on to pronounce a ringing judgment on those who would dare to crush the faith of a child who loves the Father: "but whoever causes one of these little ones who believe in Me to stumble, it is better for him that a heavy millstone be hung around his neck and that he be drowned in the depth of the sea" (Matt. 18:6) The Son of God obviously considered misleading the faith of these little ones to be a capital offense.

Do you remember the story of the one lost sheep out of a hundred? There Jesus was also talking about children who trust Him. Immediately after this story He says, "Thus it is not the will of your Father who is in heaven that one of these little ones perish" (Matthew 18:12-14).

I greatly cherish the fact that Logos School is built on this same conviction.

We are here to foster and nourish the God-given trust children have in the Father, in their parents, and in their teachers. Certainly not each of our students is a Christian. But we've seen even children from ungodly homes eagerly respond to the Bible teaching in each grade. It's almost as if they're starved for it. Consider what the world offers these same little ones. Consider, too, what the world's system of education does to the tender faith and trust of so many little ones who are told, in essence or directly, "there is no God." If we could really understand what is happening in education today, there would be a brisk run on today's equivalent of millstones!

Please remember to pray for us as we seek to build and nourish that trust and faith that so many of our students bring with them to Logos. "And whoever receives one such child in My name receives Me" (Matt. 18:5).

* * *

*As Dorothy Sayers said, "the child I know best is the one I once was." She was right. Although our childhood is a very small part of our lives, relatively, the times and experiences we have during that period form indelible memories we go back to many times. Working around children for many years, I am constantly reminded of my youth, misspent in some ways, but it's the only one I had! And perhaps others may benefit from my errors in judgement during those years...*

"A FRIEND LOVES AT ALL TIMES..."

It seemed like a good idea at the time. Dudley and I were going to give those girls a lesson in maturity. Like us, they were fifteen years old, but unlike us, they were still trick-or-treating on that Halloween night. How juvenile! So, being dressed all in black, we had been able to sneak up on them, snatch their grocery bag full of candy, and dash behind my house. We were also equipped with the means to spend a fun-filled, mature Halloween: we had pockets stuffed with cherry bombs. "Quick! Light this one and we'll drop it in the bag!", Dudley commanded, as we stood gasping over the candy bag, hearing the girls' shouts from the other side of the house. I scraped a match into flame, touched it to the fuse on the firecracker in Dudley's trembling hand. He threw it into the open bag, and we leapt for cover. The resulting blast and rain of shards of candy were all that we could have hoped for.

As you might predict, cooler, but grim, adult heads saw the act as something other than a lesson in maturity for the girls. The adults (including my parents) helped us to see the folly of our ways in short order.

## They can give my children, and their other friends, a rich trove of memories of shared, worthwhile experiences.

It didn't help my defense at all to try to blame it on Dudley (in his absence, of course). By some ridiculous, convoluted use of ethics my parents felt I was equally responsible. Imagine! If only I had been born twenty-five years later, I probably could have convinced them that I was a victim of peer-abuse, or something.

Obviously, my friends haven't always operated with my best interest at heart. Proverbs, on the other hand, speaks about the value of true friends, including their long-lasting love, the preciousness of their sometimes painful, but honest advice ("better than the kisses of an enemy"), and the richness of a man who has many friends. I once heard a wise man refer to good friends as "special gifts of God."

Most often kids take their friends, and the privilege of having them, for granted. That's not surprising; kids take most good things for granted. But as we begin a new year at Logos, I am once again reminded of one of the immense blessings these students enjoy; the vast majority of them will be able to spend the next nine months working, playing, eating, and just talking with good friends. Sure, some friends will be closer, even "as a brother" as Scripture describes, than others. But even the everyday friends will have much to offer in terms of support, laughter, and just good companionship.

I have said before that I envy the education my own children are getting. That includes the unique, warm atmosphere their peers offer them at school. I also know this hasn't come about by accident or good luck. My children's friends largely come from families who are teaching them to love the Lord and their neighbors as themselves. This translates into boys and girls who I love to welcome into our home. They can give my children, and their other friends, a rich trove of memories of shared, worthwhile experiences.

On the other hand, many times in admissions interviews I have heard of "friends" being blamed for a student's poor behavior and rebellion to his parents. I tend to think that it is very likely that the parents of those other "friends" say the very same thing about their own kids. Must be the spread of that nebulous peer-abuse, or something, so prevalent today.

I'm not unaware of the kids at Logos who are not always the best of friends, or of their unkindness toward others. Nevertheless, I rejoice in the fact the my children and the children of most of the parents in Logos will actually enjoy their time at school in the coming school year due in great measure to the good friends with whom they will share it. Believe me, Dudley and I never had it that good! Welcome back to Logos, my young friends!

# 3

## "ONE FISH, TWO FISH"—CLASSICAL INSTRUCTION AND CURRICULUM

*Adopting and understanding the idea of a "classical" education are two different things. As a school, we adopted the idea of classical education from before the doors opened in 1981. But like all worthwhile ideas, there is much more to this than we originally thought, and we are still in the beginning stages of understanding what a classical education is, not to mention how to impart it to our young proteges. Nevertheless, I trust we have at least begun to scratch the surface. The following articles reflect my own interpretation of the application of classical instruction at Logos. For a more thorough discussion of our classical philosophy, I would recommend reading Doug Wilson's book,* Recovering the Lost Tools of Learning.

\* \* \*

### "NOTHING OLD UNDER THE SUN"

Is there anything which one might say, "See this, it is new"? Already it has existed for ages which were before us. There is no remembrance of earlier things; and also of the later things which will occur, there will be for them no remembrance among those who will come later still.
~Ecclesiastes 1:10-11

"The century is turning soon. America is in the throes of a great technological revolution, the like of which has never been seen on earth. Our military can stand up to the best any other country has to offer. In fact, if push comes to shove (as it looks like it might in another part of the world where a dictator is throwing his weight around), we are able to and ready to show him what's what. Our standard of living has never been higher. The economy is strong, though many complain anyway. The great thinkers of our time are urging us to make even more progressive changes in education to prepare our students for the coming new millennium, with the cry that the world is changing so fast and profoundly that only new ideas and teaching will help our children cope in this new world ... of the *20th* century. After all, this is the 1890's!"

Sounds very familiar, doesn't it? One hundred years ago this month our country did indeed match the description above. Instead of Saddam, though, it was the Spanish dictator in Cuba we were bothered by. In fact, President McKinley requested, and Congress granted, a declaration of war against Spain at about this time. The war in Cuba was to have profound consequences for the United States (and the world) in the coming century. For one thing, it battle-hardened our greatest 20th century president, Theodore Roosevelt. (But that's another story.)

# We can and should study and learn from "earlier things," and teach our children not to despise the learning of lessons from history.

We are hearing, reading, watching the same kind of endless verbiage one hundred years later. "The century is turning, the century is turning! We must warn the people!" But if the Bible is to be believed, King Solomon was the first to essentially coin the phrase, "Been there, done that!"

However, please note that not only does he say that there is nothing really new under the sun, he also says that people will always forget what went before, i.e. not know or understand history. In other words, Solomon also says there is nothing really "old" under the sun either. We can and should study and learn from "earlier things," and teach our children not to despise the learning of lessons from history.

In Donald Kagan's excellent book, *On the Origins of War*, he compares with great insight the incredible similarities between the Peloponnesian War and World War I, as well as other wars of antiquity with "modern" wars. True, there is a lot of technical difference between the sword and shields of the Greek battles and the Precision Guided Munitions (PGMs) and satellite tracking used in the recent Gulf War. Nevertheless, Solomon still speaks truly. Technology, particularly the computer, is one of the gods of this age and culture. But like all false gods, its worship does not, nor can it redeem or sanctify its disciples. Our nature remains Adamic, and therefore in need of the Second Adam's nature.

Education, like technology, cannot save. But as Solomon points out, certain kinds of learning are valuable while some are foolish. A valuable education includes examining and learning rightly from the earlier, or former things. Even children passing into or yet to be born in the overrated 21st century will need exposure to timeless lessons, just as children did in every previous century. God's Word is not silent about preparing each succeeding generation educationally. We are not "pushing the envelope" in education or anywhere else. In fact, it wouldn't be hard to make a case that we are a millennium or two *behind* the Greeks in training the minds of our progeny for the future.

Classical, Christian education does not rely on just teaching the history of the Greco-Roman period for its strength and benefit. Certainly there is much to gain from the study of that formative period of our Western culture. But the real strength of this education comes from the synthesis that Solomon's wisdom indicated the healthy marriage of using timeless, true *methods* and *topics* for teaching, all the while acknowledging God's sovereignty and instruction in all things. While there is nothing really "new" to learn, there is nothing so "old" that it is unworthy of study by students entering the 21st century. And, by God's grace, in examining history and the world around us as it has been, and is, our children can certainly learn more that is *worthwhile* and useful than we did. That, and God's grace, will be of immeasurable help in preparing them for the "later things which will occur."

\* \* \*

## ALL CURRICULUMS ARE NOT CREATED EQUAL

To many people outside educational circles, the term "curriculum" is another word for policies or, almost as exciting, "guidelines." Even those individuals within or profoundly interested in education often misuse the term. So it shouldn't be surprising that one of the most frequent questions I am asked by prospective parents inquiring into Logos is "What kind of curriculum do you use?" And what they are really asking is, "What publisher(s) do you buy your texts from?"

> **There is a tremendous danger in relying on the texts alone to be the final authority as to what is taught in any given area of study.**

Let's set the record straight. "Curriculum," as defined by the two sources I looked at, is "All the courses of study offered by an educational institution." The word itself comes from the Latin word "currere," meaning "course," or "to run." So we see that any school's curriculum is actually made up of the entire course, or track, laid out for the students to complete.

Obviously, the materials selected as tools to implement the school's selected course are extremely important. However, they certainly do not, and should not be regarded as the final say in what principles and ideas are being emphasized. There is a tremendous danger in relying on the texts alone to be the final authority as to what is taught in any given area of study. Case in point: the recent wave of concern brought about by gross errors being found in many widely used secular U.S. History texts. The final tally, as reported in an article in the Wall Street Journal, was about 5,200 mistakes! But let us not be too hasty; it probably won't mentally destroy a child to grow up thinking that FDR died in 1944 instead of 1945; or that Napoleon won at Waterloo; or that Truman used an A-bomb on Korea in the 50's. There is far more to life than being accurate with information from history, isn't there?

A far more insidious danger in relying too heavily on any one textbook publisher, Christian or secular, is the implicit worldview found in every textbook ever published. When Logos first began, we adopted virtually all the materials we used in the school from a single, popular Christian publisher. Because of our preset philosophy on education and God's Word, we quickly became disenchanted with this publisher. Why? Simply because it taught, in addition to the basic content, that out-of-context Bible passages could be shoehorned into just about any subject. It also discouraged the application of biblical principles in approaching a subject, and instead, relied on stating opinions as truth. This served to force us to reexamine why we taught what we taught in our overall course for Logos, i.e. it forced us to develop our own curriculum guide and objectives, in addition to our philosophy and goals. Unfortunately, many Christian and homeschools blithely assume that "if it's a Christian publisher, it must be OK." In addition to the publisher's worldview, overall quality of the text is often overlooked or excused on the basis of the text's "Christian" status. But including Christian doctrine is no excuse for textbooks to have outdated data in science, or unclear charts in history, or incorrect grammar in English.

Now that I've shot at the Christian side of curriculums, let me point the gun in the opposite direction. Christian parents who have their children in a public school and, because their children appear to be doing well morally and academically, never closely examine that school's curriculum are like the followers of Crazy Horse. In the late 1800's, a number of Indians believed, because of Crazy Horse's teaching, that if they did a special dance, the white men's bullets wouldn't harm them, and, even more, the white men would leave. The wounds these students are receiving are mental and spiritual; the wounds may not bleed , but they will just as effectively cripple and maim the student's thinking for years to come. News flash: Secular curriculums today not only disregard accuracy in History, they actively ignore the biblical tradition of our country; they frequently promote homosexuality as an acceptable lifestyle; they often have a pro-abortion stance; and they belittle a traditional family structure. They do all this and more, without any warning labels on the covers!

It matters what curriculum your child is following:

> Have a care what you are after; you are teaching children; mind what you are doing. Put poison in the spring, and it will impregnate the whole stream. Take care what you are after, sir! You are twisting the sapling, and the old oak will be bent thereby.
> ~Charles Spurgeon

# DEAR PARENTS

\* \* \*

*It was Solomon who said, "There is nothing new under the sun," and that applies as much to the ageless discussion on educating children, as anything else. Which makes it all the more imperative for us to seek out the words of the Ageless One when we seek to teach these little ones.*

IN OTHER WORDS...

Every once in a while it becomes necessary to get back to the basics of what you're doing. For example, I believe it was Vince Lombardi who, after his football team had done a rather poor job of playing a game, gathered his team together and as he displayed the pigskin spheroid, said, "Men, this is a football."

I don't think we've "dropped the ball" recently; I would just like to offer some interesting quotes from rather well-known individuals who had strong views about educating children. As I hope you will notice, the debate about how children should be educated is an old one. Ideas have consequences and, depending on the ideas, the consequences can be a blessing to generations or a horror to fight against. Here is just a short offering of a variety of ideas:

> It is better to tolerate the rare instance of a parent refusing to let his child be educated, than to shock the common feelings and ideas by the forcible asportation and education of the infant against the will of the father.
> ~Thomas Jefferson

> When an opponent declares, "I will not come over to your side," I calmly say, "Your child belongs to us already...What are you? You will pass on. Your descendants, however, now stand in the new camp. In a short time they will know nothing else but this new community.
> ~Adolf Hitler

> The family was the first institution created by God, even before the state. Because it was the first, it can be considered to be the founda-

tional institution upon which all others are built. It is within the family that children learn how to worship God and how to be effective and productive citizens.
~John W. Whitehead

What the church had been for medieval man, the public school must now become for democratic and rational man. God would be replaced by the concept of the Public Good, sin and guilt by the more positive virtues of Victorian morality...
~Horace Mann

A general state education is a mere contrivance for molding people to be exactly like one another; and as that mold in which it cast them is that which pleases the predominant power in the government, whether this be a monarch, a priesthood, or an aristocracy, or the majority of the existing generation, in proportion as it is efficient and successful, it establishes a despotism over the mind, leading by natural tendency to one over the body.
~John Stuart Mill

Fathers, do not exasperate your children; instead, bring them up in the nurture and instruction of the Lord.
~God (as expressed by Paul, Eph. 6:4)

May God have the final word in all areas of our lives and the lives of our children.

\* \* \*

*I freely admit that the following two areas I choose to write on because they are my favorite disciplines. But they also serve to illustrate how your philosophy or worldview, affects literally everything. I'm very thankful for the education my children are receiving; I am also extremely thankful for the reeducation I am receiving, also.*

## "DON'T KNOW MUCH ABOUT HISTORY…"

> The religion which has introduced civil liberty is the religion of Christ and His apostles. This is genuine Christianity and to this we owe our free constitutions of government.
>
> ~Noah Webster, 1832

I truly hope that someday history books will label American education in the latter half of the twentieth century as "The Era of Foolish Experimentation With Neutrality." If our times are thus labeled, it might indicate that as a nation we had come to recognize "neutrality" in education as the absurd lie that it is. It would also indicate that the historians were desirous of passing on to future generations the painful lessons we learned from this era, in the hope of preventing a repeat of this nonsense. God repeatedly states in His Word that there is nothing outside of His domain: "the earth is His footstool." Yet, there are still many wide-eyed, true-believers, Christian and non-Christian, who hold that it is possible to teach children about the world from a "neutral" or "secular" standpoint. This is not just a bad alternative way to teach; it is wrong and compels those who teach that way to teach falsehoods.

## Yet, in compliance with the myth of neutrality, none of them taught me the full truth about American history.

Case in point: Even after thirteen years of education in primary and secondary schools, and eight years of college, it wasn't until I read some uncensored American history books on my own that I learned at least two immensely important facts. One fact was that our nation was founded on biblical principles, and founded largely by men who acknowledged God the Father and Jesus Christ in their private lives, as well as in the life of the nation. The second thing I learned was that for all those years of my education this predominantly critical truth about our nation's history had been hidden from me (and all my classmates). No doubt many of my teachers were sincere and competent instructors. Some may have even been Christians. Yet, in compliance with the myth of neutrality, none of them taught me the full truth about American history. In anticipation of some Christians who are quick to point out that "not every one of our founding fathers were Christians"—frankly, that's not the point. The fact remains that the United States of America is a profoundly unique nation due to its inception by men who, as a body, recognized the God of the Bible as their Benefactor and His truths as indispensable.

How important is this truth about our history? Imagine, if you can, any government official today, avowed Christian or not, using the language Noah Webster used in 1832 (above). This is just one quote among thousands by other founding fathers and early American government figures. I have been overwhelmed by the amount of Christian U.S. history I was never taught. John Quincy Adams, Robert E. Lee, "Stonewall" Jackson, William McKinley, even H.J. Heinz (of ketchup fame) were godly, publicly Christian men. Did that fact influence the way they lived and led in their time and culture? Absolutely! The downright scary part of all this is that, for the secularists to acknowledge and teach the significant acts of these men, without acknowledging their Christianity, the historical truth must be altered, or "revised."

And that is exactly what is happening, or being overtly proposed by diverse groups in education today. The new, proposed national standards coming out of a committee from U.C.L.A. have set up battle lines between the "revisionists" and the old-schoolers. Should these standards become truly national in scope and application, historical illiteracy will hit an all-time high. The resulting consequences in our culture could be devastating. As Lincoln said, "The philosophy in the classrooms of this generation will be the philosophy of the government in the next generation."

It matters what children are taught, who teaches them, and what those teachers believe about history, about science ... about the Almighty God.

\* \* \*

"BUT IS IT ART?"

"The kind of world God made is a model of what artists should strive to make and what all people should delight in."
"Art for art's sake!"

Far too many schools, Christian and government, have a very difficult time teaching students about art. But since Logos fits into the first category of schools, let's limit our critique to Christian schools. A definition of sorts is called for here: for the sake of this column, by "art" I mean the renderings, two- and three-dimensional, produced by people using painting, drawing, and sculpting tools. Music, drama, dancing, and other fine arts will have to wait for another day.

Christian schools usually have problems teaching young people about art because often the schools have not developed a clear idea of where to draw the line (pun intended), philosophically and practically speaking. The two quotes above illustrate two of the most frequent battle cries from opposing sides in the philosophy-of-art war. The second quote has its roots in the Enlightenment period in Europe. After man became "the measure of all things" in the Renaissance, it was a small step to all that man *does or makes* becoming autonomous from any Higher authority at all.

It might seem like a no-brainer, by looking at those quotes above, to figure out which side Christian schools should buy into. Unfortunately it is not. Unlike math or science, art is so ... well, subjective. Or so we've all been conditioned to believe. I certainly was. I grew up loving art, but heard opposing views about art all my life. My grandfather, who was a professional illustrator, as well as a talented painter in his own right, taught me that imitating the creation is an excellent way to grow in art. My art teachers, on the other hand, even in elementary school, and certainly in college, directly and indirectly taught me that art is whatever you conceive it to be. Guest "artists" at the university, while most often deriving their bread and butter from the federal coffers, slammed artists like Michelangelo for working for the Catholic Church. Standards like beauty and truth were anathema to these people. And in university art history courses, certain artists, like Andrew Wyeth or Norman Rockwell, who have been extremely popular with the "masses," are adamantly ignored or ridiculed.

> **After man became "the measure of all things" in the Renaissance, it was a small step to all that man does or makes becoming autonomous from any Higher authority at all.**

Scriptures like 1 Corinthians 10:31 teach us that nothing we do is out of God's sovereignty; all we do should be to His glory. Art is certainly no exception, then. OK, most Christian schools would buy that. "But how does that help us teach third graders art? Why isn't giving them a sheet of white construction paper and a handful of crayons and telling them to "draw something" sufficient?" Because we wouldn't do that with anything else we teach them.... "Here, kid, this is called a book. Sit down and read it! And don't ask me pesky questions like what those black marks on the page are."

When the Lord talks about art in His Word, it is always in the context of skilled craftsmen, or those gifted in design work (see the tabernacle construction account in Exodus). In Philippians 4:8, we are commanded to dwell on things of beauty and integrity. Therefore, art can and should be taught to young children initially in the form of basic skills using the whole page, correctly holding the pencil and brush, studying and practicing perspective, mixing colors, and other universal artistic elements. Many times teachers want to allow the children to be "creative," but in Scripture and in the classical method, it is understood that children naturally learn through *imitation*, copying the acts of their elders. At Logos, our in-house designed art curriculum tries to systematically train the elementary students in the requisite skills for art, and complete art projects that combine skills practice with copying from another picture, still life, or design.

At the secondary level, a relatively new art elective in the last few years has been our Painting Masters class. Here the students, after being taught some basic introductory ideas and principles, choose and copy two paintings done by established masters, such as Da Vinci, Rembrandt, Vermeer, Monet, or even Wyeth or Rockwell, to name just a few. To be honest, certain other artists like Picasso and Matisse, are not held up as worth copying because of their obvious fractured worldview and disregard for truth or beauty, as defined by Scripture and creation. The paintings these students have produced, even those with little artistic bent, have elicited many complimentary remarks from other students, staff, and parents. Even visitors have gone out of their way to marvel at the wonderful works these students have produced.

After these students learn the basic skills and imitate masters (as young apprentice artists have done for centuries in Europe), they are far better prepared to construct their own, unique renderings.

Art, just like English, math, and history, is a discipline that can and should be mastered by the average student. In a Christian setting, there is even less excuse than in a pagan setting for doing a poor job instructing students in art. After all, by imitating and relishing the Creation through art, we show tangible praise for what our Creator Father has done. What a great lesson to teach children!

\* \* \*

## REVI(SED)VED HISTORY

The autumn morning was warm, very warm, especially inside the large pavilion. The people standing in line, dressed in their Sunday-best felt the heat, but found that the excitement and anticipation were stronger feelings. Besides, the line was moving quickly into the building and along the partitioned path toward the large, jovial man everyone had come to meet. The man himself, though fairly rotund, seemed to be impervious to the stifling heat in the room. He genuinely enjoyed seeing each person and briefly, but solidly shaking each hand. He met each person's eyes and had a smile or word of welcome to share. Hundreds of people flowed by in a very short time. The security men decided to call it quits long before the kind gentleman was ready, and certainly before the many waiting to meet him were willing to leave. Just before the doors were closed, the last people in line moved forward. The shy little girl, who received a special smile, and her mother were followed by a man with a white handkerchief over his right hand.

William McKinley, president of the United States, cheerfully and warmly reached out his hand to the man with the handkerchief. Instead of extending friendship, Leon Czolgosz extended a revolver from under the white cloth and shoved it into McKinley's stomach, pulling the trigger twice...

The above could have been summed up in the brief words "William McKinley was assassinated in September of 1901 by an anarchist." And in many American history textbooks, if they mention McKinley at all, that sentence is about the amount of coverage they give such an historic event. They certainly won't mention that McKinley was a very strong Christian man who quoted hymns as he died of infection. Or that he lovingly and diligently cared for his handicapped wife, even when campaigning for the presidency.

There isn't room here to go into all the problems with how history is taught, revised, or not taught at all in many schools, private and government. Rather, I would like to share with you the excitement I have about the changes, the reviving we have given our history program. These changes will probably be most obvious in our elementary grades. Over the past year, as per the school board's directive, the curriculum committee reviewed the teaching of history throughout the entire school. This spurred a lot of thought, meetings, and work among the staff members. At the elementary level, we came up with the following basic changes to our history program:

In accordance with the classical philosophy, we will try to make history (and geography) more three-dimensional for the students, through the use of many biographies, historical novels, pictures, artifacts, models, drama, etc., and less reliance on the survey-style textbooks.

Also in line with the grammar stage of the students, we will try to use more repetition and recitation of the key, significant dates, events, and people in history. From grade to grade, these key facts will be repeated.

Each of the elementary grades will have the year broken into eight units of time, of four and a half weeks each, to study one area of history in some depth. For example, fifth graders will study the culture, people, and times of the Greeks during one unit. They will read about the Trojan War and Greek myths, see photos of the Parthenon, hear how to pronounce the names of the Greek heroes, and write their own myths, to name a few activities.

Reading, or a literature-based approach to history, will take precedence as the best way to understand and appreciate the unfolding of history.

Biblical assessments of the actions of men and nations will be easier to bring to bear as the students get a closer look at these actions and people than they do in the survey approach.

A greater emphasis on the rich, biblical heritage the United States has will be part of the objectives for studying U.S. history. Again, through reading honest biographies of godly men like George Washington, William Bradford, and William McKinley will aid toward this goal.

I believe all these, and more ideas we're implementing, will truly make history, and God's Hand in it, more memorable and thereby, more understandable to the students. We believe great books about real people and events in history are far better time machines than anything H.G. Wells could contrive.

The changes we made in our science program two years ago have reaped wonderful benefits; we are praying that our history changes will produce similar results. Your comments and ideas are always welcome and appreciated.

\* \* \*

"THE PLAY'S THE THING..."

All the world's a stage, and all men and women merely players: they have their exits and their entrances; and one man in his time plays many parts...
~William Shakespeare, *As You Like It*

The school play. That's the first thing, and often the last thing, many Christian educators and parents think of when "acting" or "the theater" are mentioned in a school context. That's not all bad, since some Christian educators are reluctant to even have students do acting in a play. Or, if a play is done in a Christian school context, the understanding is that it must be a "Christian" play. Usually these are moralistic pablum stories, full of the fluff and nonsense found in too many modern "Christian" books for children. Little wonder that by high school many Christian school students gag at the thought of being a part of the school play.

There is some historical precedent for Christians to be wary of the theater; the Puritans were highly suspicious, and sometimes outright hostile toward Elizabethan plays. Considering the low morals and ostentation displayed by many of these plays, the Puritans were often justifiably disgusted. At the same time, there is also a historical precedent for considering acting a marvelous and powerful means of communicating scriptural themes and principles. In the Middle Ages, troupes of actors, in and outside of the Church, acted out numerous biblical stories for a largely illiterate population.

A few years ago for our first Knights' Day, an in-house conference day for the secondary students, I offered a seminar entitled "the Spiritual Benefits of Drama." In the talk, I took the liberty of stating that it is my opinion that Jesus Himself in all probability did some acting as He told His many stories. Can't you picture Him using different voices and facial expressions to convey the dynamic story of the good Samaritan? There is nothing holy about a monotone, nor is there anything intrinsically secular about being animated. Jesus communicated powerful images of man's condition and nature: why wouldn't the Creator God in flesh use every tool available to capture and engage His listeners' interest? It is also true that all good gifts come from the Father; among these gifts is the talent we all recognize as acting. Like all gifts, it can be used for good or, as we see pouring out of La-la land, it can be used for evil.

Christian schools, especially classical ones, should include acting, plays, and drama techniques within their curriculum and teaching methodologies for the following very sound reasons:

## Since we are all of Adam's race, stories of human love, tragedy, comedy, mystery, etc. commonly appeal to every generation.

1. Plays, from the short skits in assemblies to the full-blown high school play, all give the students the opportunity to practice poise, confidence,

stage-presence, and public speaking (rhetoric). I have seen shy, soft-spoken first graders, through years of being on the stage, grow into confident, full-voiced actors. They will carry those characteristics with them into adult life.

2. By taking on characters, the students are exposed to other people's thoughts, attitudes, and emotions in a much more tangible way than just reading about them. This is especially true of plays done about historical figures and events. Older students, in order to play a part well, must come to understand and empathize with the setting and characters of the story. This requires them to put aside their own egos and concerns, and for a little while, live and breathe another culture, time, and event.

3. "The show must go on!" is more than a quaint phrase. Students learn that it means just that, and they find out what commitment to a project means.

4. Assuming high-quality, time-tested plays are chosen for production (and why would you chose any others?), the students learn about an important cultural legacy. In Literature class, they learn about great authors and poets; in drama they should learn about great playwrights and their works.

5. Great plays are usually considered that because, among other qualities, they communicate weighty moral themes in a timeless, memorable fashion. Since we are all of Adam's race, stories of human love, tragedy, comedy, mystery, etc. commonly appeal to every generation. We can still learn much about ourselves and see again the truth of Scripture, by watching Shakespeare or ancient Greek dramas, even in 1997. Students performing these plays, even though the pieces are considered secular, can appreciate the biblical principles and allusions found in them, particularly if the principles in Phil. 4:8 are identified.

6. Teaching, in a very real sense, is acting, and the best teachers use drama in their daily presentations. This is not done for entertainment purposes-sometimes a teacher has to really act excited because he is bone-weary. But more often a good teacher uses drama to excite the students' attention through reenactments, pretending, role-playing, speeches, etc.

As with all aspects of a Christian school, having a quality drama program means a lot of work. It should.

It mostly requires a lot of thought and planning, not to mention time, to produce the greatest benefit to the students and the audiences. And it is worth it. Our graduates may forget some of the knowledge from some of their classes, but those that participated in drama never forget it. "It's show time!"

\* \* \*

A CLASSICAL AND CHRIST-CENTERED COMPUTER EDUCATION?

Not long ago I had a personal harmonic conversion, of sorts. That is, I received two pieces of correspondence at about the same time, and addressing the same subject, only from two completely opposite views. The topic they shared was the use of computers in education. The one strongly advocated our buying into a proposed on-line classical education. It came by fax, not surprisingly. The other came from *The New York Times*.

## Are computers critical or just helpful to a quality education?

"Computers in education," as a concept, is a step beyond the initial concern back in the 80's of "computer education." Computers have become as commonplace in schools as no. 2 pencils, if just a tad more expensive to obtain. At Logos we have wrestled with how to approach this overwhelming phenomena ever since the days of buying our first (and only) Atari 400. Do we let this fascinating and growing technology guide our educational philosophy? Will we do the students a disservice in their education by not having cutting-edge equipment in each room? How much should we use computers to teach the students, if at all? Are computers critical or just helpful to a quality education?

The article I received from *The New York Times* said things about using computers in school that I hadn't read or heard anywhere else. It addressed many of those nagging questions with which we wrestle. That being the case, I would like to quote extensively from it:

Promoted as a solution to the crisis in the classroom, computers have been welcomed uncritically across the educational spectrum. So uncritically that, astonishingly, school libraries, art studios, and music rooms are being replaced by computer labs.

What's most important in a classroom? A good teacher interacting with motivated students. Anything that separates them—filmstrips, instructional videos, multimedia displays, Email, TV, interactive computers—is of questionable value.

Plop a kid down before such a [computer software education] program, and the message is, "You have to learn the math tables, so play with this computer." Teach the same lesson with flash cards, and a different message comes through: "You're important to me, and this subject is so useful that I'll spend an hour teaching you arithmetic."

Computers promise short cuts to higher grades and painless learning. Today's edutainment software comes shrink-wrapped in the magic mantra: "makes learning fun."

Equating learning with fun says that if you don't enjoy yourself, you're not learning. I disagree. Most learning isn't fun. Learning takes work. Discipline. Responsibility—you have to do your homework. Commitment from both teacher and student. There's no short cut to a quality education. And the payoff isn't an adrenaline rush, but a deep satisfaction arriving weeks, months, or years later.

Still, isn't it great that the Internet brings the latest events into the classroom? Maybe. Perhaps some teachers lack information, but most have plenty, thank you. Rather, there is too little class time to cover what's available. A shortage of information is not the problem.

One of the most common and illogical arguments for computers in the classroom is that they'll soon be everywhere, so shouldn't they be in schools? One might as well say that since cars play such a crucial role in our society, shouldn't we make driver's ed central to the curriculum? Anyway, computer skills aren't tough to learn. Millions have taught themselves at home. In school, it's better to learn how Shakespeare processed words than how Microsoft does. [I just love that one!]

In conclusion, Clifford Stoll, the author and a published astrophysicist, by the way, says that excessive reliance on using computers as teachers can encourage the students to assume that:

the world is a passive, preprogrammed place, where you need only click the mouse to get the right answer. That relationships developed over E-mail are transitory and shallow. That discipline isn't necessary when you can zap frustrations with a keystroke. That legible handwriting, grammar, analytic thought and human dealings don't matter.

Looking for simple ways to help in the classroom? Eliminate interruptions from school intercoms. Make classes smaller. Respect teachers... Protest multiple-choice exams which discourage writing and analytic thinking. If we must push technology into the classrooms, let's give teachers their own photocopiers so they can avoid the long wait at the school copier. [I know I'm going to regret including that last comment!]

Bottom line: We greatly appreciate and use computers at Logos School. But amazingly helpful as it is, even the wonder-tool of the century should be kept subservient to time-tested, good teaching by living and loving teachers. We'll keep running that premise as our main drive.

\* \* \*

*I had had for some time the strong desire to try to summarize the three stages of the Trivium, as we apply it in Logos. But, for quite a long time, I thought that would be just too boring for the readers of our newsletter. Finally, though, I figured ... why not? I found that it helped me to clarify my own thinking about what we were doing, and I hope it helps you, too.*

DEAR PARENTS

ONE FISH, TWO FISH...

You would think I could have picked up on the idea far earlier than I did. I certainly have had enough clues presented to me, especially by my own progeny over the years. It should have been obvious when Carolyn, at only three years old, "read" aloud the entire story of Sleeping Beauty into a tape player. She was able to do this after hearing her mother and I read it to her for about a zillion nights. (Actually it was probably only a week or two.)

Even with succeeding years and children, I was slow to comprehend the idea. Certainly I should have grasped it when child after child beat the tar out of me at the "Memory Game." Good grief! Why couldn't I remember where the matching animal babies were under those cards? Yet, there I'd be with my children accusing me of not trying hard and "letting" them win. Well, of course I would swallow my pride, and as a mature adult confess to them that ... well, I wanted them to win sometimes.

By now you probably know the idea or phenomena to which I am alluding: the incredible, but innate ability young children have to memorize relatively easily and recall repeated information. Actually, my poor powers of perception notwithstanding, most people recognize this characteristic of young children. Nursery rhymes, the alphabet song, and countless other childhood ditties have been passed along from generation to generation. And for countless generations of Europeans and Americans, it was the tool used by teachers to pass on knowledge to young students. However, for the past several generations in the United States (since about John Dewey's time) applying this God-given gift to educate children has been denigrated and disused. Repelled as anathema or at least as anachronistic, "rote learning," like corporal punishment, has been tossed on the trash heap of "outdated" teaching methods by modern educationists.

**At this age one readily memorizes the shapes and appearances of things; one rejoices in the chanting of rhymes and the rumble and thunder of unintelligible polysyllables...**

Nevertheless, during World War II, Dorothy Sayers observed this about the marvelous memorizing ability children normally have: "The Poll-Parrot stage is the one in which learning by heart is easy and, on the whole, pleasurable; whereas reasoning is difficult and, on the whole, little relished. At this age one readily memorizes the shapes and appearances of things; one likes to recite the number-plates of cars; one rejoices in the chanting of rhymes and the rumble and thunder of unintelligible polysyllables; one enjoys the mere accumulation of things." Otherwise known as the "Grammar Stage" of the medieval Trivium, in a child's life this period seems to last from about age four to about eleven years old. Look at Miss Sayer's description again. Doesn't that sound familiar? Consider just one aspect of her statement—the enjoyment children have in silly sounds. Perhaps Dr. Suess understood this peculiar love children have, too. In any case, he certainly charmed, and continues to charm, millions of children with his wonderful-sounding, multi syllabic words and strange stories.

As you probably already know, Logos has been committed to implementing the Trivium since we began. However, this year in the Logos elementary grades, I believe we have gotten a renewed vision of what's academically possible with these little ones. We have chanted Latin endings for years in third through sixth grades with great success. But this year, with the adoption of some new, Poll-parrot style English grammar materials, and several other teacher-created applications of rote-learning, recitations, chants, and songs, we have seen tremendous results in the kids' abilities to recall the material presented! For example, our second graders' grasp on parts of speech, attained through constant, clever recitations, has even amazed many older students. Our third graders have begun doing "State Facts" several times a day. The teacher announces, "State Facts!" Immediately the students take turns popping up and shouting out special facts about each state studied to date. It takes just a few minutes, but they obviously all know the facts by heart and enjoy the exercise.

These improvements and innovations have charged me up like few things have in recent years. We are in the process of making these and other new grammar methods a lasting part of our elementary curriculum. I am very pleased and excited for our current and future students. I believe as we study them more, and seek to apply time-proven, successful methods of teaching, that is, methods that take advantage of this God-given learning tool, we can expect even greater educational success for these young ones. It only makes sense: God has designed the world in such a way that when we use anything the way God designed it to be used, His blessing is usually obvious in the outcome.

Please don't stop praying for His wisdom to be poured out on our staff and school!

\* \* \*

### SECRET DECODER RINGS & NANCY DREW; OR TRIVIUM II

"Now it's time for Little Orphan Annie's secret message just for you kids that have one of Annie's secret decoder rings!" Many preteens in the 1930's listened eagerly for this message on the weekly radio program. Even my mother admits to having one of Annie's secret decoder rings. What was the appeal to these kids? Was this just a unique sign-of-the-times for Depression-era America? Or was this just another manifestation of a universal urge and interest of kids in that age-group?

Quite a few years later, another generation found the first Nancy Drew mysteries to be great, nonstop, page-turning reading. Again, the age group most attracted to these short books were the young adolescents of the time. They were not exactly the height of Western literature, yet these books were extremely popular probably due to the stock formulas in each: the young sleuths beating the bad adults (and thinking faster than the good adults) at a "game" of clues. Again, was this just a passing fancy?

The traits mentioned above the fascination with puzzles, the desire to "beat-out" adults, the urge to figure it all out are not unique to any generation of people. They do seem to be most evident in children of a certain age-group, however. Little children and older teens are not as enthralled with the above kinds of activities. Generally speaking, it appears that kids from about ten or eleven to about fourteen or fifteen are prime for what Dorothy Sayers calls the "Pert Stage." Here is how she described them in "The Lost Tools of Learning": "The Pert age, which follows upon this [the Poll-Parrot Age] (and naturally, overlaps it to some extent) is characterized by contradicting, answering back, liking to "catch people out" (especially one's elders) and in the propounding of conundrums. Its nuisance-value is extremely high. It usually sets in about the eighth grade."

Here at Logos, we have discovered that this Pert age frequently sets in earlier than eighth grade for most kids. Perhaps that has to do with the overall shortening of childhood we see in our culture at large. In any case, the Pert age seems to correspond nicely with our junior high program (seventh and eighth grades). These students want to know the why's and wherefore's of the material, and they have a propensity to argue and debate. Therefore, we seek to channel their desires to our own ends. We teach them formal Logic in eighth grade to give them the necessary structures for sound arguments. We try to allow debates (watching for hurt feelings) that rehash historic and/or spiritual issues. These students also possess vast stores of energy. Therefore, in the daily classes, we often use role-playing to help the kids exercise their thinking and oral skills on their feet. The junior high drama productions are also a great place to see these characteristics put into practice. Other applicable and successful teaching methods for this age include puzzles, review games, position papers, hands-on projects (such as maps and displays in geography, or experiments and demonstrations in science), and good old Socratic questioning techniques.

## These students want to know the why's and wherefore's of the material, and they have a propensity to argue and debate.

The goal, as with the Poll-Parrot and Poetic, the other stages of learning, is to take advantage of the natural, God-given traits students have and match them to the time-proven process of teaching and learning, i.e. the Trivium. Done well, this method of learning can be at least as interesting to the kids as a decoder ring, and a lot more useful to them in later life.

\* \* \*

## WOODSTOCK AND PAUL THE APOSTLE, OR TRIVIUM III

"Going up to Yasgar's farm, gonna join a rock-and-roll band, gonna get back to the land and set my soul free".... So sang Crosby, Stills, Nash, and Young in celebration of the biggest, muddiest, campout ever seen. Over a quarter of a million young adults spent three rainy, drug-hazed days in a field in upper New York, having their hearing and most other senses threatened, if not destroyed, at the rock concert of the century. (And, no, this isn't the voice of experience!) Woodstock was held in August of 1969, symbolically the nadir (or zenith, depending on how you look at it) of the hippie movement that began in the sixties and burned out in the early seventies.

Aside from the plethora of bizarre and immoral manifestations of that era, some observations can be made about the basic, similar characteristics of those young people. I would submit that the majority of them (us) were smack dab in the midst of what Dorothy Sayers would call the "Poetic Age!" I know I was and I don't think I was alone. Harken unto Miss Sayers' description:

> The Poetic Age is popularly known as the "difficult" age. It is self-centered [!!!]; it yearns to express itself ["All we are saying..."]; it rather specializes in being misunderstood ["People try to put us d-d-down..."]; it is restless and tries to achieve independence ["Born to be wild..." But there's hope.] and, with good luck and good guidance, it should show the beginnings of creativeness, a reachingout towards a synthesis of what it already knows, and a deliberate eagerness to know and do some one thing in preference to all others.

She goes on to say that a fair amount of latitude should be given these students to pursue an area of special interest, while encouraging them to see the overall integration of knowledge. Individual subjects, as such, now meld into a wider view, a biblically-based view, of the world.

**It is during this age, then, that Rhetoric—the skill of speaking and writing well and convincingly is so suitable for mastery.**

It is during this age, then, that Rhetoric the skill of speaking and writing well and convincingly is so suitable for mastery. Every former "subject" becomes a form of grist for the mill of expression. These students now delight in expressing their thoughts and opinions. It has been the work of prior teachers and training to equip them with ability to recognize supportive facts (Grammar), and the appropriate connections of those facts (Logic).

Now they are trained to use that prior work and skillfully express a synthesis of knowledge. At Logos, during their Rhetoric classes, our juniors and seniors are required to research, write, and then defend several theses before a committee of teachers. They are assisted in the construction of the papers by those teachers who have expertise in the topic chosen by the student. But the topical premise must stretch across more than one subject or field.

In Acts we see Paul the Apostle using his rhetorical skills for the glory of God; "And according to Paul's custom, he went to them, and for three Sabbaths reasoned with them from the Scriptures, explaining and giving evidence ... and some of them were persuaded and joined Paul and Silas...." (Acts 17:3-4). Our senior, elective Apologetics course is a very popular class. It very nicely combines the skills of rhetoric with the knowledge needed to proclaim the truths of Scripture, as Paul did. Some of our graduates have remarked on the applicable benefits they have used in the "outside" world, from the skills and knowledge they obtained in their Rhetoric and Apologetics classes.

In addition, while the school maintains a standard number of required credits for our seniors, as young people eager to do "some one thing in preference to others," they are allowed to choose among a number of classes. This choice includes the option of university classes and/or an approved independent study. Many of the independent studies take the form of apprenticeship with professionals in the community. We have heard many positive comments about this aspect of our high school program, from students, parents, and the business community.

So, the Woodstock generation notwithstanding, there is a lot to gain from and offer to students in the Poetic Age. We are very delighted to see that our graduates regard and emulate Paul the Apostle more than Peter, Paul, and Mary!

\* \* \*

## HOW FIRM A FOUNDATION?

It has been said in various contexts that you can't make a good omelet with rotten eggs. Along the same lines, C.S. Lewis stated that no matter how much or how good the wine is, if you pour it into a mud puddle, you still have a mud puddle. Jesus Himself referred to the same kind of predicament, i.e. wasting something valuable on an unworthy or unready recipient. He called it "casting pearls before swine."

Classical, Christian education is a valuable commodity and to gain the fullest possible benefit from it, students need to come to it with a home-developed foundation. Put another way, there are certain intrinsic characteristics of the families whose students do well in this kind of education. When these characteristics are absent, it is very likely that in spite of the best efforts of the school and teachers, the student will gain little. The following is not intended to be the exhaustive compilation of those characteristics, but they should serve as examples to illustrate the point. The order of their presentation is rather random, since they all relate.

"Moral training" is the big "E" on the eye chart of prerequisite characteristics. Put even more plainly, children coming from homes where God's Word is honored and obeyed will see a profound similarity in the expectations at school regarding their behavior. Homes that identify sin as sin, expect cheerful obedience, show love and forgiveness consistently will find the school's standards will reinforce those biblical principles.

> **Listen to how students talk; if the subject of parents comes up at all, it takes very little astuteness to determine the health of the student's view of his parents.**

But how does that kind of training practically look at school? What are some even more precise evidences of a firm foundation that enables a student to get the most out of the school's program? One very obvious evidence is the student's view of authority in general, and his parents' authority in particular. A good measure of the student's regard for authority is the love boys show to their mothers, and the respect girls display for their fathers. Listen to how students talk; if the subject of parents comes up at all, it takes very little astuteness to determine the health of the student's view of his parents.

Another related characteristic is old-fashioned etiquette or manners. In the past, good manners were referred to as the "oil" of maintaining good relations with others in public. It is not a sin, per se, for a boy not to hold the door for a girl, but it is probably an indicator that his training in being a gentleman is not complete. The way a child speaks to an adult, the way he sits or slouches in his desk, and other numerous little acts that show respect for others, especially the elderly, speak volumes about that student.

A firm foundation also shows up in the way a student "filters" the plethora of cultural messages. Is there evidence of growing biblically-based discernment, or does the student generally accept almost every attractive, popular theme at face value? Legalistic rejection is not biblical discernment any more than is a wide-eyed, "I-wanna-be-hip" attitude. Biblical discernment takes a lot of study, time, and a willingness to stand alone at times. "Wise as serpents, innocent as doves" sums it up quite well.

A student's appearance billboards both his respect for others and his family's training in discernment. Even in the secular world, appearance is recognized as the message-sending device it is. Dress should not be THE means to determine success, but it is a lie to tell children that it doesn't matter at all. Even young children understand the difference "dressing up" makes in how they are to regard their activity. All little girls want to look pretty at a wedding, and all young boys want to wear their team uniform with pride. A student who supposedly doesn't care about his appearance actually cares too much for himself and not enough for those who have to see him. This attitude profoundly affects his teachability.

A firm foundation provides a student with a solid work ethic, i.e. standards of doing a job well. This goes beyond just being honest and not cheating on the test. Doing their work "as unto the Lord" practically means they don't have a "is-this-going-to-be-on-the-test?" mentality toward the acquisition and value of knowledge. Most often the students with a strong work ethic, who sweat bullets for every B they get, will fair far better in the adult world than those gifted students who breezily accept their A's.

Finally, parents will improve their students' opportunity to gain much from a classical, Christian education by ensuring that they (the parents) understand, value, and teach the purpose of this education. It is not enough to send the kids and pay the tuition the parents must be able to articulate the reasons they are doing this and help their children understand it as well. Otherwise it will only be one more program dad and mom sign their kids up for, like summer swimming or piano lessons. Do you want this type of education for your *grand*children? If not, or if it doesn't make any difference to you, then consider going with something cheaper and easier. If so, than it must be understood to be valuable by your children. They will pass on only what *they* value, for all else will drop away with the passing of their parents' generation.

How firm is the foundation? As we look at the students here at Logos, there are evidences of many, many deeply sunk pylons; may God be pleased to allow us all to build upon them well.

\* \* \*

MARIO ISN'T SO TOUGH

Long after most of the civilized world became obsessed by it, our family decided to invest in the infamous Nintendo game machine. It was just the plain old Mario I kind, before Sega and even before the now virtually antiquated 64 version. We even used a TV to play it on! (For you grandparents, this is the equivalent of recalling days of walking to school five miles each day, up hill both ways.) The problem came when anyone over thirty tried to play it. At least that's the logical assumption I came to, since *I* was over thirty and didn't stand a chance of doing nearly as well on it as even my youngest child. Therefore, I assume ALL adults had trouble with it.

But my kids, particularly Seth, could and did repeatedly whip right through it. I think he mastered it as I was taking the game box packaging out to the garbage can. But he was patient when I played it and would point out why I got shrunk once again. "You forgot to jump and bump that spot with his head," he would calmly point out. "But there's nothing but blue SKY there!" I would mildly respond, as Mario cheerily leaped to his death yet again. "Well, you just have to KNOW where to jump," was Seth's confident reply.

The computer age has probably generated more comments and anecdotes like the one above than there are blonde jokes. Who *hasn't* heard a parent say, with some obvious pride in his voice, "Yes, junior figured out our new 3,000 gig, 900 meg ram, artificial intelligence-loaded PC much faster than we could. So we're letting him do our taxes on it this year." Or words to that effect.

Is this phenomenon unique to mankind with the advent of computers? Or do parents always respond with incredulity when seeing their kids do more than they did at the same age (or even older)? I submit the latter is universally true. Whatever we as parents experienced in our tender, formative years naturally, but unfortunately, becomes the template we hold up to our own children's experiences. It's natural because that was the only childhood we knew; it's unfortunate because our children may just be able to do and learn more than we did, but we can discourage them in our comparisons. For instance, the classic, "When I was your age..." can have a particularly negative effect when applied to educational standards. Yet, we say we want more for our children then we received, but do we really?

The classical, Christian school resurgence has spawned a rather strange but predictable side-effect among parents. In most places where the idea of starting a school based on this philosophy takes root, there is, as in the parable of the sower, an almost immediate enthusiastic embracing of the idea. Parents spring up and cry with joy when they see and hear the first fruits of their children's learning in the grammar stage. The rhyming, chanting, singing, and memorization seem to almost work miracles of instruction. "That's my Johnny parsing that sentence!" We're so very proud! Gee, we think (or actually say) that the only Latin I ever learned was 'pig-latin!' But after a few years, an ominous change seems to take place. "Hey, they're making my little Johnny WORK! *I* sure never had to do that much homework or study so hard for a test or write such a long paper or..." (Exactly!) What was initially welcomed with joy now seems burdensome and possibly repellent to us.

## This type of education is much harder on the parents than it is on the children.

Certainly classical schools can, in their zeal to excel, place too great a burden too quickly on the backs or minds of young students. But I have to be candid with you; after observing our own as well as many other similar schools across the United States, the conclusion I have come to is this: This type of education is much harder on the parents than it is on the children. As parents, we are compelled to protect our children from all sorts of aches, pains, illnesses, and burdens. So it is natural to be concerned for them when schoolwork seems overwhelming. The problem is that we have not resisted the laziness of our age to the shedding of blood, to re-phrase a good verse. Or, in other, less dramatic terms perhaps, our threshold for the pain of academic work is often much lower than that of our own children. Remember: this is the only childhood they know. They have no experience with anything different from what they are receiving. If they are loved and consistently supported through the years, this will be as natural to them as the pets they own. Whereas, when we compare our memories with their current experiences, we tend to forget that children can frequently rise to expectations never presented to us. Classical education, like anything truly valuable, does require work to acquire, and lots of it. The wonderful advantage of such an education comes because not only do children naturally accept it but classical education, taught well, also naturally fits the child. Grammar techniques appeal to young, eager learners, logical instruction challenges and channels young teens' feistiness, and rhetorical skills equip young adults to be confident and knowledgeable in front of others-a matter of some concern to that age.

Classical education is not "fun," but it fits. It isn't easy, but it does cut with the grain. It is work that over and over again is proving its worth. Ask our grads and their parents. The patient hardship endured by the parents over the years has been of great benefit to their children, as it should be. Such are the blessings of one generation to another. For these young ones, Mario is nothing compared to what they are capable of, if *we* can hang on!

\* \* \*

COMPELLED TO MATURE

> For though by this time you ought to be teachers, you have need again for someone to teach you the elementary principles of the oracles of God, and you have come to need milk and not solid food.... But solid food is for the mature, who because of practice have their senses trained to discern good and evil.
> ~Hebrews 5:12, 14

One of the most delightful traditions Logos enjoys is Alumni Day. I love to see and hear from our graduates. Inevitably, when they visit the school, we will hear one or more of them comment on the changes we have made since their tenure. "It figures! You guys wait until WE leave to do X!" Every graduating class seems to think we purposely wait for their particular class to graduate before we try to make any improvements in the programs or the facility. What nonsense! That's only true with a few classes...

## Institutions are not exempt from the inevitability of change.

Someone has said the only constancy is change. We all know that, but we still often resist change for a variety of reasons, many stemming from the fear of the unknown future. Where will this change take us? Every adult can look back on his transition from childhood to adulthood and recall the tremulous times of change that, hopefully, resulted in maturity.

Institutions are not exempt from the inevitability of change. Logos School is housed in a physical environment that certainly has seen changes, and those are probably the easiest changes to identify. But families and staff members who have been with the school for a fair number of years know that Logos has changed greatly in many ways that have nothing to do with the facility. I recall our first and early years with a great amount of fondness. There was indeed something special about the intimacy and excitement of working with a small group of students and families. But just like the brevity of a honeymoon compared to the day-today, year-to-year work of a solid marriage, Logos had to grow and mature past its cozy beginnings to become the full-scale school its planners envisionedInstitutions are not exempt from the inevitability of change.

Logos has a two-part motto: "A classical and Christ-centered education." Both aspects of that motto compel us toward maturity. For the first aspect, we must constantly seek to understand and apply the benefits of a classical education. To do that we must address and apply the answers to questions like: What did a historical classical education look like in its prime? Are those expectations realistic for our students? How should/can we modify certain 20th century content to fit into the classical model? How many of our cultural ideas of education are worth retaining? How quickly can we realistically expect to recover what has been lost? Are parents willing to exchange "modern" views of education for older, proven methods? These are just a few of the questions that we consider as an institution. The answers will continue to directly affect the kinds of work the students do in the classrooms every day, from kindergarten through twelfth grade.

The second aspect also compels us to change and mature. As the passage in Hebrews directs, all Christians are to be maturing in their understanding and application of the Word. There is no plateau for spiritual grazing. The men and women who work, teach, and lead in Logos School are to be Christians in training. They should be growing in their discernment of God's Word and seeking its blessings for themselves, their students, and the school as a whole. Being a non-denominational school does not mean being a static, biblically immature institution. If the individuals who work here are growing more Christ-like, as they are commanded, then the school should recognize and reap the benefits of that growth. Therefore, Logos should call for and illustrate more spiritual maturity through its staff and program now than it did in 1981, or 1987, or 1996.

Changes in either or both of the above aspects, classical and Christian, have caused concern in families and patrons of Logos School. "Where will these changes take us?" Some may legitimately question whether the changes are necessary or right: Will the kids get burned-out if we go too fast, or make the program too hard? Why is Latin given so much emphasis? Is the school becoming Reformed in its view of Scripture? Is there enough (too much, too little) emphasis on the kids' spiritual lives? Good questions and all requiring an increasing amount of discernment by those leading Logos School. We can and must be constantly looking to the One who compels us to maturity for the wisdom to practice that maturity. Change will come; the only options we have are being surprised by it, or planning by and with God's grace to implement change to His glory.

Please keep us in your prayers as we strive to grow in discernment.

\* \* \*

A MILITANT, CHRIST-CENTERED EDUCATION

Eighty-three years ago this month almost all of Europe's kingdoms determined that war with their neighbors was necessary to defend their respective honors. Each monarch envisioned a war in which their brave, noble young men would gallop into a blaze of glory and bring home the victory. Interestingly, the monarchs all also believed that the Almighty God was with them in their cause, and they roused their people to fight for Him and the Mother or Father-land.

The survivors of that war called it "the Great War." We call it just World War I. Rather than the glory envisioned by rulers from the previous century, World War I slaughtered almost an entire generation of young men, not to mention millions of innocent civilians. It brought down almost every monarch involved, even the "victorious" ones, and set the world stage for the next, inevitable, larger war.

One of the many reasons WWI was so catastrophic is that even the "enlightened" British, not to mention the anachronistic Russians, ordered wave after wave of men on foot or horses straight into the sights of German machine guns. One Teutonic soldier so armed could mow down hundreds of British "Tommies," regardless of their grand and glorious purpose.

There are thousands of Christian schools in the United States alone, not to mention worldwide. Yearly they graduate hundreds of thousands of students who go out into a God-hating culture. But is the "invasion" of these students similar to the Allies' on D-Day, 1944, i.e. hard fighting, but a victorious first step toward recapturing lost territory? Or is it more similar to the guns of August, 1914? I would submit that a lot of Christian school graduates quickly disappear into a kind of societal "no-man's-land." That may sound a bit dramatic, but if measured in terms of making marked inroads, arresting our culture's decline, I think it's an appropriate comparison. Victory doesn't seem any closer.

Dorothy Sayers saw the same sad condition in her day:

## Because while these students *may* be taught generally WHAT to think, they are not being taught HOW to think.

For we let our young men and women go out unarmed in a day when armor was never so necessary. By teaching them to read, we have left them at the mercy of the printed word. By the invention of the film and the radio, we have made certain that no aversion to reading shall secure them from the incessant battery of words, words, words. They do not know what the words mean; they do not know how to ward them off or blunt their edge or fling them back; they are a prey to words in their emotions instead of being the masters of them in their intellects. We who were scandalized in 1940 when men were sent to fight armored tanks with rifles, are not scandalized when young men and women are sent into the world to fight mass propaganda with a smattering of "subjects"; and when whole classes and whole nations become hypnotized by the arts of the spellbinder, we have the impudence to be astonished. We dole out lip-service to the importance of education-lip-service and, just occasionally, a little grant of money; we postpone the school leaving-age, and plan to build bigger and better schools; the teachers slave conscientiously in and out of school hours, till responsibility comes a burden and a nightmare; and yet, as I believe, all this devoted effort is largely frustrated, because we have lost the tools of learning, and in their absence can only make a botched and piece-meal job of it.

Miss Sayers was talking primarily about students from the British government schools. So, why is adding "Christian" teaching not making enough difference to be noted on our American cultural gauge? Why do the students she described in the 1940's sound so similar to many Christian school graduates today? Because while these students *may* be taught generally WHAT to think, they are not being taught HOW to think. They are simply unprepared and unequipped to make a difference or to be different.

The Scriptures clearly invoke the image of Christians being prepared for battle (Eph. 6:10-17). This battle is not just relegated to our hearts; it is to extend to our minds, and from there, to the effect we have on the world around us (Romans 12:1-2; 1 Cor. 2:6-8; 2 Cor.10:3-6). In short, rather than preparing students who just become (like the stated goals of government education) "good, productive citizens," Christian schools should graduate students who are able to engage and do successful battle with the "wisdom" and philosophies of this age. They should cause a good kind of trouble, not be troubled, when they attend secular colleges. They should be able to identify and attack falsehood in the political, business, and religious sectors. Through training in the "lost tools of learning," they should know where they came from and how to think about the future. They should be well-armed; spiritually and intellectually, to do battle with those powers and influences who are certainly not reluctant about pursuing their side of the war. There is no neutrality, and we are commanded to avoid appeasement with the world.

As we begin our seventeenth year, I can assure you that we are even more committed to, impassioned by, and informed about the potential of a classical, Christian education than we were in 1981. The task is also more daunting because we understand it a bit better. But we have seen many, many victories, by God's grace in the lives of the students who have left us and their families to stand on their own in our culture. We once again beseech you to remember us daily in prayer this year. May God continue to use Logos School and many other schools to help bring the equivalent of a VJ (Victory in Jesus) Day in the educational, cultural, and spiritual battlefields of our country.

\* \* \*

## PAUL THE MAN FOR ALL REASONS

Early in his ministry the Hebrew known as Saul could be found on a typical Sabbath in one of a number of Mediterranean synagogues, reasoning for Jesus as the Messiah and Lord. His apologetic came from a strong knowledge of the Scriptures, his own background as a Pharisee, and his trained skills in rhetoric. During those debates in the warm, moist climate, the listeners' tempers often flared into red-hot anger and frustration. He endured more than one pain-filled stoning for his scriptural, well-reasoned attack on the Jewish misinterpretations and warping of the Law. His enemies were so incensed and jealous that they followed him from city to city, and even resorted to a frustrated ambush.

But the Roman citizen known as Paul was called also to the Gentile Greeks to bring them the Gospel of Jesus the Christ. His methods? Persuasive argument, reasoned debate, knowledge of the Greek and Roman laws and culture, logic, grace-filled wit, and godly love. He spoke a variety of classical and Hebrew dialects. At times he was soft-spoken, at others his voice thundered for attention, but rarely was he a "silent witness" to the authority and Gospel of his Lord. And he did indeed learn, as the Lord foretold, "how much he must suffer for My Name's sake."

## God prepared Paul for his life's work through an intense classical, scriptural education.

Paul was a fascinating compilation of traits and training. He became the apostle to the Gentiles through God's direct appointment. God prepared Paul for his life's work through an intense classical, scriptural education. Paul had had his own zealous plans for using that education, specifically the crushing of the new Christian religion but the Lord used it to bring countless others into the kingdom of God. His skills in writing persuasively were used to pen most of the New Testament, evidencing a profound knowledge of both the Old Testament writings and the history of the vast Roman culture. He seemed to write as much from inside a Roman prison as from outside of one. But his knowledge and application of their laws about citizens not only saved him from one unjust beating, he even evoked an apology from the local Roman authorities for illegally imprisoning him at one point.

A classical, Christ-centered education is not an oxymoron. The integration of the two can be a powerful weapon for the Kingdom, as is clearly seen from Paul's life. Paul knew his spiritual, as well as his historical roots, which included times and peoples beyond the Jewish race. He was wise enough to see that, even though he was thankful to be a Jew.

Sadly, some American Christian educators make the mistake of thinking Christianity and even all good education started in 1776, in Philadelphia (a Greek name). One group of otherwise well-intentioned Christian educators recently published an article in response to Dorothy Sayer's *The Lost Tools of Learning* and the growing classical education reformation in general. The article stated: "We never lost our tools they're not medieval; they're Biblical and governmental. And they're uniquely American." They also asked: "Why look to medieval Europe for classical education when the pinnacle of classical education was reached in our own nation with a Biblical and governmental mission two centuries ago? The tools of learning are not 'lost.' They're not medieval, they're Biblical and governmental. *And they're uniquely American*"[1] (Emphasis mine).

At Logos we certainly want to teach an accurate and appreciative view of our nation's history, but at no time do we want to leave the students with the impression that the United States has the corner on all that is good. Rather, we are the beneficiaries of all that God has seen fit to pass down to us from antiquity, including the almost lost heritage and blessings of a classical, godly education. Numbered among our educational forefathers, therefore, are Homer, Herodotus, and certainly Paul, in addition to Washington, Adams, and Madison. The former group laid the foundations for the latter. Our government schools and, sad to say, many Christian schools have ignored one or both groups to the detriment of the students' best understanding.

Our culture desperately needs more Pauls, classically educated Christian men and women who through God's grace persuade others to see Christ in the Scriptures and to avoid lawlessness. They will not always be lauded or popular—Paul certainly wasn't—but they won't be overlooked either. They should disrupt, attack, and reason against the wisdom of this world. Paul went to Caesar; who knows before whom our young "Pauls" may testify?

---

1. Nordskog Publishing, "American Classical Education: Biblical and Governmental the 'Found' Tools of Learning," F.A.C.E. 5, no. 1 (Spring 1998), available at nordskogpublishing.com/american-classical-education-biblical-and-governmental-the-found-tools-of-learning/.

# 4

## BAD MOON ARISING—
## MODERN TRENDS IN EDUCATION

*More and more of our families at Logos are starting their students in our kindergarten, or other early elementary years, and are, therefore not necessarily aware of what is happening in the government schools. I don't spend a lot of time in them, either, but I hear a lot from families who come to apply at Logos. Also, I receive a number of news magazines that alert us to the latest nonsense, or worse. So, even though our families may not be directly affected by these trends, I think it's very important that they know about them. Their children, when they graduate from here, or before, will face a very different peer group than the one they are seeing at school. It would make sense to let them know ahead of time why and how this happened.*

### A BAD MOON ARISING: A BRIEF TALLY OF RECENT TRENDS IN EDUCATION

Have you ever had the unsettling experience of being totally immersed, heart and mind, in a really good novel for an uncertain block of time, then looking up, you find your surroundings had unaccountably changed? People who were in the room a "moment ago" are long gone, the sunlight in the room has altered noticeably, and your mind races to get "caught up" with what's transpired while you were preoccupied.

That has happened to me too often, and on a broader scale than just reading a good book. As you may have noticed in the last few newsletters, we have had lots of encouraging events at Logos to tell you know about, and that we have been totally immersed in, such as graduations, the A.C.C.S. conference, and the all-consuming accreditation process. While catching up on some reading on educational issues, both Christian and governmental this summer, it occurred to me that, like myself, you may want to be aware of how the educational "surroundings" in the U.S. have altered recently.

With a very brief reference to each, allow me to bring you up to speed on just a few of the more ominous trends in recent years that are affecting immense numbers of children in our country. Some you may have heard of, others may be new to you. In any case, I urge you to be on your guard and critically and biblically examine how they are affecting kids and families.

1. Whole Language: This is the most recent rehash of the old "see-say" method of teaching reading. That is, instead of concentrating on phonics, the sounds letters make in an alphabetic system of language (like English), this method teaches children to try to identify the "look" or "appearance" of a word. Students are encouraged to bring their own "interpretation" to what they read vs. deciphering each word and interpreting it literally. Another name for this method is the deconstruction theory of reading. Don't be fooled by the use of actual, popular children's literature being used with Whole Language; having good titles does not mean children are able to read them or understand them as the authors intended. At its base, this program is destroying the validity of the written word for numerous children. Also, consider how students taught this way would approach the reading and understanding of the most important Book.

2. Outcome Based Education, Alias "O.B.E." or "Mastery Learning": This is, in many opinions, the worst, most destructive thing to happen to education since John Dewey was given a podium. It is insidious because not only does it dress itself in positive sounding ideology, it is rather amorphous: it changes shape from school to school and state to state. In spite of the rhetoric it's dressed up in, it amounts to the same thing: a sweeping plan to redefine what constitutes an education. In its initial presentation it sounds refreshing: a return to concentrating on students

mastering certain objectives as the means to evaluate whether or not the students have received a good education. But the baggage it includes is staggering: grading and objective evaluative criteria are removed; instead of traditional academic knowledge, "behaviors" and "feelings" are taught and assessed. O.B.E. pushes egalitarianism (leveling of individuals) to an Orwellian level. "Political correctness" is the rule and requirement for determining a "successful" student, or "world citizen." There is not space here to adequately outline all O.B.E.'s problems. Suffice it say, it is the most popular and far-reaching movement in education today, similar in scope to the changes made after Sputnik's launch in 1957.

3. Goals 2000: These are a list of outlandish, idealistic goals for all U.S. public schools, developed by national leaders in politics and education (that should scare you right there) that President Bush supported, and President Clinton is pushing. They include the necessity of implementing O.B.E. to accomplish "correct thinking" about such things as the environment, solving "interpersonal problems and conflicts," and "appreciating diversity." For example, just one goal is, by the year 2000, all U.S. schools will be free of drugs and violence and "offer a disciplined environment to learning." That's less than six years away. Who is going to do this and how will it be accomplished? Parents are mentioned in these goals, too ... as "partners." Any problem with the diminished authority implicit in that?

4. Children's "Rights" Programs, e.g. the United Nations "Children's Rights Declaration," D.A.R.E. (drug abuse resistance education) programs, etc.: There is not space or time to go into all the aspects of these programs. The bottom line to consider in examining these types of programs, aimed primarily at children, not their parents, is ... what are they saying about families? And how does that compare with what the Bible says? The common element they contain is, at the very least, treating the child as an autonomous being. Yes, even the very popular D.A.R.E. program. Out of the seventeen program objectives, parents are included in one, and there just as one of many "support" people for a child. The attempted destruction of the biblical family is rampant. A slogan I've seen sums up the "new" definition of the family being inculcated... "A family is a circle of friends who love you!" God help us!

DEAR PARENTS

\* \* \*

*Christians differ on a lot of things, which is not too surprising, I guess. Even Paul and Barnabus had a falling out of sorts. But Christians today are differing over what should be rather plain for all to see, and not just the more obscure doctrines in Scripture. One of these issues is the view of the "environment," or as we used to call it, nature. God's Word is very clear about how we are to view and consider His creation.*

PANIC OR PROMISES: WHAT ON EARTH ARE WE TEACHING CHILDREN ABOUT "THE ENVIRONMENT"?

Man belongs to the earth; the earth does not belong to man.
~From a backpack patch)

And God blessed Noah and his sons and said to them, "Be fruitful and multiply and fill the earth.... Every moving thing that is alive shall be food for you; *I give all to you*, as I gave the green plant."
~Genesis 9:1, 3, emphasis added

In response to several unrelated inquiries and comments we have received in the past from patrons, I would like to address the topic above with as much objectivity as possible.

The thrust of the comments we have received was that it is "common knowledge that Logos is not into the environment", i.e. we don't have active programs promoting a "save-the-world" agenda. Instead of arguing for or against the validity of each proffered program that comes along, it may be wise to hear from a quarter frequently ignored in the rush to cleanse the world of man's presence. That "quarter" was written by the One Who created and sustains the earth. (Remember when it was simply called "earth," or "nature," and not the nebulous "environment"?)

Let's compare what Scripture says with the basic philosophies screaming at us from everything from cereal boxes to Barbie dolls to movie stars:

"OVER-POPULATION"

Fear says: Man is crowding himself off the planet. We are overtaxing all the natural resources and will bring death by starvation to us all. Planned families (read: abortion-on-demand) and some form of equal distribution of resources and food are the only solutions.

Scripture says: Every man is a unique creation by Almighty God. Man is to be fruitful in procreation, and children are a gift from Him. The clear implication is that no limits on numbers of people "allowed" on this planet would ever be condoned by God. Resources are abundant for those willing to work in accordance with scriptural principles of work. (See Leviticus and Proverbs, for starters.) Sin (individual and corporate), more often than scarcity, produces a lack of basic necessities.

## Let's compare what Scripture says with the basic philosophies screaming at us…

"ANIMAL RIGHTS"

Fear says: We are all animals. Man is therefore not more important than the other animals; he is just farther up the scale of evolution, with the possible exception of dolphins. Man should learn to live with all animals and treat them as brothers. And, of course, you would never use your brother for medical research (unless he is a human in utero).

Scripture says: Man is a unique creation; he is not an animal. Animals are here to serve Man; as food, servants, companions, and evidences of God's creativity.

Cruelty toward anyone or anything is forbidden; this includes animals. Extinction is an example of the sin of selfishness and greed.

"ENVIRONMENTAL COLLAPSE IMMINENT BECAUSE OF GLOBAL WARMING, ACID RAIN, DEPLETION OF RESOURCES, POLLUTION, _____" (Fill in the blank.)

Fear says: If we keep _ing (fill in the latest threat), we're all going to die! This is all we have, so let's save it from ourselves! Er … that is, we need to save it for our children! Yeah, that's it!

Scripture says: "While the earth remains, seed time and harvest, and cold and heat, and summer and winter, and day and night shall not cease" (Genesis 8:22). Though man is evil, God is faithful to His Word. No one can thwart His plans, through "good" intentions or overt evil ones.

What should we teach children about God's wondrous earth? We teach the scriptural principles above, along with the basic truth that since God gave the world to us and He sustains it, we are to be grateful. If that is our attitude, we will care for it and use it as Adam was commanded to and we are not to fear. With awe and respect for our Creator, we seek to help raise a generation that will marvel at, appreciate, and use to the fullest, the rich blessings by which He has promised to sustain us. He is sovereign.

\* \* \*

*This column, like quite a few others, came out of hearing more than I wanted to about the topic. But since it is affecting the way parents and teachers are treating vast numbers of children, even in Christian schools, I wanted to put forth the approach we are taking. Learning disabilities, a very recent term itself, are creating quite a fog in education. There is so much hype and nonsense that it is hard to see through it all to determine if there is any real substance there. So, as with everything else we come across, we need to examine the basic premises in the clear, fog-dispelling light of Scripture.*

WHO'S GOT THE RIGHT DIAGNOSIS?

> They interrupt...they don't follow directions. In short, they do what seizes them at the moment without thinking through the consequences.... Accept the fact that it is a handicap...don't expect your child to behave like others."
> ~Sandra Doran, on children with "ADHD"; *Focus On the Family*

> Even a child is known by his deeds, whether they are pure and right.
> ~God, on children with sin natures, Prov. 20:11

> Children, be obedient to your parents in all things, for this is well-pleasing to the Lord.
> ~Col. 3:20

When I was doing my student teaching at Moscow High School a "few" years ago, as part of my experience I was assigned to regularly teach art to a group of handicapped students. I grew very fond of these students and we had an all too short time together. We were able to complete a pretty nifty wall-mural, though. Among these students were kids in wheelchairs, kids with Down's Syndrome, and others with a variety of mental and physical problems. However, the one thing they had in common was a generally cheerful and compliant spirit. I had few discipline problems with them, after the class rules were made clear.

In the years since then there has been a Mississippi River-sized flood of previously undetected "disabilities" afflicting our newest generation of students. FDR's "alphabet soup" of programs doesn't hold a candle to the burgeoning list of labels issuing from the educationists today: LD, ADD, ADHD, to name just a few. The truly sad aspect to this is that all these recently revealed "handicaps" are being brought to us by the same establishment that has produced over twenty million functionally illiterate adults in the last twenty-five years. Doesn't it strike you as odd that we are able to simultaneously produce the most poorly educated generation in our country's history and yet "discover" all these inherent learning and behavioral problems that previous generations failed to notice? How can we know so much about children and their learning capabilities and yet have a lower proportion of reading adults than 100 years ago?

## Who would take their child to a doctor whose success rate was less than 50%?

When one of our children is having problems, whether it is difficulty learning the multiplication tables or a cough that won't go away, as loving parents we will seek a way to help this little one. What parent can sit by and calmly watch their child suffer? But before we act, doesn't it make sense to try to diagnose the real problem? We don't put a band-aid on a child's sore throat or give them vitamin C for a scraped knee. Today, all sorts of "experts" will tell us what is best for our children, especially when it comes educating them. Doesn't it make sense to listen to someone who has not only vast experience, but successful experience with solving problems like the ones we see? Who would take their child to a doctor whose success rate was less than 50%? Yet vast numbers of parents, even Christian parents, seek advice on raising and educating children from "professionals" who have an even worse rate of true accomplishment. What about seeking out non-"professional," but very successful godly parents and grandparents for advice that has meat in it?

The real sinister aspect of this plethora of misdiagnoses is that what used to be considered just plain bad behavior is now considered part and parcel of a learning disability. As such, therefore, the child should not be disciplined for having an "LD". Frankly, parents of such "handicapped" children are often just having their ears tickled. A recent cartoon strip showed a couple whose terribly unruly child had been so diagnosed. Upon leaving the doctor's office, they leaped in the air and gleefully shouted, "It's not our fault!" This trend really shouldn't be that surprising since we live in a culture that is actively seeking new names and causes for old sins. Drunkenness, homosexuality, even spewing foul-language has now been "linked" to genetics. God calls them sin; the world calls them syndromes. And the Christian church marches right behind the world, a few steps back, but precisely in the same footsteps.

God loves our children even more than we do; wouldn't it make sense to consistently, not sporadically, trust and practice His methods? It is ludicrous to imagine that we in the late twentieth century, for all our technology and degrees, have discovered fundamental things about training our children that our blessed Father forgot or neglected to tell us in His Word. True, the Bible does not tell us directly how to help a child struggling with math, but it does directly tell us why children misbehave the way they often do. It also clearly tells us parents what to do for our children. When consistently heeded, God's diagnosis and prescriptions will never fail to produce lasting benefits for our precious children. He promised.

\* \* \*

## STATE ACCREDITATION VS. EXCELLENCE IN EDUCATION

I considered entitling this column "State Accreditation: The Golden Cow of Education," but upon reflection felt that that would be inappropriate and unkind.

Cows get enough bad press as it is.

It is rare, when I interview new families, that one of the parents does not ask about our accreditation status with the state. It is also very common that they inquire about the certification requirements we place upon our teaching applicants. Understandable questions, given the conditioning to which we, as a culture, have been subject. We have been told, both directly and subliminally, that state accreditation is to education what the FDA stamp of approval is to food quality, i.e. the guarantee of rigorous scrutiny by knowledgeable experts. The only problem is that if the FDA's stamp indicated the same "quality" in food that state accreditation does for schools, salmonella and hepatitis would be as common as the cold and we'd all resort to raising our own food. Not too surprisingly, many people have done just that in education; they've started their own schools!

## The State has been given no biblical authority in education.

The idea of holding educational institutions and their instructors accountable and ensuring they maintain high standards is very appropriate. However, at least two things need to be carefully considered:

1. WHO or WHAT is the superior and responsible agency to which the institution is accountable?
2. WHAT STANDARDS are used as the yardstick against which the institution is being measured?

It's very disappointing to me to see so many Christians become schizophrenic (Latin "split mind") on this issue. On most other issues involving children and their training, most Christians resort immediately to the scriptures. To cut to the chase, the Bible clearly and without apology says parents are the primary educators (Deut. 6; Ephesians 6:1-4). They are the "WHO" to which any institution educating children must be accountable. The State has been given no biblical authority in education. Doesn't it then follow that the "STANDARDS" are also up to the parents, within certain, specified biblical principles? For example, it is just as wrong for parents to disregard God's command to thoroughly educate their children, as it is for the state to use force to ensure that parents do so.

If all this isn't convincing enough, consider two other points: is state accreditation (a relatively new idea on the block, historically) consistently bequeathing us better and better educated citizens, or just the opposite? In other words, is state accreditation any type of guarantee of quality? Further, the actual accreditation process gives barely a nod to the academic performance of a school's students. Instead, the process and tool itself majors on the physical plant and faculty numbers.

At Logos we not only believe we operate directly under the collective authority of our families (as prescribed and enforced by our school board), a large percentage of our staff is comprised of parents. The standards we hold all our staff members to, and the school at large, come from the Bible. Therefore, loving the children and modeling the Christian life to them are enforced standards. On a more administrative, but still significant level, as a school we sought and received accreditation from A.C.S.I. (the Association of Christian Schools, Intl.), of which we are also a member. Their standards, both for staff and the school, incorporate both biblical and strong academic standards for education.

In the end, the excellence of any education is discerned by the quality evidenced in the lives of the students, not by state-approved, meaningless certificates.

\* \* \*

*I knew that sooner or later we would have to deal with the topics below, and let our families know the way we would handle these hot items. Here again, Christians disagree on the level, type, and extent of educating children in these matters. I found out, right after publishing this first column, that even within our own constituency there is a fair degree of diversity of thought. Nevertheless, we have always deferred and will defer to the parents, whether they assume their responsibility or not.*

SEX AND DRUG EDUCATION AT LOGOS...

"New Survey Indicates Significant Increase in Premarital Sex Among Young Teens." "Resurgence Of Marijuana Use Among High School Students." Sound like articles you've seen recently? These had the same bottom line; they both were bemoaning the fact that *in spite of the great numbers of new sex and drug education programs aimed at young people,* the problems are getting much worse, not better. Here's the punch line ... what was the answer proposed? MORE programs!

Last year our community, with the help of our local police department, hosted a major antidrug program. As a local school, we were asked to participate. Among other things, we were asked to hand *out* red ribbons *to* all the students. The ribbons boldly proclaimed "My Choice Drug-Free!" We cordially declined the offer. Nevertheless, red ribbons were draped everywhere around town to encourage kids to "just say no" to drugs. To the best of my knowledge, the local junior and senior high schools did not report a dramatic (or even noticeable) drop in drug-use among the kids following this blitz of bunting.

As I pointed out to a Christian police officer who came to invite us to help in the campaign, these programs are, at best, a waste of time and money. If God Himself knew that He would not stop people from sinning by declaring the Ten Commandments accompanied by fire and smoke, what makes us think that handing our pathetic red ribbons or sex ed. brochures will stop young people from sinning today? What audacity on our part. The Law condemns and illustrates our sinful nature; it certainly doesn't change it. Grace alone can do that.

## The Law condemns and illustrates our sinful nature; it certainly doesn't change it.

Logos School doesn't provide sex and drug education for the same reason we don't give marriage counseling or do brain surgery ... it's not our job and we would be unequipped to do either. If students come to us after many years in a godly home, and they "need" a ribbon to remind them to avoid drug abuse, the battle has already been lost. By the same token, if our teenage girls aren't secure enough in the physical love of their dads to not need a boy draped over them, there are no lesson plans my teachers can use to fill that void. If our teenage boys haven't been raised to respect (an under-used word) and cherish their mothers and sisters, telling the boys how girls become pregnant will hardly increase acts of courtesy and kindness. More often (as substantiated by history) sin increases when knowledge is not accompanied by morality. As has been said elsewhere, "If you educate a devil, you don't get a saint; you get an educated devil."

We teach human reproduction in biology and, when appropriate, we will tell students the effects certain drugs have when used incorrectly. At no time, however, during these presentations do we try to convince ourselves (or the kids) that this instruction will somehow change the hearts of the students.

Sadly, many Christians have bought the heretical lie that schools, Christian or public, can *create* a desire to be moral in children. Education, even excellent education, is *not* the Savior. God commands most parents to be the first and best teachers for their children. For good or ill, children will learn the most about families (both making and raising them) from their parents' examples. They will also learn through obedience and trust in their parents about respecting their own and others' bodies.

We support and encourage, not *usurp*, this God-given role of parents. Primarily because of their homes and Christ's work, we daily see and build up many students who, even without any "programs," will never be a cultural statistic.

\* \* \*

## SEX AND DRUG EDUCATION AT LOGOS…THE SEQUEL

*"Does he mean Logos ignores the whole issue?"*
*"What do they do when sex is mentioned in the Bible?"*
*"But Logos has a unique opportunity to teach the kids the right information."*

The above were just a few of the comments I received mostly indirectly (not many people actually came to me) from my last column. Ironically, after writing the column, I had mentioned to my wife Julie that I wasn't sure if anyone ever read my ramblings, besides my parents and some long-suffering friends. But the reaction to the last column made it clear that others do read these ramblings. What a great feeling to know *someone's out there!*

I'd like to drop the other shoe regarding this weighty topic but first let me briefly restate the points I was attempting to make in the first column:
- Sexual activity and illegal drug use are moral decisions, not intellectual ones.
- Education, of any kind, can never be a substitute for moral integrity.

- In fact, sin increases when knowledge is not accompanied by God's law written on hearts of flesh, not stone.
- Families are the first and most important place children will, for good or ill, learn how to treat the opposite sex and how to regard and care for their own bodies.

So what do we do here at Logos regarding these incredibly hot topics? First, some definitions are in order. By "sex and/or drug education," I mean comprehensive programs that are part of a school's curriculum. These programs include training in everything from basic body parts, reproduction, sexual life-styles, AIDS, drug identification, and the effects of drug abuse. About the only thing these programs leave to the imagination of the students is what God says about the issue. Logos School's curriculum does not, nor will it, include these kinds of programs.

## The Bible depicts real people, in all their raw, sinful conditions.

The Bible, on the other hand, does have a major role in our curriculum. One of our school goals says that all subjects are related and find their common source in God's Word. We use it, therefore, at all levels of our program. Yet, if someone were to rate the Bible as movies are rated it would likely earn an R rating. The Bible depicts real people, in all their raw, sinful conditions. Its characters frequently commit sexual sin and get drunk (inseparable from abusing other drugs), to mention just two among a plethora of other horrific acts. The students, from first grade to twelfth, read the unadulterated Word, not a cleaned-up, condensed version.

Nevertheless, we use the Bible at all levels because it also contains God's answer to the common source of sexual sin and drunkenness, i.e. being filled by His Spirit. In addition to the frequent reference to Scripture, on these and other matters, we instruct by example, as do our parents. Logos School's second goal states that we will "provide a clear model of the biblical Christian life through our staff and board." This cannot be passive. It means that all our actions, comments, attitudes, life-styles, and relationships are to be biblical in character. Those of us who are married are teaching, by word and action, what a godly marriage is to be like. Those of us who are single are teaching about relations with other single people. We've had romances, engagements, marriages, and births within Logos School, all teaching the students about God's design. We've had several pregnant teenage ladies come to us since they were unwelcome in their own schools. We accepted them so that they wouldn't consider abortion. Even our kindergartners were told why the girls came, that what the girls had done was wrong, but that we loved them anyway. Talk about audiovisual instruction!

Finally, in our secondary Bible classes, few holds are barred. If it comes up in the Word, or even by a student's question, we will answer questions regarding sex, drugs, music, dancing, etc. as best we can with two things in mind:

- Staying safely within the written Word;
- Not teaching secondary doctrines as primary (i.e. not encouraging divisiveness).

We expect that by the time our junior high students come into our Bible classes, they will have already learned, from their parents ideally, all the basic elements of bodily functions and human reproduction. We do not want to be the first *or* only place these topics are discussed with the students.

Pray for us as we seek to reinforce and build on the good training most of these kids have already received in their homes.

\* \* \*

*As with many Christians, I find the most upsetting aspect of our American cultural flight from morality to be the abortion industry. Therefore, I find it extremely disturbing to read about government school programs that foster that industry. This column came as direct result of reading about one such local program. Interestingly, and additionally disheartening was the discovery, after publishing my critique, that the local school's administrator was a believer who disagreed with my assessment. Oh really.*

"YOU MUST HAVE BEEN A BEAUTIFUL BABY"

Without doubt the intentions (as usual) were sterling. Unfortunately the thinking (as usual) was flawed, to put it mildly. This fall a local middle school went to the expense and trouble to purchase a number of computerized, six-and-a-half pound "babies" for a health class. These were state-of-the-art, high-tech infants. They were programmed to cry at unpredictable times, and the only way to get them to stop was to insert a special key into their backs. The keys were attached to a hospital-type bracelet worn by the "mother" or "father" students. The bionic bambinos could even register any "abuse," such as being stuffed in a locker for an extended period.

## This kind of program will do for the abortion industry what recreational dating has done for the divorce courts.

The news article reporting this latest crusade against student promiscuity quoted the reactions of the students packing their plastic progeny. "It was fun at first," said one young lady. "But after a while I just wanted to throw it out the window." It seems that, just like the real McCoy, these toy tots would cry at night, causing frustration and irritation in many homes. Wonder what the parents of these short-term, young "parents" thought? One real mom was a bit put out at the loss of sleep, but figured "it's for a good reason." The "good reason" or intent, according to the teacher, was to let these kids know what it's "really" like to have a baby at their young ages. What folly! It is ludicrous to think that carrying around an electronically-exasperating doll can teach young people anything about the love, security, and, yes, constant care real babies require. Nor can it teach them the heartfelt, often inexpressible joy that sweetsmelling, soft-skinned babies bring to a home. And, not surprisingly, no one thinks to bring in the idea that God ordained the structure of marriage and family specifically for the best nurturing of children.

But such a program is not a complete waste of time, it will teach the students one fundamental lesson. While it won't teach them to abstain from sexual activity, it will certainly teach them to "throw it out" should a baby be the result of their fun. This kind of program will do for the abortion industry what recreational dating has done for the divorce courts. Dating has virtually removed any concept of the commitment and covenant marriage requires, and replaced it with numerous, disposable relationships. Sex ed. classes, such as the one above, remove or ignore any reference to the biblical view of childbirth or childrearing.

Ironically, on the same front page featuring the fake baby story was an article on a local real-life tragedy wherein a young, angry father shook his three-month old infant to death. Perhaps this living child had also cried once too often in the middle of the night. This man is accused of murder, as he should be. But his criminal view of the inconvenience of children is being advocated and paid for by the same taxpayers who want to see him punished. Ideas have consequences, and bad ideas have bad consequences.

"Behold, children are a gift of the Lord; the fruit of the womb is a reward" (Psalm 127:3). Viewing children as a blessing instead a curse also has consequences wonderful ones. Recently, we have experienced the vicarious joy of seeing several of our Logos alumni become mothers to some of God's cutest gifts. In recent months, Michelle (Smith) Fickle ('96), gave birth to Jonathon; Jade (Kohl) Miller ('95) gave birth to Audrey Paige; and Ashley (Lucas) Neukom ('92) gave birth to Georgia Renee. Then Bekah (Wilson) Merkle ('94) has let us know she won't be back to teach high-school Latin next year, since she'll be busy caring for Doug and Nancy's first grandchild. We rejoice with these young families. Some of us recall these mothers as little girls in grammar school, and to see them as godly wives and mothers is the fulfillment of the hope we had for them during their school days.

Logos School has been and, I pray, always will be boldly affirming of the view God has of children. I don't say "pro-life" because that has come to mean many things to many people, and not all the meanings are founded in Scripture. But we will continue to teach these children that they are unique creations of a loving Father, and that only from Him can we and they learn the true value and purpose of life.

\* \* \*

*History reveals the Solomonic truth that "there is nothing new under the sun." The idea of children acting as "salt and light" in the government schools is not a new concept, in its application. Parents have been wrong-headed about this idea in the past, as they are today, with obvious, disastrous results.*

### THE LOST CRUSADE

Without doubt there was anguish. No parent with a heart of flesh could have borne their decision without much fear and trepidation. But the purpose was one with a higher calling for most it was regarded it as "the will of God." Therefore, though the parting was more tearful than joyful, especially for the mothers, the children went forth. The older ones, that is, those twelve years old and above, assured their parents that they would look out for the "little ones." So, they marched off, the older ones herding the younger ones in groups of a dozen or more, their heads high, proud that their mission was one that God would undoubtedly bless. From across the entire country, hundreds of children, with their parents' heart-rending acquiescence, responded to the call.

The mission, now a holy crusade, was indeed one fraught with great danger, but surely with God's blessings the children would be victorious. They were marching to wrest the Holy Land from the hands and presence of the heathens. Where the adult knights had failed, these children would succeed. They would be the "salt and light" of which our Lord spoke, to the pagan peoples who had taken Jerusalem. There was no need for training with the sword or shield, no need for battle-hardened veterans; these children with full hearts and innocent eyes would conquer with soft words and gentle hands.

Actually there would be two children's crusades, one from France and one from Germany, around 1212 AD. The children were given little, if any provisions, protection, and transportation to travel from their homelands to the far-off, mid-east countries. Not much is written about their pitiful, sorrow-filled journeys. What became of them? Did God indeed bless their sincere, but horribly misguided purpose? We do know that hundreds of those who set out never returned home. Many died of exposure, starvation, abduction, and murder. Others returned half-alive to their homes, with tales of horror. Some got as far as the Holy Land, only to become slaves of the Muslims. The "glory" of the these crusades wasn't even a memory that could be distorted to legendary proportions in the years to come. They were best forgotten, if possible.

# They would ask: Is this truly children's work? Will my child be nourished and protected as I would want?

Someone said that "the only thing we learn from history is that we don't learn from history." But surely today thinking, loving parents would never knowingly send their children en mass into a situation that is so dangerous that even adults need good training and protection there. Even when presented with the glowing admonitions to consider it a "higher calling," or being "salt and light," parents would certainly consider carefully all aspects of any "crusade." They would ask: Is this truly children's work? Will my child be nourished and protected as I would want? Will my child come home to me stronger in the Lord, or will his faith be attacked and his spirit crushed by heavy-handed adults? Will he be victorious or taken captive? And most importantly: Does God, in His Word, really require this of my children?

What would have happened if all those French and German parents had examined the "call" of the crusade in the above light? At the very least their children would not have been lost, for they would not have gone. The Holy Land would have remained in the hands of the Muslims, as it did anyway, crusade or no. Let's not indulge in more lost crusades. And let us be extremely cautious and biblically discerning, with whom and to what we entrust our precious children.

> "And whoever receives one such child in My Name receives Me; but whoever causes one of these little ones to stumble, it is better for him that a heavy millstone be hung around his neck, and that he be drowned in the depth of the sea."
> ~Jesus Christ, Matthew 18:5-6

\* \* \*

## GUNS & BUTTER

The hard-won victory (actually a series of victories) that the United States enjoyed in World War II could very legitimately be credited to the Homefront. The United States literally out-produced its enemies and not only supplied our own troops with the food, medicine, weapons, and other necessary material they needed, we also helped supply our allies. Considering our general state of war-readiness, or lack thereof, prior to Pearl Harbor, the production amounts by 1945 were barely short of miraculous.

A critical contributing factor to this outpouring of material was the attitude of the general American population toward the war effort. Rationing, scrap drives, and basically going without many of the niceties of life became the norm. Typical of this approach of sacrificing for the greater cause was the surrendering of butter by the average citizen. Butter became a luxury at home because its ingredients were needed by the troops for their weapons. "Guns *or* butter!" became one of the many slogans from this era. The implied point being that the war couldn't be won unless the folks at home were willing to give up a bit of their high standard of living. (As a side-note, margarine was created to fill the vacuum butter left at home during the war. Initially it was a clear paste, but that looked disgusting on toast, so "artificial coloring" was added to make it *look* like butter much better!)

During the war in Vietnam, President Lyndon Johnson discarded the lessons of sacrifice and homefront support we learned in World War II, and tried to have "guns *and* butter." He tried to support and supply our troops without having the folks at home feel the pinch. Like many other ideas of that war, it backfired. It wasn't the only reason we lost, but it contributed to the distance that was evident between the average citizen and the soldiers coming home.

In the past several years, but with increasing regularity in recent months, we have opened our newspapers or turned on the TV (or internet) and heard about another student shooting at a school. There was almost an audible sigh of limited relief heard across the United States when schools were let out this spring: at least the kids won't be at the same risk as they were while in class. Each succeeding tragedy was like another slap across our corporate face. As expected the cry went up, and will increase in volume as the many trials become news events, "What can we do to make schools safer?"

I have had several families applying for next year, as well as some of our teachers, ask me "Could such a thing happen at Logos?" The fact that all the shootings so far have been in government schools is cold comfort to worried adults. Christian schools do not have any greater physical protections (certainly far fewer security measures) than the average government school that would deter a raging or vengeful student with a gun.

But is this trend like lightning hitting anywhere, anytime, destroying without any warning? Or, are there real reasons why this is happening *now*, with such frequency, being done by "good" kids in middle-class schools? (Shootings in inner-city schools have been happening so frequently they don't get front-page news status.) Is it possible, to change the above euphemism, that we have indulged ourselves with "butter" for so long, that now we get the guns?

According to God's Word, things happen for a reason—one of those is that God is not mocked, "what a man sows, that will he reap." As a culture we have actively lied to ourselves and our children for at least the last fifty years, saying that if God exists He doesn't matter and we can educate better without Him and His Word. Our "butter"—our man-centered, live-for-yourself education—has tasted so good to us that it takes the literal shedding of children's blood to make us sit up and notice that something is wrong. "Where did these angry, lost children with guns come from? Something must be done!"

## "Where did these angry, lost children with guns come from? Something must be done!"

My predictions for the short term? As usual, instead of looking for the widespread reasons for the guns, i.e. morally bankrupt families and churches, there will be calls for more security guards, more metal-detectors, more gun laws, and above all else, more PROGRAMS in schools to "help kids channel their aggressions in a positive way, and feel better about themselves." School counselors will go to training classes specializing in responding to kids who are talking about shooting people. Children will be expelled who continue to just talk about violence. And, in all probability, like most trends, the shootings will abate after a while. We will all congratulate ourselves that the crisis is past and probably even hand out awards for those who made the programs this time.

But the "butter" will not be sacrificed. And, since our God is just, what will be the next level of "guns?" The battle against God and His Word is hardly

over in our nation. But He is already the Victor and those individuals and families in His army have nothing to fear, especially not fear itself. Let's continue to pray for repentance and the resulting peace in our land.

* * *

BOOMER CROSSROADS, PART I

In the vast history of mankind, it is arguably the most pampered, healthy, well-fed, rich, lazy, ungrateful, and self-centered generation to come along. In the history of the United States, it is without question the largest generation to make it past infancy as a group. They are the babies, the sons and daughters, of the World War II generation. They are lumped together because so many were born at about the same time, shortly after American soldiers and sailors came home from the fighting that stopped world-wide in September of 1945.

The "baby boom" began in that year and, since many of the new parents back then didn't think four or more children were too many, the boom lasted until about 1963. During that period, over fifteen million of us came into the world, more specifically, into the culture and history of the United States. It would produce quite a shock to the national system.

> **Our parents, even if they were Christians, naively assumed that we were growing up as they had, learning the same knowledge in the same way they had.**

Where our parents had endured both an unparalleled depression and a world war with great grace and self-sacrifice, we grew up expecting that our every need, from health to entertainment, would be met without delay. That's because our parents worked hard and we reaped the benefits. Then we had the audacity to whine and protest against the hands that fed us. We also learned more from TV than we did from school. After all, just about everything that made the news was recorded on camera, then shown on TV. Even in our tender years we saw it all, from the first manned U.S. flight into space, to JFK's death, to the moon landing, to Kent State, Woodstock, and Watergate. Our schools, on the other hand, were turned into "secular" training grounds to prepare us for our future vocations, not to give us a quality education, as previous generations had assumed schools were supposed to provide. No surprise, then, that as group, we found TV far more interesting and entertaining than the teachers ever could be.

Our parents, even if they were Christians, naively assumed that we were growing up as they had, learning the same knowledge in the same way they had. They were very sadly mistaken. And we, being rather clueless ourselves, assumed that this was the way things were supposed to be, since we had nothing else with which to compare our experiences (not being taught actual history in school, either).

We grew up. Our parents aged. We had technologies and medicines that we took for granted while they boggled our parents' (now grandparents') minds. Our cynicism, especially after the sixties and Watergate, was part of our worldview. Where our parents had naturally, unquestioningly put family first, for us the job and position were everything. Making the grade and the bucks were the prime motivators for working, not any sense of duty or obligation to others, even our children. To "make it" required Mom to work, full-time of course, so day cares boomed, too. Yet we had more luxuries and vacation time than our parents every dreamed about. Home entertainment centers became immense, filling a good portion of our living rooms. Our material wealth wrapped us in a mindless, soft existence, which even our churches didn't challenge, much less condemn.

So, Christian boomers looked, acted, and believed pretty much the same way all their pagan peers did. One of the worst parts of this is the downstream effect this came to have on our own children. We hadn't been taught to really think, especially biblically, about our culture, our government, our money, but most of all, about how to raise our progeny. We assumed that when the Bible talked about raising up children in the admonition of the Lord, or teaching them His Word, that this could mostly be done through our churches, with some help at home, as time allowed. In our defense, we honestly didn't know what or how else to think about educating our children. Not knowing our history, particularly the history of the Church, we have assumed that every other generation of Christian parents had to make similar decisions for their kids. That is, we actually assume that Christian parents have always had to capitulate to the surrounding culture to a great degree, i.e. send their children to the local schools, expose them (without biblical preparation) to the existing mores, and then just pray the kids somehow survive intact.

Yet there is hope, even for us self-centered boomers. We can still learn from the Word and the past and pass that marvelous legacy on to our kids. It will be harder for us than it will be for them since we have a lot of baggage to pitch, a lot of reading to do, and some tough decisions to make. But I frequently hear fellow boomers, Christian and otherwise, complaining about the current culture and, of all things, the coming generation of significantly self-absorbed kids. Gee, how did that all happen? Look in the mirror.

Swimming upstream is never easy but that's exactly what we are doing each day at Logos. The staff and parents here are largely boomers. We are equally victims and perpetrators of a criminally mindless, God-hating culture. By God's grace, we are taking baby steps in the opposite direction, trying to understand and, at the same time, teach about the antithesis that God tells us about in His timeless Word. More on those baby steps next time...

\* \* \*

BOOMER CROSSROADS, PART II

The post-World War II generation of babies born between about 1945 and 1963 is the largest generation in U.S. history. About seventy million of us (I incorrectly put fifteen earlier, mea culpa) comprise "the" Baby Boom. We were experimented upon educationally (after Sputnik caused a revolution in American schooling), we were spoiled, undisciplined (Dr. Spock's baby book frowned on spanking), spent hours in front of the new TV babysitter, and were very healthy (thanks to Dr. Jonas Salk's miracle, other vaccines and fluoride).

Boomers grew up in the midst of a technological wave that continues today. So profoundly has this wave affected every part of our daily lives that at least two mental assumptions are religiously held by all of us (and now our children):

- *The wave will continue unabated.* We just have to wait and what is incredible today will be in Office Depot tomorrow, and then cost even less a year from now.
- *The technological innovations reflect an intrinsic moral upward movement as well.* In other words, we are "improving" as human beings because we have increasingly efficient gizmos.

That second idea may look ludicrous on paper, but think about it. How many times have you heard people say something like, "How can anyone think X? This is *2003*, after all!" "X" is usually some old-fashioned idea such as premarital sex being wrong. Putting this belief in starker terms: "New is good, old is bad, or at least unimportant." Roll over, Beethoven!

While our culture became more and more materialistic, post WWII, what happened to the churches as we grew up? When we were "teens," we demanded (!) that worship services, music and sermons be more "relevant" to us. So, we put "Christian" lyrics to *The House of the Rising Sun* and *Bridge Over Troubled Waters* and youth groups conducted very hip evening services.

Largely, American churches in the 1960s and 70s were swept along with the wave of modernity instead of standing firm on the rock of Christ's Words to answer our rebellious culture. As goes the Church, so goes education.

It's no wonder at all that, for all intents and purposes, Christian boomers look, act, work, talk, marry, divorce, and largely think, like the non-believing culture around us. We are in and of the world up to our eyeballs.

But what about our children? Rejecting the old for the new was fine as long as we were the "new." Now we are the "old." Nevertheless, as Christians, we want our kids to value what we value, particularly Christ and His Word. But our children's generation have indeed learned well the lessons we've taught them or allowed them to be taught (same thing), i.e. this is just a material world, the past is dead, and life is living to please No. 1. We never seriously brought those same assumptions into the harsh, revealing light of God's Word; why should our kids?

## When we repent of our self-absorption, study His Word, and commit to act on what He shows us, He will not fail to teach and guide us.

Praise be to God, He is kind, even to stiff-necked people. His Word promises that He will not forsake us. When we repent of our self-absorption, study His Word, and commit to act on what He shows us, He will not fail to teach and guide us. He will pick us up where we *are*, not abandon us because we are not where we ought to have been.

So, by God's grace and leading, some Christian baby boomers are taking baby steps back to what works and matters. First things first: Having a willingness to admit that we need to draw from more than just our own understanding and experience is a good start. Frankly, we had a lousy education, to put it mildly. We need lots of help. That recognition should lead us to re-examine all those verses about children and parents in the Scriptures. Maybe they really mean what they say: it really *is* the parents' responsibility to train and teach children! Not only that, ALL of what our children learn should be from God's viewpoint, not man's. "All" means everything a child is taught, from the alphabet to zoology.

That should overwhelm us to the point where we call for oxygen and then, if we are smart, we ask what in the world did Christian parents do in the past? Ah, the past! Maybe old is not dead and unimportant. We start cracking open old books, or at least ask others who have, and discover that there was indeed a time when parents understood, practiced, and required biblical instruction of their children, even in schools. A time when an educated (i.e. well prepared) young person knew the Scriptures, ancient history, classical languages, and how to identify truth, as well as effectively refute falsehoods. They exulted in beauty and rejected ugliness. And the kids worked very hard, with wonderful results, i.e. tangible blessings for themselves and their posterity.

It can be done! The old ways and paths are not so overgrown that we can't find them again. Our children can have an answer to the materialistic, hedonistic culture, and it needn't be "Leave us alone, we just want to be Christians privately!" Instead, with grace in their speech and actions, they can refute ungodly professors, please their employers by their work ethic, not be fooled by political "saviors" promising the "American dream," and establish homes that resound with the laughter of secure children. They may even be more prepared than their "salt and light" peers to stand up to the growing persecution of Christians and the Church in the United States. Our Savior promised that this would happen to those called by His Name; we may forget that promise, but it is nonetheless true.

For all our hip-ness, we boomers have missed out on a great deal that we need to recover, for our children's sake, if not ours. If studying our own times teaches us anything, it should teach us that modernity, as a whole, has failed us and is failing our children horribly.

From this boomer's view, the kind of education these students at Logos are getting is profoundly unlike what I received. And it goes far beyond the valuable,

DEAR PARENTS

rigorous assignments; it is evident in the very look and attitude of the students as they live, talk, and interact at school each day. They express a joy in living and learning that no "flower child" could ever understand. May God bless this next generation, insofar as we, their parents, reject our self-centeredness and embrace His Word.

\* \* \*

GIANTS IN THE LAND?

No doubt they sure looked big, really big. That's just because they were probably upwards of nine feet tall. As the twelve Hebrew spies checked out these huge people, possibly from a safe vantage point behind some shrubbery, their feelings of despair would be very understandable. These monstrous people were dominating and living in the land that was supposedly to become the sole property of the Israelites. God had told Moses that, anyway. So, what's the deal with these giants? What are the people of God supposed to do now?

Ten of the spies figured that what they should do was forget that piece of property and shop elsewhere. But two godly men, Joshua and Caleb, stood firm. Their thinking: God said the land is ours, so let's lock and load. God's word was enough for these two. Giants were not a problem if God said they weren't. The sad upshot was, in a typical human response, the majority of the people (democracy in action) went with the judgement of the other ten spies and were ready to cower. That is, until Moses told them that God would send them on a very long trip through the wilderness. Suddenly, the giant problem was not so big and the people (without God's blessing) tried to take the land on their own. You know the result Giants 1, Israelites ... a big 0. And they got the wilderness trip for a consolation prize.

## The giants moved into a land that God had given only to parents.

Now for the analogy you knew was coming. After the War Between the

States, federal control over education in the United States kicked into high gear. Where education had formerly been a private relationship among families within their homes and their own communities, now by some bizarre form of eminent domain, it became the business of the national government. A number of elements contributed to this, including the way the fourteenth amendment was interpreted over time and its application to education among the states. The giants moved into a land that God had given only to parents. That is, the rich, wonderful landscape of educating children. Talk about a land flowing with milk and honey! Not only is it a promised land for parents, there are promises attendant regarding the blessings godly parents may look to enjoy: "The father of the righteous will greatly rejoice, and he who begets a wise son will be glad in him" (Prov. 23:24).

How the giants came to control this land is not as important as the recognition by God's people that the giants are there, that they are indeed big, and that ultimately they need to leave. They make their presence known in a number of ways, from overt tyranny to subtle but real intimidation. The tyranny takes the form of making Peter pay for Paul's children to be educated by the government. If Peter doesn't want his children educated that way, that's fine, he may choose another option, just as long as he still pays for Paul's kids' schooling. If this illegitimate taxation were enforced anywhere else in our free market system, there would be wails and gnashing of teeth by all concerned. Imagine being heavily taxed to pay for someone else's car or divorce or TV cable service. Considering that the national average cost for government schooling is approaching $6,000 per student, that's a high price to pay for a less than superior product you don't want or use. Then add to that amount the cost Peter pays for opting out and having his kids educated elsewhere.

The giants' reason for charging Peter when he doesn't use the service he's paying for? "An educated society is a good society. Educated citizens make better citizens. Therefore, it is in the interest of the State to ensure that everyone receives a good education, regardless of their ability to pay for it. Besides, if we left it up to just the parents, we might get poorly educated citizens and then where would we all be?"

The truth or not of these arguments has been billboarded for all to see.

The giants also intimidate even God's people through the rhetoric of edu-terminology, making anyone who challenges the conclusions of "professional" educators feel like dolts. "Of course millions of children need Ritalin to drug them into compliance. How else can we control them long enough to teach the anti-drug classes?" The population explosion in the special education field is a further testimony of the giants' intimidation. Physical ailments were not enough. The message is plain to the parents: Your child needs special (additionally funded) help because of his obvious inability to read, write, count his toes, stay in the lines, focus, sit down, come in from recess on time ... etc, etc.

Lest this all sound too negative, there is good news. There is growing dissension even among the ranks of the giants. Rebellion is in the air. Charter schools, vouchers, tuition tax credits, and now even the new president encouraging choice! But more constructively, many of God's people are sounding and, better yet, acting like Joshua and Caleb. They are not killing the giants; they are just moving into the territory that is rightfully theirs. And God is blessing their land-taking. A clear example is the way classical, Christian education, as practiced by parents in schools and homes all across the country, is challenging the right of the giants to occupy sacred ground. Perhaps this may encourage other Christian parents who too long have lived in fear of the giants, or worse have believed the false promises of the giants, to gird up their loins and join the conquest.

There are "giants" in our land. They are big, for now. May God allow us to see the day when: "There shall no man be able to stand before you; the Lord your God shall lay the dread of you and the fear of you on all the land on which you set foot, as He has spoken to you" (Deut. 11:25). To Him be the glory!

\* \* \*

EDUCATIONAL PREPAREDNESS: WILSONIAN OR BIBLICAL?

> By teaching them to read, we have left them at the mercy of the printed word. By the invention of the film and the radio, we have made certain that no aversion to reading shall secure them from the incessant battery of words, words, words. They do not know what the words mean; they do not know how to ward them off or blunt their edge or fling them back; they are a prey to words in their *emotions*, instead of being masters of them in their *intellects*.
> ~Dorothy Sayers, *The Lost Tools of Learning*

# We have "tolerant" churches who seek appeasement with tyrants.

When the over-inflated pride of self-centered European monarchs was pricked and the long-expected war of national egos finally broke out in Europe in July, 1914, President Woodrow Wilson urged Americans to be "too proud to fight." Not many argued with him since, after all, the fighting was far away across the vast Atlantic. Even after over a hundred Americans went down with the Lusitania, Wilson's response was to urge us to consider the idea of "preparedness," as though good intentions could adequately prepare our doughboys for what they would face in the mud and blood of Verdun or the Somme or the Argonne Forest. But they went anyway, with the president's empty theme of "making the world safe for democracy" as their battle-cry.

From the time our Lord walked the streets of Jerusalem until now, the people of God have been told by their King that they face a world-wide war of ideas. On one side is the Truth: the Word in flesh and in a book. On the other side, our enemy concocts a plethora of ideas that have one thing in common they exalt the pride of man. There is no neutral territory. And the enemy has no compassion on the unprepared.

But urbane, sophisticated Christians of the present time (fill in the blank with any year, it doesn't matter) don't hold to such harsh contrasts. We have "tolerant" churches who seek appeasement with tyrants. Christians using war themes sound so, well, crusade-ish. Therefore, every spring thousands of Christian high school graduates pour into American culture, with no more clue of their purpose or the battle they face than did our boys landing in France in June of 1917.

So, what happens to them? To continue the battlefield metaphor, in this world war of ideas, it seems one of three possible scenarios await these young recruits: Most of these young zealous believers actually know a few scriptures and, with a white-knuckled grip on their Bibles, charge over the top and into the face of the merciless machine-gun bullets, bullets comprised of humanistic philosophy, fired with deadly, accurate aim by pagan professors. Like so many British Tommies marching smartly in rows against the enemy, these young believers are mown down, collapsing back into their college classroom desks with the sound of mocking laughter around them. They will never rise again, and later, as adults, they will disappear into the muddy fields of post-modern culture, joining the hundreds of thousands of American Christians content to go along to get along. But they'll go to church.

Other graduates, like many of their parents, choose to ignore and write-off any talk of preparing well for a war of ideas. And so, like most Americans in early 1941, these young people make plans for college, for work, for marriage, for comfortable lives, with the firmly held notion that such a war will never touch them where they live. But then there is a Sunday morning in December in Hawaii or, in these students' lives, perhaps plans fall through or they're required to vote on an issue or children are born and need to be educated or a dear friend needs counsel or a parent dies or a church splits.... Then, as with the British at Dunkirk, their unpreparedness compels them to flee, to retreat from the battlefield by any means at hand. Any boat will do, just take them away; they can't fight anymore. And they too fade into the culture, joining the list of casualties. (OK, for history nit-pickers, the British DID come back after Dunkirk. Thank you.)

A few graduates, prepared by God's grace through the means of a thorough, intensive training in how to battle ideas with Truth, make a beachhead even in enemy-held territory. The guns are certainly firing at them, but for them it's June 6, 1944, and they won't be turned back. Because they know what they are facing, they can keep moving forward, in spite of taking a hit here and there. All authority and territory belong indeed to their Commander, and the empty philosophies of the enemy are not strongholds enough against the Truth. These students answer back, politely but ably, to their professors and their professors are confounded. They haven't seen Christian graduates who could think and reply like this! Bosses haven't seen such honest, respectful workers like this. Newspaper editors haven't had to deal with letters and arguments like this before. Communities haven't had to be concerned about the challenging influence of a church before. Neighbors haven't seen marriages and beloved children like this before. And, ultimately and surely, the culture is won and the victory is Christ's.

What kind of preparation are our kids getting? It's got to be all-encompassing, 24-7, founded on the Word of God and historically, philosophically sound. The war is very real and on-going; we long to have God bless us and you with the grace and wisdom to prepare these future combatants very well.

\*\*\*

IN SO MANY WORDS...

One of my favorite quotes from Doug Wilson is his comment that, in response to those who accuse him of all sorts of inflammatory rhetoric on various issues, he would like to have his tombstone engraved with the words, "He was holding himself back!" Amen.

There are times when, due to reading the local newspaper or a news magazine or watching the news or just listening to parents who have been there, I hear what's happening on the other side of the chain link fence, so to speak. In other words, I read or hear about the latest doings in the government schools. And I chafe and wouldst rend mine garments if I was either strong enough or dumb enough to I'm not sure which. Anyway, I don't, but I'm provoked to often. However, I have been given very good counsel from godly people for years who have encouraged me to not "bash" the government schools. Instead I should focus my writings on what is good and important about Logos School or just classical, Christian education broadly. I believe the record shows I have, for the most part, followed that good advice. And I intend to continue to follow that advice in this column. For instance, it may seem overly negative for me to say anything about how our current God-hating, government educational system is similar to the former Soviet system of education. So I won't do that. Rather, I would like to allow someone with more knowledge and clout in the public sector make that and other rather blunt points.

John Taylor Gatto was a public school teacher for thirty years in some of the toughest schools in America located in downtown Manhattan. He not only was a long-term teacher: he was awarded again and again with prestigious honors for his brilliant teaching abilities. These awards included those from the New York State Education Department, Encyclopedia Britannica, and the New York Public School Alliance. In addition, he earned the New York State Teacher of the Year in 1990 and 1991, after being named New York City Teacher of the Year for 1989, 1990, and 1991. In other words, he was no slouch of a teacher. But he resigned in a very public fashion in 1991 by publishing his resignation in the *Wall Street*

*Journal.* In a recent interview with *School Reform News* he made some enlightening remarks (watch for references to the kind of teaching he would endorse I was pleasantly surprised by them, too).

People who are well-schooled in government schools have a low threshold of boredom. They need constant novelty to feel alive because they have only the flimsiest inner lives. Here's how schools pull the trick off: They destroy the inner life. They do this by training poorly in history, philosophy, economics, literature, poetry, theology, music, art—anything that is known to develop a personal inner life.

# "My personal bias is towards the classical schooling technique because the little bit of what I had has stuck with me and served me very, very well."

There is no way to fix them (the government schools). It's an enormous system where no individual has very much influence, and the system has built-in protections against change. Even the current standards movement is certain to be only rhetorically realized because the system has its own structural logic, and that does not include excellence. To say that you're going to produce high standards by putting money, or pressure, or tests at fourth through eighth grade—that is just Pollyanna nonsense. The American education system is a Soviet-style system, and just because we live in the United States is no guarantee that it's not a Soviet system. It destroys people wholesale while it provides for the world's most reliable domestic economy. That was in the original design of the system ... and it has achieved those purposes perfectly.

It's interesting to note that in the Presidential election of 2000, four of the final six candidates were from private boarding schools that had a collective graduating class yearly of under 2,000 people.

It's significant that when the British owned North America, they took steps to prevent the development of the active literacies of writing and public speaking in the colonial population. If you can read well, and fluently, you can get access to the best minds that ever lived. But you can't change things unless you can convince others, and you do that only by writing and speaking. I would absolutely concentrate on the rhetoric and debate stages of classical education.

My personal bias is towards the classical schooling technique because the little bit of what I had has stuck with me and served me very, very well. But these techniques have been understood for a long time by people who wanted to do the best for themselves and their children. And the secret of all the successes I won as a school teacher was that I adopted those procedures.[1]

As a school, we don't exist to topple the government school system. That's up to the holy and just One. God has been very kind to allow us to see wonderful educational successes in hundreds of children's lives through the work of Logos School. We pray He will continue to open the eyes of greater numbers of Christian parents here and abroad to the mandate of a Christian education and the benefit of a specifically classical education for their children and future generations. We won't "hold back" on expressing that desire. Thank you for your continued interest and support!

---

1. Interview by George A. Clowes, "Masters of their own souls: John Taylor Gatto," The Heartland Institute, August 1, 2001, heartland.org/news-opinion/news/masters-of-their-own-souls-john-taylor-gatto/.

# 5

## EVEN A CHILD IS
## KNOWN BY HIS DEEDS

*What does it mean to be a "Christian" school? Sit twelve assorted Christian school administrators down and ask them that question, and I'll bet you'll get twelve assorted answers. There are certain obvious, predictable answers: "A school that is founded on God's Word." "A school that seeks to glorify Jesus Christ in all it does." "A school that trains children up in the way that they should go." All true and appropriate answers, but of the same ilk as saying that an espresso stand sells coffee; no doubt, but the answer begs even more questions. Such as what kinds of coffee, what do they taste like, how is the coffee different than all the other espresso stands, or is it different? In other words, it is not enough definition to say that you're a Christian school, and define your mission only by one of the above answers.*

*We certainly didn't start out with a fully-operational definition, either. In fact, we're daily learning what we are and aren't as a Christian school (not to mention a classical school), as God grants us a bit more insight. Some of the various bits we've obtained are recorded here.*

ALIENS

Excerpts from a commencement address for a sister ACCS school:
Greetings to you parents, families, grandparents, friends, board members, fac-

ulty and staff and not least of all, greetings to you, our graduating aliens.

Lest you think I am being disrespectful to these sharp-looking young men and this young lady whom I barely know or, heaven forbid, that you think I am trying to appeal to the tastes of the current, sci-fi pop culture, allow me to explain myself. You ARE aliens in two very significant ways.

The first way is an alien is a person who finds himself in a land where, due to the differences in his upbringing, appearance, culture, language, education and religion, he is regarded as a foreigner, a stranger in a strange land. Even with the little I know of you and your school, you most definitely fit this description of an alien. Pause and consider with me:

First, your origins or upbringing. I'm going out on a limb here, but I'd guess that you were raised by loving parents who, against the will and inclinations of our culture, insisted on standards of respect, behavior, cleanliness, and nutrition now largely considered anachronistic. Right was right and wrong was wrong, regardless of the current year or even your personal feelings.

Second, judging from your current appearance, if purple hair and pierced tongues were ever part of your anatomy, wisdom, maturity and taste have won the day. Again, this most likely reflects well on your parents' patient, long-suffering training, as they swam upstream, fighting forces larger than themselves.

Third, how about the culture and language you have been exposed to? Alien to the max. Beauty is like the gleaming flecks of gold barely perceptible in a mountain stream at the best of times. Today it is almost impossible to discover beauty under the muddying effects of the ugliness in our pop culture. But, through the godly efforts and persistence of a growing number of Christian folks, beauty is being rediscovered and rescued and set upon its rightful pedestal again, probably even by your teachers. For instance, I believe you have been privileged to see and experience the richness of real artists, poets, authors, and musicians through the ages. You have also been trained in a wonderful ancient language fools now declare long dead, even as they use its terminology to reason, analyze, categorize and finally pronounce the death sentence.

Fourth, your education. Ah yes, your education. It is tempting to spend the rest of my brief time with you just on the unique, dare I say, classically applicable education you have received. Even though your school, like ours, is just out of the starting blocks in the race to recover an ancient prize, i.e. a thoroughly rigorous education, it has already affected you in ways you are just discovering. One of those ways is to put you rather significantly out of step with your peers. While a unqualified blessing, your education just wasn't the pragmatic means to a high salary and maximum lifestyles, but rather the preparation for continued learning about God's good earth and Himself. An alien concept indeed.

Fifth, and finally, your religion. This actually leads to my second reason for calling you aliens at the outset. But first what may seem like a diversion, but is nothing of the sort:

I will make a prediction here and now about each one of you that you may find a bit chilling, but I promise it is meant to comfort and inspire you. My prediction is this: I think it highly likely you will each die. No matter what paths, choices, moves, jobs, etc. that you take after you leave this place, death will one day find you. Now, lest this sound too macabre, I now move to my second reason for calling you aliens: the Bible says you are in Hebrews 11:8,9 and I Peter 2:11, among other passages. Christians are, by their very redeemed natures, strangers in a strange land. Death will one day take us through the door, across the chasm, into the river, (all wonderful literary analogies for death, by the way) and we will find ourselves, really find ourselves for the first time, and for time beyond time, resting in our final home glorious heaven. Or as C.S. Lewis wrote in *The Last Battle* describing our arrival in heaven, "The term is over, the holidays have begun, the dream is ended, this is the morning."

## Christians are, by their very redeemed natures, strangers in a strange land.

As believers in the risen Lord, you are sojourners here. You will only have time to put up a tent, at best. Your time on earth, according to Scripture, will be like a morning mist, a wisp of smoke, like the brief time a flower blooms. But it is all before you now. Life awaits. How will you invest in that brief lapse of time before death calls you to your Creator, to give account for these years facing you now? Scripture says you will not only be held accountable for your actions, but there will be eternal rewards—eternal, mind you, for what you did while here. What will your obituaries read like to those left behind? That matters. And they will just be read by people. Even more, then, what will your Lord say when you face Him? What will His assessment be of what you did with the talents, gifts, blessings, He has already bestowed and will bestow on you?

Here's my two cents for you as you, I hope, ponder the weight of death and heaven a bit: love wisely and love well.

Love wisely: choose with wisdom the studies, the books, the music, the entertainment, the friends, the jobs, and certainly, the spouse you will love. For where your treasure is, there will be your heart. Love wisely that your Master in heaven will approve and have pleasure in your choices. And your parents will also be very proud, by the way.

Love well: Don't love lightly. Give all you can to what you love. If you have chosen wisely, love well. Love with teeth in it. Study well, work well, play well, read well, exhaust yourself in doing good. Practice now loving with commitment to a goal. Love your family well: you should know by now the value that has. And should God give you a godly spouse who has also loved wisely in choosing YOU, you will be more prepared to love him or her well. That means until you are parted by death. We keep coming back to that death deal don't we? That's because in the world God made, cursed by the fall now, death is what we will all come to, except for those fortunate enough to be here when the Lord returns. So, I say again, love wisely and love well.

Revel in your alieness: Delight in the unique ways you have been prepared by this school for the world you will soon be a part of. You may be alien to those around you, but, and here's the wonderful irony, you are actually more attuned now to this world, as it really is, than those who love it for the wrong reasons and in the wrong way. For you have been told the truth about it and its Creator! The "real world" has not been hidden from you, nor you from it, popular myths to the contrary. Evil, perversion, and ugliness are not more real or important or strong than goodness, unsullied pleasures, and beauty. Even in this fallen world, grass and flowers, given enough time, bloom over Auschwitz. Love trumps hate, ugliness fades, beauty endures, the bad guys lose, the good guys win; God says so.

And so, please regard your alieness as Abraham your father did he looked beyond his circumstances of sand and heat and tents to a city whose builder is God Himself. Love wisely and well here, and by doing so, you will be investing in the home you will enjoy forever. And don't take yourselves too seriously. Congratulations and blessings to each of you! And from one alien to others...Soli deo gloria!

EVEN A CHILD IS KNOWN BY HIS DEEDS

\* \* \*

CALLING OUR SHOTS

One of my favorite past-times is target shooting with Seth, my son. We move the car out of the garage and set up a box at the far end. The box's interior is then ringed with burnt-out light bulbs of various sizes. We save them up for several weeks and then have a shoot out with pellet revolvers. As we take turns, we frequently ask each other, "What's your target?" Frankly, it would be hard to *miss* hitting one of the bulbs; so to make sure we are being precise, we call our shots. And unlike paper targets, it's not only obvious *where* you hit; it makes such a satisfyingly cool explosion! Calling our shots keeps us accountable to each other and ensures our shooting improves.

In a similar way, Logos School is self-consciously aiming in some direction all the time. In light of our philosophy and goals, we need to be aware of not only where we are heading broadly but also how that direction compares to other institutions' directions. Putting it another way, we need to know and communicate to our supporters what the differences are between our aims and those of other educational options. Because, for good or ill, we are constantly being compared to these other options and, on occasion, under pressure to change our aim to be more like theirs. So, before we either succumb to or resist such pressures, it would be helpful to examine their aims.

## What does learning about Aristotle have to do with my job interviews?

The two other options, largely speaking, are the government schools and modern (not classical) Christian schools. (Home schooling and tutorial services are not being considered here since they do not have the same corporate nature schools share.) What general, philosophical aims do these other options seem to have at this point in time? What do they consider worthy philosophical targets and thereby set their direction? If they are worthwhile ideas, we need to be willing, at least, to consider them for possible adoption. If the ideas are dangerous or a waste of time, we need to recognize that and have an answer ready for those who would want to move us in that direction.

Generally speaking (of course), the government schools have adopted an unmitigated, very pragmatic view of the purpose of education. This is most evident in the widespread, new gospel of "School-To-Work" programs. In the past, it was pretty much just school counselors who encouraged kids to plan their course work with an eye toward getting "a good job." Now the gloves have come off, and throughout the land it's a no-holds-barred scramble to prepare young people for the marketplace. It should come as no surprise then to hear the students constantly question whether their assigned school work has any utilitarian value. What does learning about Aristotle have to do with my job interviews? Why should I learn about Andrew Jackson if I am just planning to be a (well-paid) mechanic? Answers to these questions are getting harder, so instead the curriculum of these schools is becoming more utilitarian all the time. Lofty-sounding, euphemistic educational ideals are fading fast under the harsh glare of making a buck. These young people will be trained from kindergarten to graduation to become good workers for our great society. Karl Marx would be thrilled to know his ideas are being resurrected on another continent.

A growing practice among modern, American Christian schools is, in the name of "character emphasis" or "spiritual training," to belittle success in academics or intellectual pursuits. Instead, climbing to the moral high ground, they espouse "just loving Jesus!" Numerous magazine articles written by Christian educators recite this mantra over and over again: "We should encourage the students to just love God and not be concerned with good grades or emphasizing academics!" It has gone far beyond the biblical warning that "love builds up and knowledge puffs up." Good grades, strenuous intellectual work, and classical studies are seen as almost antithetical to students' Christian growth. The gnostics would heartily agree: spiritual is good; material is bad. This has the appearance of wisdom but denies the reality of scriptural mandates that make *no* distinction between a humble *heart* and a *mind* seeking to be transformed biblically. Jesus placed loving God with ALL that we have, including our minds, above all other commandments. We are to "work heartily, as unto the Lord" (Col. 3:23). Good, hard work, done with the right attitude, gives glory to God. These schools seem to forget their role of trafficking in ideas and instead take on the role and even the appearance of churches.

Preparing kids to enter the workplace is not a worthless idea. Encouraging the students to consider all their learning as nothing compared to the knowledge of Christ is not a bad idea either. But neither goes far enough. Let's aim higher yet. How about this: "As you therefore have received Christ Jesus the Lord, so *walk* in Him, having been *firmly rooted* and now being *built up* in Him and *established* in your faith just as you were *instructed* and overflowing with gratitude. See to it that no one takes you captive through *philosophy* and empty deception, according to the *tradition of men*, according to the *elementary principles* of the world, rather than according to Christ" (Col. 2:6-8). Notice the italicized words imply a balanced grasp of our foundation in Christ along with the *rigorous* study of ideas, worldly and biblical. Ideas have consequences, as any good study of history will show. And we must study history well. That implies standards, grades, accountability ... solid, academic work.

The classical, Christian philosophy Logos is seeking to implement doesn't ensure a bull's-eye in all that we aim for every time; only God's grace sustains our direction day-by-day. But we do believe that this time-tested philosophy makes it easier to know *what*, *how*, and *why* we are shooting. If anyone asks, we can tell them what we are aiming for; we can call our shots. Please keep praying that by His grace we will get to be better shots through humble, rigorous practice.

\* \* \*

## THE TIGHTROPE OF BEING A NONDENOMINATIONALCHRISTIAN SCHOOL

> Now I exhort you, brethren, by the name of our Lord Jesus Christ, that you all agree, and there be no divisions among you, but you be made complete in the same mind and in the same judgement.
> ~1 Cor. 1:10

Discussion of controversial issues which the Bible does not specifically address, or which divides real Christians, should be on an informative, nonpartisan level. Teachers should be careful not to bias the attitudes of the students in a manner that would cause offense to the parents.

> Presentations of all sides, with an encouragement to the students to confer with their parents, is the best approach.
> ~Logos School Policy Manual, Personnel Policies Section

The policy above is often referred to as our "Secondary Doctrine policy." When it was formulated along with dozens of other policies back in 1981, it seemed like just a good, practical plan. Now, almost eleven years later, it stands out as one of the most often referenced and cherished policies we have.

Because we hold to the biblical principle behind the policy, we have asked every teaching applicant, during the board's hiring interviews, if the applicant understood and could comply with this policy. Practicing the principle also means that we recruit and hire teachers and staff from a wide range of evangelical churches.

However, I used the term "tightrope" in my title for a good reason. Although I've never even dreamed of being a circus aerialist, I know a few things from watching some professionals. First, you better have a really good rope! It has to be tight and strong enough to hold you, even when you jump up and down on it. Then, because it's usually a long fall to the ground, it doesn't matter too much which side you err on; it's a big mistake either way. So, you need to have an extremely well-developed sense of balance, which can only come from constant training and familiarity with the rope.

## Secondary doctrines could be defined as those things which potentially (and often substantively) divide Christians from Christians.

The "rope" in my analogy is our school's Statement of Faith. As I tell new families and potential staff members, the statements it contains, since they come from the scriptures, do divide Christians from non-Christians. We call them primary doctrines. Secondary doctrines could be defined as those things which potentially (and often substantively) divide Christians from Christians. The former doctrines, essentially the Gospel, will be vigorously taught and emphasized in Logos School. The latter doctrines are addressed by our policy above. We don't consider secondary doctrines unimportant, but our Lord placed a high value on our unity as believers. Frequently He commanded it and He even said the world would know the truth of His salvation by the way in which we love one another (John 13:34-35).

Even after quite a few years it's not easy to stay on the rope all the time. It means having to 'bite your tongue' on occasion, when you're anxious to dump the "right" way of viewing things on the students or even parents. But God, by His grace and mercy, has kept the number of heavy confrontations to a small number. This is truly amazing, when you consider the number and range of backgrounds our many staff members and families have had. The blessings of being a unifying element in the Christian community have also been numerous. By concentrating primarily on what God has done for us through His Son, we have experienced the joy of real fellowship, both individually and collectively. Please pray that we stay steadfastly on the tightrope.

* * *

*There are so many assumptions and attendant baggage regarding Christian schools, that sometimes it's just plain overwhelming to try to sort through it all. One of the more prevalent pieces of luggage I came across early on was the idea that Christian schools naturally have only Christian kids in them. Further, not only are Christian schools supposed to ground the students in a solid academic education, the school is also largely responsible for the spiritual growth of the students. What a task! No wonder so many parents, having those assumptions, become unhappy with many Christian schools, including Logos. If the child frequently sins at school, then the obvious conclusion is that the school is not doing its spiritual training adequately. I have actually had parents say, upon hearing about another child's sin, "I wouldn't have expected that kind of behavior in a Christian school!" As though our doors are sin-impermeable.*

*We are "in loco parentis" as Christian educators, which means that all of our duties, including any spiritual training, are delegated. The parents retain, like it or not, all the responsibility for their children's education spiritual as well as academic. That's as it should be.*

## A CARDINAL SIN OF CHRISTIAN EDUCATION

Perhaps you've heard the expression that runs something like this: "There are more hypocrites behind hymnals than anywhere else." Unfortunately, judging from the general condition of the Church today, there is a lot of truth in that statement. When the Lord God in His Third Commandment prohibited His name being used meaninglessly, the ramifications ran far deeper than the pagans using it as an oath when they stub their toes. In fact, strictly speaking, the Lord wasn't directly addressing the command to nonbelievers; the direct hearers of the command were His chosen people.

Over the years I've had occasion to see many Christian school's entrance requirements for their families and students. It seems most have some version of a requirement that either one or both of the parents "have a clear Christian testimony," and oftentimes if the student is entering junior high or high school, he too must espouse a relationship with Christ. The reason for these requirements is obvious: the schools want students and families who share the common faith. If achievable, this would certainly make the work of Christian educators far simpler.

## A spoken confession does not equal a new creation.

The sad, but irrefutable truth is that having a requirement does not ensure a redeemed student body. It doesn't even guarantee a predominantly Christian enrollment. A spoken confession does not equal a new creation. However, there is one thing that such a policy will ensure. It ensures that there will be students at that Christian school who, by being granted admission and jumping that hoop, will assume, possibly to their eternal detriment, that they are Christians, when they are most definitely not.

I believe that one of the cardinal sins of Christian education is the widespread practice of treating all students as though they are Christians. (I specifically used the term "Christian education," vs. just Christian schools for a reason. Vast numbers of homeschoolers have also committed this mistake of the assumption of the salvation of their children.) I am not saying that Christian educators should call a child's precious account of his conversion experience into question to his face. Over the years Logos has existed, I am very happy to state that numerous children have told us of their coming into the kingdom. Our response has been and will always be to rejoice with those young ones. At the same time, we remember the many scriptures that say that "he that endures to the end will be saved." Christ said to watch and wait for fruit that will testify to a person's true nature: redeemed or rebellious.

Our Reverence policy was formed for this very purpose. It states, among other things, that teachers are to avoid "implying directly or indirectly that all the students are Christians." It also stresses the kind of awe and reverence we are to give to our Lord's name. It specifies avoiding trite songs or other references to God or mocking angelic powers, good or evil. This has real, day-to-day ramifications in what kind of songs we sing, how we pray, the kinds of skits we do for assemblies, etc. It certainly affects the way we discuss things pertaining to believers. For example, instead of saying, "As Christians, we all know God hears our prayers." Instead, we ask the teachers to rephrase that same statement to remove the implied collectivism: "If you are a Christian, you know God promises to hear your prayers." A small, but significant difference. One that won't continue to inoculate a child against Christianity by "giving" him just enough to think he has had it all and can later in life say, "Yeah, I tried that Christian stuff and it didn't make any difference for me." Too right.

As always, we need your prayers to discern how best to love and encourage these precious students to have a lasting, real relationship with our heavenly Father.

\* \* \*

CHRISTIAN SCHOOL TEACHERS:
WARRIORS AGAINST THE DARKNESS

I can almost hear some folks saying, "Getting a bit cliche with our topics, aren't we, Tom?" Bear with me. A warrior, according to my American Heritage Dictionary, is "one who is engaged or experienced in battle." If you don't think teachers are daily fighting battles, allow me to acquaint you with the reality of this profession. To cut some fast thinkers off at the pass no, I am not alluding to the need for consistent vigilance in the area of classroom discipline. I am not so far gone as to think that, even on the toughest of days, keeping third graders under control is the equivalent of real warfare. Then again....

The reality I am alluding to can be illustrated by an example from our Western culture's colorful history. Courtesy of the U.S. Navy, I had the opportunity to visit Rome and other ancient cities in Italy. Even in ruins, the architecture was truly incredible! The aqueducts, for instance, were a technological marvel, even by modern standards. These mortar and brick structures carried water to Roman cities over dozens of miles, from the mountains streams to the towns, gradually decreasing in height to allow gravity to do its work. Within many Roman cities, this water system linked up to street water fountains and even some basic indoor plumbing! After the fall of Rome as a world empire and the coming of what we call the Dark Ages, not only did we as a civilization lose our moral and civil bearings, we lost the ability to even make cement. Think about it. In less than two generations men went from daily living with fresh water from aqueducts to filthy, contaminated squalor and rampant pestilence.

True education—thorough and moral education, was lost for a time during our culture's Dark Ages. I am not doom-sayer, but others far more insightful than I are posing the question, "Are we on the verge of another cultural Dark Age?" Look around. Read the papers. Watch (if you can stomach it) what passes for entertainment on TV, in the movies, in popular music. Listen to what is being taught to young people in the government schools and in college classrooms. Never in our history have we seen such blatant evidence of darkened minds and souls ( see Romans: 1 and 2). In 1983, President Reagan commissioned a group of well-known professional educators to take a serious look at education in America. Their report, which they titled A Nation At Risk, has this statement: *"If an unfriendly foreign power had attempted to impose on America the mediocre educational performance that exists today, we might well have viewed it as an act of war."* (Emphasis mine.) Then came President Bush's plan for educational reform, America 2000, which states: "Our challenge amounts to nothing less than a revolution in education."

## Can those who brought us to this brink save us from going over the edge?

Can those who brought us to this brink save us from going over the edge? Christian school teachers, by God's very abundant and powerful grace, daily strive to prepare and gird up young lives and minds against a very real, threatening darkness. Working together with many godly parents, these teachers (I work with some of the best) are in a real battle. Real lives, hearts and minds can be won or lost.

Our Father commanded us to love Him with everything we have, including our minds. Romans 12:1, 2 considers the "transforming" of our minds as an obvious evidence of God's regeneration of our lives. It is not enough to teach our children to have warm feelings toward their Creator; they must be equipped with biblical knowledge, through years of intensive study and application, to know the Truth and use it not only to withstand the darkness, but to have victory against it. Please pray for the Christian schoolteachers you know; with God's strength they are in the front lines, preparing future warriors against the darkness.

\* \* \*

LOVE VS. KNOWLEDGE...OR...LOVING KNOWLEDGEABLY?

Knowledge puffs up, but love builds up.
~1 Cor. 8:1b

In what context have you heard the above verse quoted? Like me, you have probably heard it used numerous times in arguments that run something like this: "Knowledge and learning are OK, as far as they go, but remember," (warning tone in speaker's voice)... 'Knowledge puffs up, but love builds up!'" The conclusion in such arguments is usually that knowledge is, at best, a second-class citizen compared to love, and at worst, if too much time is spent on attaining it, knowledge can become a hindrance to love. To be honest, up until a couple of months ago, I would have written much the same argument in this space. Being involved in education for most of my adult life, every time I heard someone put forth the above persuasion, I would feel a pang of pseudo guilt. Here I had been thinking that educating children toward a biblical worldview was a tremendously important thing to do, all the while unwittingly disregarding the importance of love!

During several recent events, I have heard some very wise, godly men explain and demonstrate that love and knowledge are not at odds. In one instance, the speaker quoted Charles Spurgeon who, when asked how he would reconcile Faith and Reason, said, "There is no need to reconcile them. Old friends do not need to be reconciled." We had our first Knights' Day, a conference day for our secondary students last month, and a main speaker encouraged the kids to use knowledge to the glory of God. He also spoke of the danger of arrogance when knowledge is considered more important than love.

## It seems even many Christians believe that the world and Scripture mean the same thing by "knowledge."

Then in studying the scriptures further to see what they said about love and knowledge, I thought the following verse from Colossians seemed applicable: "See to it that no one takes you captive through philosophy and empty deception, according to the elementary principles of the world, rather than according to Christ" (2:8). So there is a kind of so-called "knowledge" that the world offers: its "philosophy" and "elementary principles." It seems even many Christians believe that the world and Scripture mean the same thing by "knowledge." But if we think that, then we are accepting the big lie perpetrated on the last couple of generations; specifically that knowledge can be "secular," i.e. without religious content. The Bible never asserts this; just the opposite, it asserts that all true knowledge (vs. the false kind described in Colossians) and wisdom come from, and lead us back to, the Father.

A number of conclusions and applications appropriate to formal Christian education may be drawn from this view:

- There is no antipathy between knowledge and love, between faith and reason. Rather, as our increasing faith should increase our ability to reason biblically, so too our love of Christ (as Christian parents and teachers) should increase our hunger for knowledge.
- Our students, our children should be taught in light of the above truth.

They should see and understand it is our love for them and our Lord compelling us to equip them with more and more knowledge.

- This knowledge, by means of instruction and content, can and should equip the students to identify and counter the world's philosophies, "empty deceptions," and "elementary principles." They come to understand that only by applying biblically trained reason, in Christ's love, will they be able to effectively and knowledgeably counter the false "knowledge" of the world.

This is not at all hypothetical or wishful thinking. Everyday, in the lives of real students I see the fruit of their being trained at home and at school to love God and His gift of reason. I also look forward to seeing the effect these students will have when they go into a culture which has too few who can express Christ's love effectively and knowledgeably.

\* \* \*

SETTLING FOR "SURVIVAL"?

An advertisement I've once heard on the radio seems to epitomize the spirit of this age. It's for some brand of beer and has as its theme "It doesn't get any better than this!" What they mean by "this" is meeting your buddies at the local bar drinking lots of the named beer and eating large quantities of red meat, all the while ogling the ladies.

Not too many Christians I know would overtly subscribe to that lifestyle of philosophy. Yet over many years of talking with parents and students I've repeatedly heard variations on the following theme "I think he/she will probably do all right in the public schools." Upon further discussion it usually turns out that "all right" means not becoming pregnant, addicted to drugs, or generally becoming a juvenile delinquent. Should a child from a Christian home survive in the public system without totally compromising his faith, he is considered a success. In other words we as parents can't and don't expect any more than that type of success. "It doesn't get any better then this!"

## Our children can and should be "more than conquerors" in the world.

Obviously I believe it can and should be better than merely surviving. At our 1990 Eighth Grade Promotion ceremony one of our co-valedictorians was Bekah Wilson. In her speech Bekah spent a fair amount of time speaking of her gratefulness for the creation of Logos. She ended her talk by saying "Thank you, Papa!" to her father Doug Wilson one of the founders of Logos School. That is the kind of success that the Bible promises to parents who follow God's guidelines for raising children.

The measure of success I'm referring to here is not just academic. There is a significant difference in the teaching and content of what we consider academic work here at Logos, but that is a topic for another time. The moral development of a child can't be measured in the same way academic growth can be and it is the moral development of a child that will make the biggest difference in the long-term. The fact that a student got an "A" in Algebra will not have the same effect in his life that an embracing of the command to love his neighbor will. Not many people would disagree with that statement, but what do we really do? Consider how much time energy thought and money goes into most Sunday School programs which make up one or two hours of a child's week. How many Sunday School teachers would be allowed to spend that time encouraging the kid, toward an unbiblical humanistic view of the world? Not many! But what about the 30+ hours a week that same child spends in a school setting? Why should we settle for "surviving" the time there and trust that the one to two hours of formal moral training will be sufficient for training in godliness? Even coupled with whatever time of formal training is done at home this will not come close to the amount of time at school.

The children described in Proverbs who "rise up" and praise their parents receive a thorough, consistent, round-the-clock biblical training. Anything less will be insufficient. Our children can and should be "more than conquerors" in the world. That's not just a vision we're seeing real conquerors here. They're growing stronger daily under the nurturing of their parents and teachers. A far cry indeed from merely "surviving!"

# 6

## IT'S NOT JUST A JOB...

*Teaching and administering in a Christian school, especially one that seeks to be classical, is not something I was trained to do in college, or anywhere else that I remember. Yet, here we are and, even though there isn't anywhere or anyone I know of to turn to for some sort of blueprint, I have seen certain common patterns develop within our professional work at Logos. Some of those patterns are no doubt similar to and even inherent in any teaching situation, Christian or secular, like setting up staff manuals or having in-house training. But other patterns have also developed, and these we have had to muddle our way through to become part and parcel with what we do, such as identifying and institutionalizing the authority structures within Logos. Dull as that may sound, having everyone parents, board members, administrators, teachers, students know how they fit into the invisible lines of submission and respect within the school has been a long, pain-filled process. Policies and guidelines have been carefully written after flesh-and-blood people have been fired, offended, and otherwise disturbed, yes, even in a Christian setting.*

*Professional protocol and ethics matter a lot. Here a few collected and diverse aspects to the professional work we try to do at Logos.*

## AN OPEN LETTER TO A PROSPECTIVE CHRISTIAN SCHOOL TEACHER

Dear Roderick,

Thank you for your enthusiastic letter of inquiry. I am pleased and humbled that you would ask for my opinion on whether you should pursue a career in teaching at a Christian school like Logos. Your last comment.... "I believe your opinion is worth getting since you are my uncle, no matter what my mother has told me about you!" was also insightful. Your confidence overwhelms me. Anyway, here are some thoughts for your consideration:

You didn't specify whether you are interested in teaching at the elementary or secondary level so I will try to generalize my comments to fit either level. Also, I am glad you're thinking about this in your freshman year at Polly T. Korekt State University. Many students (like your favorite uncle) didn't consider the need for a serious career choice until their senior year. College can seem like a warm bath, at times, until you realize you have to get out and put your bare feet on that cold-tiled floor, called the real world.

The first thing you should start doing now, if you are intent on being a Christian school teacher after you graduate from P.S.U. is to study the Scriptures daily and evaluate everything you hear in the light of God's primer. Also, read the books on the list I am enclosing. They were written by Christian scholars far more knowledgeable than myself (a hearty "Amen", no doubt will emanate from your mother). The one by C.S. Lewis is especially applicable to your questions.

Regarding the university training you are now subject to, consider that much of what you're taught, especially in your "ed" classes will be as useful to you as a solar-powered flashlight; interesting concept, but not very applicable to real life.

Seriously, Roddy, it is no coincidence that the vast bulk of my teachers here at Logos are either parents with children in the school or come from families where Christian education was highly valued. We have had numerous fresh-faced youths come to us straight from college, anxious to start their first year of teaching, only to be told by me that they have to relearn most of what they were taught by their professors about children, discipline, the teaching process, and the curriculum, and the world. Other than those minor problem areas, these young teachers were somewhat prepared. I hope this doesn't discourage you; so what if you're wasting thousands of your parents' hard-earned bucks? Just kidding.... Anyway, our current teachers, many of whom have been with us for quite a few years, have carefully weighed the differences between the way the world teaches children and the way God instructs parents to have their children educated. These teachers have come to the conclusion that God's truth is worth the investment of their time and efforts.

> These teachers have come to the conclusion that God's truth is worth the investment of their time and efforts.

Here is a list of a few personal characteristics that, if you have them or can attain them, will greatly assist you in this career:

1. A strong, loving heart that can withstand the temptation to withhold needed discipline for a sweet-faced little one, and yet pour out consistent, overt love toward the unlovely, disruptive hotshot.
2. A lead-lined stomach that can endure stories of, and close encounters with, gruesome childhood injuries and diseases, as well as consume and enjoy a full spectrum of treats. (There must be more recipes for birthday cupcakes and cookies than there are languages in the world.)
3. A rhino's skin to allow children's and parents' potentially pain-inducing comments to just bounce off. Be assured, my boy, if you have any quirk, feature, blemish, habit, no matter how personal, some student will point it out to you and to the world at large in double-digit decibels. Not to mention that your decisions regarding everything from pencil-sharpening procedures to test days will come under the parents' scrutiny. Just keep smiling and exude that ol' confidence.
4. A computer-quick mind and a restrained tongue which, when used in conjunction, will keep you learning how to stay at least one step ahead of your students, and will keep you from attempting to reveal the Mind of God to them in one sitting. These characteristics will also help you think of loads of snappy comebacks to ridiculous questions, but the wisdom not to say them.
5. Finally, and most important, a teachable and humble spirit without which you'd be better off selling "mint" Edsels, sporting a phony grin and

a plaid jacket. The majority of parents you might be working with see their children as the most precious gifts of God given them, second only to the gift of the Lord Jesus Christ. And they will be right. Plan to practice your craft tenderly and cautiously; these are eternal beings for whom the Savior gave His life and their parents would gladly do so as well.

Write again as often as you wish. Greetings to your folks! Tell your mother I still love her, in spite of that last birthday card she sent me.

Love, Uncle Tom

\* \* \*

*Sometimes a peek behind the scenes is really interesting, like finding out how they did that special effect in Star Wars. Other times, when someone tries to share a unique, or humorous view behind the scenes, there is an assumption that the viewer knows all the intimate details that make this expose so funny ... and three people end up laughing. I hope you can appreciate the following couple of columns, even if you haven't been at Logos recently.*

LOGOS' BELIEVE IT OR...DON'T: STRANGE, BUT TRUE, UNIQUE FACTS ABOUT LOGOS SCHOOL!

Since 1982 when Logos purchased its first school bus, all of its buses have been named after one of the tribes of Israel (Issachar, Zebulun, Dan, Naphtali, etc.), representing traveling groups of little nomads. *Hundreds of children have traveled on these buses, yet not one has complained about too much manna!*

Among the teaching staff currently at Logos, there are at least three married pairs of teachers. *Yet no official complaints of violations of the No-P.D.A.s (Public Displays of Affection) policy have been registered!*

Beth Everett, a former Logos student, was hired to teach sixth grade in 1992. Her mother, Mary Lou Busby, a first grade teacher at Logos, did not object and seemed to understand her daughter was now grown up and on her own. *Nevertheless, on one cold, wet day in winter, Mr. Garfield received a note excusing Mrs. Everett from recess duty, signed by her mother!*

In October, 1987, the remodeling of a former roller rink to become the home of Logos School was almost complete. On the exterior, the school sign was up, proclaiming the new name in letters eighteen inches high, and twenty-three windows, and several new doors had been added. One day a group of would-be roller skaters came into the office to inquire as to times the building might be open for them to enjoy their favorite indoor sport. *The school representative not only refrained from sarcasm, he did not charge them an entrance fee!*

It has been frequently observed by reputable individuals that often a notable transformation happens to normally very shy or even withdrawn children upon spending a relatively short period of time at Logos School. Shocked parents relate that some of these children have contributed to class discussions and even *appeared on the school stage, in front of masses of people, wearing bizarre clothing and reciting in bold voices!* (To date the state department of Health and Welfare has not made any formal investigation.)

If you put all of the current Logos elementary teachers in a small room and lobbed in a full water balloon, you would most likely dampen a teacher who has not only taught for several years at his/her grade, but *is a parent of some Logos students as well!* If you did the same thing with the secondary teachers, you would likely soak a man with an affinity for writing and literature, and has also taught at Logos for at least several years. In either case, you would not only be struck by the Logos staff's professionalism, *you would also be struck by their retaliatory strike of water balloons!*

Unbeknownst to many people in North America, Logos School not only has the only private, nonsectarian junior and senior high programs (sharing the same building as the elementary program) in the Moscow, Idaho community ... *it is also the only school in that community with a Greek name! ("Logos", not "School")*

Even after serving at Logos School since its inception in 1981 and seeing numerous school-year endings, *Mr. Garfield, Logos' superintendent, will miss all of the students (and staff) something awful while the school is out for the summer!* (Editor's note: Mr. Garfield became quite sentimental and emotional after entering the last strange fact for this column and gave this writer the following quote to enter: "I'm very proud of all the kids and their work this year ... and I will be praying for them over the summer. Please ask them to come by and visit me!")

DEAR PARENTS

\* \* \*

## I CORINTHIANS 13 IN TRV (TEACHERS' REVISED VERSION)

*(with apologies to brother Paul)*

If I speak with the tongues of Latin, Greek, and all other Romance languages, but do not have love for my students, I have become as the sounding of the class buzzer or recess bell.

And if I have the gift of knowing a student's chance of passing my class just by looking at him, and know how to explain all mysteries, even the purpose and working of the electoral college, and all knowledge, without relying on my teacher's editions, and if I have all faith to move the entire NEA to a conservative stance, but do not have love for my students, I am nothing.

And if I give all my tape, chalk, and pens from my desk to help equip poor students and poor teachers, and if I deliver my body to frigid temperatures and high winds at recess duty, but do not have love for these precious students, all that sacrifice profits me nothing.

Love for my students is patient, enduring all sorts of strange behaviors; it is kind, not delivering an incredibly applicable, but nevertheless, snide comment when tempted; love is not jealous of my "private, personal" time; love for my students means I model humility to them, even though I do know more than they do, and I encourage them to be open to correction, too, for love is not arrogant.

Love for my students shows itself in my classroom decorum, it means I seek no glory for myself, it is not easily provoked, even by the umpteenth time that little guy has done that! It does not make a big deal out of what could be interpreted as a personal offense; it does not rejoice in teaching about pain and suffering, even if the "bad guys" are the ones on the receiving end; it does rejoice in teaching about God's truth and real justice toward all.

Love for my students draws on God's grace to bear countless antagonisms, it believes the best is possible from any student, and does not doubt a student's word without good reason each time; it hopes that each student will succeed and endures many setbacks to that hope, without giving up on the student.

This love never fails, by God's grace alone, in providing the strength and stamina I need to show these students love; but if I rely on my fantastic teaching ability or immense knowledge of the subject, these will be done away with and probably forgotten by the students; if I rely on my quick wit and large vocabulary, they will cease with every dumb cold or sore throat I may be afflicted with; if I rely on even my knowledge of how to integrate the material, even this will not last as long as love.

## For the time being my students will see, as in a hazy picture, the Master Teacher teaching through me...

For all that we may know as teachers, we still know only part of God's revelation, and even in our best teaching times, we are teaching poorly and partially compared to the Master Teacher;

But when all truth and real knowledge in Christ is revealed in the Eternal School, our "best" teaching will be done away with.

I need to remember that I, too, was once a child like those looking up to me now. I, too, perceived life as a child, seeing my teachers as demigods; I spoke, acted, and, yea verily, even thought like these students; I grew to adulthood, these students will, too. I did away with the thoughts, actions, and speech of a child, through the hard work and loving training of my teachers; these student, too, will one day lay aside these childish ways.

For the time being my students will see, as in a hazy picture, the Master Teacher teaching through me, but, Lord willing, when they come into the Eternal School, they will see Him face to face. Now I teach from my limited understanding, but then I will be able to learn and know, as I have am now known by my Teacher.

But for now the best characteristics expressed through my teaching should be: my faith in my Lord and His Word; my hope in my students expecting the very best from them, and my love for my students as an obvious channel for God's love; these three characteristics, but the greatest of these is love.

\* \* \*

*As I mentioned earlier, a novice teacher can be taught in a secular college of education how to assess students' work and issue grades (although this is becoming "outdated"). What cannot be taught, even in a Christian teachers' college, is the way to handle parental concerns or expectations regarding their children's grades in school. I would submit that Christian parents, in a Christian school, are profoundly more interested in their child's grades, and how they are determined, than the average parent in the government schools. This has certainly been our experience. There is nothing wrong with this, just the opposite; if a Christian parent wasn't interested I would question their commitment to their child's education. However, sometimes these parental expectations (and the teacher's) can be slightly out of perspective. Hence the motivation for the following...*

GRADE EXPECTATIONS

A few years ago, while at my parents' home in Portland, I had some strange impulse to view my elementary report cards. Being good parents, my folks had of course saved them in a box, tucked away with my name on it. We dug it out and, amidst old school photos that should never be seen by other humans, I found a packet of envelopes containing report cards summing up my entire elementary career. With a touch of reverential awe, I gently unfolded and read each card, anticipating sage-like observations on my tender, growing character. And I was not far wrong; year after year, even with several different schools represented, the teachers' comments bore incredible consistency "Tends to talk too much, but loves art!" That said it all, or rather, that was about all that was said. Sheeesh. The grades themselves bore no consistency, since each school had a different system of marking. I guess I passed, though.

Now that I have four children in school, three in the secondary and one in the elementary, grades and teachers' comments mean far more to me than they did when I was in school. And from my years at Logos, I know that that is true of the other parents here as well. Our hearts frequently beat with the rhythm of the successes and failures our children experience at school. Their delight with a good grade thrills us, too. Just as their tears at a poor grade can tempt us to become vigilantes ready to string up the teacher that dared to "hurt" our child this way.

Logos School is not an easy school in which to maintain an 'A' average. In fact, for many students, being at Logos means a lot of hard work just to maintain passing grades, not to mention being on the honor roll. That fact has caused a number of parents and students real distress over the years. Some parents have been tempted to resent the standards, or to assume that Logos just wants, and appeals to "smart" kids, while not caring about the success of "average" or slow students. We have had families leave Logos because, though they may not have said so at the time, they felt the school was too difficult for their children. That may have been true, too.

Our expectations as parents for our children and our children' school, teachers, daily work, grades, behavior standards, etc. will necessarily vary from family to family. That's a fact that has contributed to my loss of hair and sleep, as no doubt it does to other administrators. Some parents come close to destroying their children's childhood for the almighty 'A'. Others put school work lower than laundry on the priority scale. Nevertheless, Logos was, and still is being formed to offer a certain kind of education Christian, taught in a certain way classically. Through years of trial and error, we have come up with the program we currently offer to families seeking this kind of education. Admittedly, it is not a "one-size-fits-all" program.

## Admittedly, it is not a "one-sizefits-All" program.

Therefore, while experience has taught us that the vast majority of students from families committed to a Christian education will, with varying degrees of effort, succeed at Logos, there are students who will find it very difficult. My heart, just like our teachers' hearts, goes out to the student of any age who, year after year, struggles to do his best, and pulls 'B's and 'C's at best. However, because those grades represent consistent, gut-it-out work, in the long run they will be worth far more than the 'A's of the kid who earned them without much effort at all.

School is not all there is to life; in fact it is a very short part of it, relatively, as we adults have discovered. The students who, in their homes and at Logos, learn to work hard for everything they get, will take gain much more from their school years than the students who breeze through school with little or no effort. We as parents need to remember that, just like my long-forgotten report cards, our children's grades will have little impact in the adult world for which we are preparing our children. Grade expectations need to be kept in perspective, by the school and the families. After all, we are primarily in the business of raising godly children, not GPAs.

\* \* \*

*We all frequently construct strongly-held ideas or opinions about people, businesses, churches, etc., even when we have very little real information to go on. For example, for many years I suspected that Mexican restaurants served really disgusting food, even though I had never actually eaten at one. I just thought the particular fare looked and sounded gross, so of course they would taste that way, too. It wasn't until after I was married that my wife was able to convince me to put aside my prejudice against those restaurants one time, and try having a meal in one. I acquiesced, and found, to my great surprise, that I had been right all those years! Yuck, give me shrimp or steak any day.*

*The point here being that I shouldn't have been surprised that people would construct ideas and opinions about Christian schools, particularly Logos, even when they had limited knowledge. But I was surprised, and decided to share some of the more frequent misconceptions...*

### POPULAR MYTHS ABOUT CHRISTIAN EDUCATION

Over the years I've been involved in Christian education, I've had the opportunity to talk with many individuals and groups. It's always surprising to me when otherwise intelligent, informed people have solemnly repeated common misconceptions about Christian education that have no basis in fact. Yet, because it is easier to adopt someone else's views than research the truth ourselves, the myths continue.

Let me repeat a few I regularly hear:
1. Christian schools have good discipline because good children go there. Following this logic, people are restored to health in hospitals because hospitals only admit patients who are already recovering. This myth as-

sumes that the treatment, i.e. applied biblical discipline, in the Christian school has little to do with the resulting good behavior. As every parent knows that is absurd. Children are sinners; only through God's grace and years of consistent, biblical training will children's hearts and actions be changed for the better.

2. Christian schools have good academic results/scores because they only admit very intelligent students. Sounds like a variation on the theme above, doesn't it? It is. Like the applied discipline above, it assumes that the time-tested (and in our case, the classical) teaching methods play no part in how well the students do academically, regardless of where they come from. Nevertheless, I hear this very often, especially from public school teachers and administrators. There is an a ironic twist to this myth. When Christian schools or Christian home schools do have academic problems, the same people accuse the involved teachers or a parents of incompetence. Any stick is good enough, it seems.

3. Christian education keeps Christian students from being "salt and light" in the public schools. I hear this most often from Christian parents of elementary-age students. Unfortunately, at the junior and senior high level, I hear Christian parents saying something different. At that point, the parents will often settle for their kids "surviving." That means graduating without becoming a drug addict or pregnant or otherwise being seriously damaged by the system. Nowhere in all of Scripture are we, as parents, commanded or even encouraged to send our little ones out to be "missionaries" in an overwhelmingly evil environment. In fact, just the opposite is true: from Genesis to Ephesians we are commanded to train our children up in the Lord and His word. I've seen children at Logos who are real missionaries for Christ to their unsaved fellow students. The difference is that here those young missionaries are supported and taught by adults who share the same Lord. We may even train and nurture future, mature adult missionaries.

4. Christian education shields children from the raw, ugly facts of our society. Whoops. That isn't a myth; it's true. That is, we do shield, but we don't lie. The children do learn the truth, both the ugly and the beautiful facts, as seen from God's viewpoint and with His solution.

DEAR PARENTS

# I've seen children at Logos who are real missionaries for Christ to their unsaved fellow students.

Thank you for examining these myths with me. I encourage and welcome your comments at any time, especially if you think I mythed the point.

\* \* \*

SHOULD THE BIBLE GET AN "R" RATING?

*Or "Should Christian Schools "Cleanup" the Bible?"*

> All Scripture is inspired by God and profitable for teaching, for reproof, for correction, for training in righteousness, that the man of God may be adequate, equipped for every good work.
> ~2 Timothy 3:16

A study in contrasts: a Precious Moments Christmas card, showing a cherubic, preschool looking Joseph and Mary, holding a baby Jesus, who appears to be barely a few years younger than His earthly parents, versus the biblical account of Herod's act of infanticide on the little boys of Bethlehem, and its environs, causing widespread, indescribable grief because the children "were no more." Which illustration is more in keeping with the way the Bible as a whole presents its message?

What impression of God and His Word would someone get from just a walk through the average Christian gift store? Or, for that matter, from the typical flannel-board, Sunday school stories? Would he be impressed by the overwhelming wickedness of man, God's wrath, and yet His mercy through His Son's sacrifice? Or would he come away with the impression that if only he joined some group called Christians, he, too, could buy, wear, and listen to all sorts of neat stuff?

I still recall the shock I got from reading the uncensored version of some of my favorite Old Testament Bible stories. In fact, it would prove my point, as stated by the above title, if I just put in here, verbatim, the "rest of the story" about Noah, or Lot, or Abraham, or even Tamar, Jael, Jacob, David, Dinah, Samson, and the beat goes on. Just in that little list we have drunkenness, incest, adultery, murder in various forms, rape, lying, mutilation, and other forms of violence that most Christians would turn off, understandably, were it on TV. (Believe it or not, by some fluke, I was 18 and in Navy boot camp before I got around to reading the entire book of Song of Solomon. Wow!)

## In a very real sense, the Bible was not written for children.

Christian schools too often take the very same Reader's Digest approach to the Bible. During our evaluation for accreditation with ACSI, we were encouraged to put "spiritual" posters and displays in our halls. That's somewhat understandable. Bible posters and innocuous choruses are easier to deal with and still give a "spiritual" atmosphere, than trying to explain circumcision to a class of first-graders. Lest I be misunderstood, I am not advocating that the rape of Dinah, and her brothers' bloody revenge on a whole city, be taught in gory detail to kindergartners. But neither should we Christian school teachers present the Bible as though it were a nonfiction book of fairy tales, where heroes slay giants, mighty men beat up lions, and the good guys escape deadly floods.

In a very real sense, the Bible was not written for children. Therein lies the problem for Christian educators. The Bible is, well, just too adult. People are presented as they are, in all their sinful, disgusting nature. Yet, we are commanded to teach God's law to children. That means some form of discernment is necessary for adults to practice as they introduce raw, real-life themes to tender consciences and wide eyes. It does not mean we have the right to water-down and dilute the power of the Word. Every medicinal drug comes with a recommended dosage for children. It is always a fraction of the amount adults should be able to handle. In other words, rather than weaken the good medicine, to carry out the metaphor, we need to administer the truth in smaller, but still potent doses.

As soon as the students are independent readers at Logos, usually around the middle of first grade, we start them on a course of reading various books of the Bible, both the Old and New Testaments. In a planned schedule, each grade reads through at least one book of the Old Testament, a Gospel account, and a couple of the Epistles. That includes first grade. Granted, the New Testament is seemingly less 'colorful' in its stories than the Old, therefore it could be argued that we should just use those books. But then, as he is safely reading about Jesus' ministry, a second grader asks, "What is adultery, and how'd the woman get caught in it? Is it like a trap?"

Whoa. "Out of the mouth of babes..."

Christian school teachers must present the Bible as it presents Itself. No fairy tales, no Precious Moments, no trivializing. If we come across some "medicine" that is too strong for the age-group, then we allow the parents to administer it at home. We do that frequently. But out of respect for the Word, and to encourage our children to mature in their respect and love of it, we must not rewrite it or obscure it in any way. And when it is presented honestly and carefully, He will use it to "divide and pierce" souls. God says His entire Word, even the uncomfortable parts must be taught, without shame, and it will not return void.

\* \* \*

## VIRUSES THAT ARE KILLING CHRISTIAN SCHOOLS

> "virus" n., a poison, 1. Any of a large group of tiny infective agents causing various diseases, 2. Any harmful influence

One of the tangential, but significant results of our four national A.C.C.S. conferences has been to make me painfully aware of the sorry state of Christian education in the United States. We hear from parents, teachers, administrators and board members from literally all points of the compass at these conferences. The most recently completed conference in Raleigh, North Carolina, had more than four hundred attendees, most coming for the first time. (Not too surprising really, considering the accessibility of Moscow, Idaho, to the rest of the nation!) As at the three preceding conferences, these delegates shared with us (unsolicited) sad to awful stories about the Christian schools in their locale. One of the most common comments I've heard far too many times goes like this: "We would be happy to send our children to the Christian school near us, but it is little different than the public schools. Biblical convictions and worldviews are not practiced or even promoted."

After hearing numerous accounts of Christian school problems, and seeing some firsthand, I've compiled just a few of the more severe illnesses often afflicting these schools:

Admission Fever: Evidenced by a low grade of student morale, and constant, chronic problems with discipline and poor attitudes among the students. Behaviors typically seen in government schools are also evident in Christian schools with this illness. Most often brought on by administrators and boards succumbing to budget pressures and admitting problem students. Can also be brought on by the lack of a restraining, definitive statement regarding admission standards, i.e. a clear picture of the kind of students desired. Some Christian schools even deny the disease by thinking they are "being a godly influence on needy kids." TREATMENT: Immediately establish precise, consistently high standards for student acceptance, behavior, and expulsion. Follow those measures up with expelling the students that will not comply with the standards. And for the future, be ready to "just say NO" to an unhealthy application.

Verbiage Disorder: Most often evidenced by parents and staff members not being able, or possibly not knowing how to control their speech. Can produce extremely irritating rashes or outbreaks of discontent among all school members. Watch for hotbeds of talk about school or class issues that upset people, but no positive and biblical action is advocated by any of the participants. More delight seems to come from discussion than real treatment. This is sometimes excused by the fear of confrontation, or thinking that they are just "sharing concerns." Other terms for this affliction are: Gossip, Discontentment, Lack of Submission to Authority, Spreading Strife, Loose Tongue Disease. TREATMENT: Repentance is always a good medicine for this illness (and many others), followed up by creating and adhering to prescriptive policies that allow for the biblical addressing of concerns.

Biblical Botulism: Certainly one of the most virulent diseases afflicting Christian schools. When manifested in a school, it has been known to breakdown the resistance even Christian students have to wholesale pagan thinking. Often allowed to enter under the guise of "spiritually training the students" without adequate regard to the biblically-established authorities, i.e. the family and the church. Evidenced by an abundance of "Christian" posters, stickers, banners, flags, songs, and themes, and little substantive emphasis on biblical thinking and living. This mishandling, or poor preservation of the pure gospel is readily apparent in a school when students and teachers speak and think lightly of the Lord's Name, His Word, biblical apologetics, and consistent Christian behavior in all situations (see Admission Fever). TREATMENT: This is so serious that it calls for a complete reexamination of the school's philosophy, goals, mission statement, admissions policy, etc. in light of Scripture. A realignment of recognized authorities and the school's primary purposes may be necessary. Otherwise the school may be inadvertently inoculating many students against Christianity.

As I stated above, these are just a few of the more serious viruses. There are many others, but these are presented out of a real concern for our sister schools who labor in our Lord's Name. May we all be blessed with the ability to see our work and its results in a right, biblical manner. Your prayers and constructive input for any Christian school you know are critical for its life and health.

\* \* \*

## MATTHEW 18 APPLIES EVEN IN LOGOS

> And if your brother sins, go and reprove him *in private*; if he listens to you, you have won your brother. But if he does not listen to you, take one or two more with you, so that by the mouth of two or three witnesses every fact may be confirmed.
> ~Matthew 18:15-16

There. It had happened again. Though hopefully unnoticeable to the person on the other side of my desk, my knee had definitely jerked. Worse, my knuckles were whitening—surely I couldn't hide that. Breathe deeply, relax those muscles. Now, focus on what she is saying...

"...and after talking to all those other moms, I found that I'm really not the only parent in the class who feels this way about Mrs. Burkstock's science test last week. In fact, after I told them my concerns, several of them said they felt exactly the same way, but were not sure if they should say anything to her. I mean, nobody wants to hurt her feelings, you know what I mean?"

## But surely there was no slander intended; she only wanted to see if others "felt the same way."

Yes, I knew what she meant. With the kindest of intentions, what she really meant was that gossiping is a whole lot easier and less awkward than individually confronting a teacher with her concerns. Gossip? Surely that is a bit harsh, isn't it? "He who goes about as a slanderer reveals secrets, therefore do not associate with a gossip" (Prov. 20:19). But surely there was no slander intended; she only wanted to see if others "felt the same way." And what "way" was that? Eliminating all the hyperbole, these parents believed the teacher had made a poor call, a significant lapse in judgement, in giving the test.

So, what's wrong with a few parents comparing "notes" about a teacher's (or administrator's or board's) actions, without consulting her? Don't they have the right to do that? After all, the teacher is teaching *their* children. A number of years ago I was asked to go to another Christian school to "troubleshoot" and give them some advice. Oh boy. After arriving at the school, it took me all of half-a-day to ascertain two facts: 1) this school had the worst problems I had ever personally seen, and 2) that a great portion of those problems stemmed from parents, staff, and board members all "just talking" to each other; they just hadn't bothered to confront the *right* people (i.e. those that could do something) about the problems. It had been far easier and more gratifying to talk behind each other's backs. Among other suggestions, I urged their board to adopt the principle of Matthew 18 in their school.

Certainly in Matthew 18 our Lord is directly addressing a suspected sin, vs. bad judgement calls, but as with many portions of Scripture certain principles can be derived from the direct teaching. Gossip or slander is addressed frequently in the Bible, from Proverbs to James. (James devotes all of chapter 3 to just what damage the tongue can do!) If the purpose of our Lord's directives in Matthew 18 was *not* to avoid groundless rumors and slander, what is the point of going to the person privately? By going first to the person under suspicion, gossip (a real sin) is avoided.

Besides, by going first to the correct person, both sides of an issue are then heard, and it often turns out that at least part of the concern was based on inaccurate information. (For example, kids don't always give all sides of a story.)

I have seen far more damage than good done, even when a specific "sin" was not the initial problem, by people discussing the concern with everyone except the person who could do something positive. As one of our own "prophets," Bob Dylan, has said, "If you're not part of the solution, you're part of the problem." Christian school staff members, like most folks, are susceptible to the hurt that comes from discovering others have been talking behind their backs. Almost always an immediate feeling of betrayal of trust and friendship results. (At the school mentioned above, peace was not restored before almost the entire staff had been fired or resigned.)

On the other hand, many parents feel they should apologize when they do bring a concern directly to me or a teacher. They feel that they may be regarded as "complaining" or being a nuisance. Nothing could be further from the truth; by coming directly to the "source," they have done the right thing and avoided complaining to others, which is a real nuisance. Confrontations are about as fun as a trip to the dentist, but usually they are just as necessary. They can also be even more productive for all involved.

When a common spirit of trust and application of the *principle* in Matthew 18 exists in a Christian school setting, rumors and gossip rarely get a toehold. When the opposite happens, that is parents and teachers slandering others in the name of "concern," even Christian schools can be destroyed. It has happened and happened too often. The enemy of our souls frequently works to poison a Christian institution from the inside out, not from the outside in. Our Lord's wisdom still works well today, because He is in authority over all our schools and private lives.

\* \* \*

ARE HEROES ANACHRONISTIC?

Or *"Why Johnny Can't Relate To Great Men"*

Hero: any person esp. a man, admired for courage, nobility, etc.

We need heroes. Paul Bunyan, Pecos Bill, Big John, Superman, Robin Hood, Zorro, and others that fill the pages of comics or folk tales are the stuff that dreams are made of. Everyone, even those of us who lived at a time when these characters' stories entertained us for hours, knew that they were just paper heroes. Then we learned of others who were real flesh and blood men, but, through time, elaboration, and discrete editing, they became legends of mythical proportions for daring and boldness: Jesse James, Sir Walter Raleigh, John Paul Jones, Wild Bill Hickok, Babe Ruth. When we first learned of them, they seemed literally larger than life, but like the Greek gods, their all-too-mortal failings became apparent with some honest scrutiny. Instead of noble men of daring-do, while certainly bold, talented, or just unusually audacious men, they tend to shrink in our estimation the closer we look at their characters. Not too dissimilar from Impressionist paintings, these men are best viewed from a bit of a distance.

If you ask just about any history major at a typical post-modern university, "Who are the truly admirable men of history?", you would likely discover that through being very carefully taught, the students can name nary a one. Further, they would likely castigate you for thinking such a thing were even possible, or worse, desirable. And regardless of it being a hypothetical question, why did you chose just *men*?, they might inquire, nose-to-nose with you. From Watergate on to the present day (especially the present day), the baby-boom generation has been taught and is now teaching generation X that "all have sinned and fallen short of any glory." The bottom line being that "glory" has never been possible. Therefore, we must not have heroes. We have never really had any heroes if we look hard enough one finds dirt on every man, even Washington, so the mantra goes. By definition, great men have never existed, just powerful or talented men.

Are we then to conclude, along with our cynical age, that not only are there no more heroes, there never were any? More importantly, does the Bible discourage making distinctions of this sort among men and espouse the egalitarian spirit? The answer to both questions is an emphatic "No!" There have indeed been men we can and should hold up as great men heroes. King David had, among his immense contingent of warriors, a group called "the Three" and another called "the Thirty" (2 Samuel). These men were exceedingly valiant warriors, renowned for their incredible, super-human feats. They also served David loyally, and, if we can deduce from Scripture, they must have been upright men or else David would have not endured them for long.

DEAR PARENTS

## Are we then to conclude, along with our cynical age, that not only are there no more heroes, there never were any?

So what makes a man great enough to be worthy of emulation? No man can be truly great without being good, as Scripture defines good, i.e. godly, not perfect, but characterized by godliness. Certainly there have been, thank God, many godly men through history who lived their lives out with only their families bearing witness to their goodness. Heroes are made when God in His wisdom, takes otherwise "ordinary" godly men, endows them with special gifts, puts them in extraordinary circumstances, and gives them the grace to emerge victorious. There are a few found in the Bible: Joshua, Daniel, Joseph.

But how about in our American history? The secular world, as noted above, not only doesn't believe in heroes, it has no definition for honor, nobility, or even goodness. However, God has raised up many men who became great enough that even in 1998 we can point to them in our classrooms here and say, "These men are worth your attention, admiration, and emulation." Men whose characters stand up to the necessary scrutiny of history. In a Christian and classical context therefore it is a profound joy to introduce especially our young men to George Washington, Patrick Henry, Stonewall Jackson, Robert E. Lee, Theodore Roosevelt, Orville and Wilbur Wright, and Alvin York, to name a few of special note. These men were real, not just myths. They lived in times of great difficulty, and temptations to take the easy out, compromise, and sin were just as strong as they are today. But they stood strong in the Lord, and their example should not be forgotten. Such is part of the hope and work we have as Christian educators, seeking to raise young men who believe in, and may even become, heroes in God's world.

> We make men without chests and expect of them virtue and enterprise. We laugh at honor and are shocked to find traitors in our midst. We castrate and bid the geldings be fruitful.
> ~C.S. Lewis, *The Abolition of Man*

## NOT VERY "STREET SMART"

> Behold, I send you out as sheep in the midst of wolves; therefore be shrewd as serpents, and innocent as doves.
> ~Matthew 10:16

It most likely happened in the small (why are they "small?") hours of Saturday morning. The Saturday night following the University of Idaho's graduation ceremonies ("That, Dr. Watson, is worth noting.") Of course, we didn't discover it until Sunday morning when one of our teachers arrived at school well before the church services held on our campus. He called me at about 7:30 am. That is not particularly noteworthy. According to the police, it appeared that at least one (!) person had taken a baseball bat to our glass front doors and, not thinking that enough fun, had also smashed portions of our stained glass windows on each side of the doors. All the glass in the doors was strewn in very small pieces inwards for thirty or more feet. However, for some strange reason, the perp. ("perpetrator") did not actually go through the glass-less door frames and into the school. Had he (they?) done so, the large, glass trophy case just inside the foyer would have made for even more batting practice, san dut. Therefore, the officers suspect the person(s) may have been interrupted in the act and left the premises in a hurry.

This actually was the second act of vandalism we had experienced this spring. Less than two weeks before our front doors were shattered, someone(s?) had used many of our classroom windows for paint-balling practice, breaking two outside panes in the process. Was it the same unknown person or persons? Do we have someone out there who doesn't like us, or maybe just our windows? (Maybe they accidentally ran into a school window as a young child...?) Anyway, we had no leads to offer the officers in either situation.

All this made us feel rather vulnerable, though. Were there any measures we could or should have taken that would have made these incidents less likely to happen? Well, no, probably not in these cases, short of my secret fantasy of having several, extremely well-trained, sharp-fanged Dobermans prowling the grounds of the school all night long. The key there being "well-trained." ("*Logos School has an immediate opening for a second grade teacher due to our late teacher's attempt to retrieve items from her classroom at 1:00 am.*")

## Our basic system of discipline throughout the school is founded on one, very intangible element: *trust*.

But there are numerous, less violent ways we are vulnerable to being abused, or at least taken advantage of as a school. We are not very "street smart" when it comes to preventing a host of small crimes, such as: items being taken from lockers (we don't have locks on them); students lying about why they are in the halls during class (we don't use hall passes); students' absences from school for questionable reasons (we don't grant "excused/unexcused" absences: we just defer to the parents' statements and keep records). And we may not always be very astute in determining when or exactly how a student may be cheating in class or lying to us. Our basic system of discipline throughout the school is founded on one, very intangible element: *trust*.

We certainly know the Adamic nature we share with all the students here. We know that we all sin in many ways. And we know not all the students here are Christians (as though that would negate them sinning). We simply don't know how to build a system worth living and working within that is based on anything less than trust. Would we be shrewder, as our Lord defines it, if we did have locks, bars, security cameras, even police officers in the school? Is "shrewdness" better served if we assume guilt on the students' part when there is *any* doubt, or require more proof of their innocence? Should our administrators have the street smarts and hard-boiled savvy of some TV-world, NYPD detectives? By the nature of my questions it is probably obvious that I don't believe the above approaches are what Jesus would consider obedience to His command. Paul has a parallel command in Romans 16:19: "... but I want you to be wise in what is good, and innocent in what is evil." Wisdom and shrewdness, biblically speaking, certainly call for not being blind to or ignorant of the forms of evil, but our thought life is better spent dwelling on what is good.

Trust is good. Turning the other cheek is good. Even being defrauded can be good, rather than returning evil for evil. So, instead of growing hard and seeing the students in the school as little sinners just waiting their chance, or viewing those outside the school as potential enemies and vandals, we are to trust the sovereign Lord of the universe to do what's best. What can man do to us outside of His will? Praise God for His protection, praise Him for our constant vulnerability that reminds us of His 24-hour care. Trusting Logos to His care is far better than the Dobermans, too.

We had a wonderful, God-blessed, twentieth year! Thank you and blessings on your summer!

\* \* \*

## EDUCATING FOR WORSHIP

Formal education is inescapably a religious exercise. This little news item came as a bit of a surprise, I think, to a class of education majors I addressed a few years ago at the University of Idaho. They believed what they had been taught (of course) which was the myth that you can and should separate church ("religious activities") and state ("educational, sectarian activities") within schools.

In fact, that first statement may be one that even some Christians would take to task. But consider what fundamental questions are presupposed in formally educating a child? Even though very rarely stated, what primary questions are being addressed by virtually any general form of educating children, past and present? They are profoundly religious questions. At the very least the list includes the following:

1. Where did I (the student) come from?
2. What relationship do I have with all these other people?
3. How did the world come to be here?
4. What is authority and who wields it?
5. How should I respond to the rules of behavior authority presents to me?
6. What is my purpose in life?
7. Is there something, anything "out there" greater than me to which I must answer?

If those aren't religious questions, i.e. those concerned with a set of beliefs about life, then what are they?

Study any curriculum in any school that sets out to teach young children through their young adulthood and the content will necessarily address the above questions, one way or another. Again, it is inescapable. There is simply no other place to start in educating children and, sooner or later, all those questions (and more like them) will come up, requiring some kind of answer from the teachers and the school.

The Christian response may seem as obvious as dirt, but sadly even Christian schools can and do lose sight of their reason for existence. Far too often they adopt some barely diluted version of the State's answers to those questions. What are their answers? Put in the most positive light the State says this: "You (student) are here and being educated so that you may be a good citizen and achieve the maximum amount of personal comfort in your short, meaningless existence." But the Christian school answer is frequently not that dissimilar: "You (student) are here and being educated so that you may be a good, "Christian" citizen and keep your personal nose clean while you seek the maximum amount of personal comfort before you die and go to heaven." Lest that sound a bit cynical, I am sincerely putting the best light on observing the Christian school movement over twenty years or more not what's *said*, but what is done.

So, what's the "right" answer? And, no, Logos doesn't have either the corner on it, nor the clarity of purpose I pray we may have some day. The point and purpose of education is to encourage the right worship of the Holy Creator and Sovereign Lord of the universe (Deut. 6:13; Romans 12:1-2). All the questions above should be answered in light of *that* primary, unchangeable reason for man's existence. Put another way, any answer that doesn't point to why, how, and who we *worship* is meaningless. Even the pagans encourage worship ... the worship of the creature man, vs. the Creator God.

> **Put another way, any answer that doesn't point to why, how, and Who we *worship* is meaningless.**

Therefore, for example, as we daily teach math, science, languages and logic, we teach the wonder and awe of God's marvelous attention to detail, complexity, order and balance awe that inspires, compels and identifies specific reasons for worship, just as the Psalmists did. As we teach the Bible, history, literature, and the arts, we teach reverence and fear of the God who made and redeemed the world, raises and destroys entire nations, and who gives good and beautiful gifts to man to be used to glorify His Holy name. This reverence compels worship through discerning purity and growing wisdom, rejecting ugliness and foolish trends, as He does. Bodily discipline in exercises and athletics reminds us of how we are flesh as well as spirit, so we worship Him for our strength and health and we worship Him for reminding us of our physical frailties and limits. And in all our in-house rules, discipline, dress, and decorum in the school, we constantly remind ourselves and the students that we cannot worship and love our Lord if we think only of ourselves and wrong our brothers.

Man was designed to worship. History shows us that the only question really is who or what he will worship the living Triune God of the Bible, or some form of the created order Nothing so strengthens and blesses a people (within a church, a nation, or just a school) as the right worship of the God of heaven, and nothing more surely destroys a people than the worship of anything created (idolatry).

As we begin a new year of educating students formally, our twenty-second for those counting, it behooves us to remember we exist, move, and have our being for His glory and worship. That's it. May God grant us increasing wisdom as we seek to give these students even more profound reasons and motivation for worshiping and loving the One who made them. Pray for us!

# 7

## THE JUNK DRAWER

*I have a drawer in my desk that I firmly believe mirrors at least one drawer in almost everybody else's desk. That is, if people were honest, they would own up to the fact that they have such a drawer. Some might self-righteously deny it, and the worst of these people are usually right, which just shows you how off balance they are! Others would say their entire desk is made up of such drawers. To these I say, "Get your act to gether ... good grief!". You know the drawer I mean, the one with things like the piece of a flashlight you're saving to, uh ... fix another flashlight, yeah, that's it. This drawer also has your in-office hand-tool collection: the small sized version of pliers, screwdrivers (Phillips and slot), an adjustable wrench, and a small hammer. Wire pieces of various sizes, an almost-gone roll of duct tape, burned out light bulbs, various batteries that may just have some life in them, and countless screws, nuts, nails, tacks, paper clips, and cookie crumbs multiply on the bottom of this drawer. Mine also has a cowboy toy gun, a clipboard, about a zillion tiny compasses (that don't work), a Happy Birthday banner, and handcuffs (I'll leave their purpose to your imagination).*

*In other words, I have a junk drawer. That title also seemed appropriate for a chapter I had to include in such a volume as this. For every issue I have written a column about in our school newsletter, there is usually at least one other issue that I wish I could write on, but for a variety of reasons decide it wouldn't be a good idea. These reasons range from not wanting to whack the proverbial bees' nest (my most often-used reason), to figuring I'm the only one who thinks in such a strange vein, to just thinking it's not the right time to get into this issue. So, for these reasons, and others, my potential, partially constructed column ideas get tossed into a mental junk drawer. As I toss the idea in, and shove the drawer shut, I often think, "Well, someday I may get around to using that ... someday."*

*Since this is a rather different format and, possibly, a different audience than what our newsletter offers (i.e. it's my book, for goodness sake), I thought it might be a chance to dig out some of the ideas from the "junk drawer," dust them off, and see how they look in the harsh light of day. And as with all the stuff from such a drawer, you'll notice that not all of them are complete and in one piece.*

*By the way, "The views presented hereafter are solely the thoughts and opinions of the author; they do not necessarily reflect the beliefs, goals, or policies of Logos School." There. That should take care of any potential concerns.*

\* \* \*

### "I JUST LOVE A STUDENT IN UNIFORM!"

*Scene 1: Interior shot of average home on any weekday morning:* "Mom! I can't find my purple pants!"

"They're in the dirty clothes, honey. Find something else to wear."

"But I CAN'T wear anything else! Nothing else matches, and I really wanted Sandy to see my purple pants with my new blouse!"

"Sandy won't care what you wear...!"

"Oh Mom! She ALWAYS notices and tells me if I wear something weird!"

(Huge sigh.) "Ok, ok ... dig them out of the hamper. But you'll have to at least iron them before you wear them!"

"But I'll be LATE if I iron them!"

And the scene degenerates from there. From personal experience, I know this is not a hypothetical, nor a rare scenario in many households. Even in godly, loving homes, sometimes the pace of preparing for a school day can produce severe temptations to frustration in the most solid saint-of-a-parent. There are just a lot of things to think about, from lunches to homework, to needed books for that day, to after-school plans to double check on. Knowing precisely what clothes will be worn the next day might just lift one major burden from the backs of the students and the parents alike.

*Scene 2: Interior shot of much-beloved Christian school on an average weekday:*
The students, albeit with many smiles and friendly attitudes, move from class to class dressed as though they had dropped in on their way home from a four-day hike through uncharted wilderness. Rumpled sweatshirts, t-shirts, and semi-clean blue jeans, supported by well-worn sneakers or scuffed boots abound. An untucked sports shirt flaps over a dull-colored t-shirt, the attire of the student slumped in the desk at the front of the room. She is a bright, friendly student, as are most in this school, so no one comments on her combat-weary demeanor.

Meanwhile, the teacher in front of the room wears his tie and jacket everyday, and hoping, somewhere in the recesses of his mind, that his "modeling" of maturity in dress will somehow affect the students' understanding of the adult life.

*Scene 3: Exterior shot featuring the selfsame female student from scene 2:*
Dressed in matching mauve top and pants, and sporting a quaint cap with a monogrammed yellow letter, the young lady dashes a hot food order to a waiting car in the parking lot. She doesn't see any disparity of thought between her unique attire for the few hours she weekly puts into this fast-food restaurant, and the daily grungy appearance she flaunts in school most of her waking hours.

**Had uniforms even been mentioned, I am confident that all present, self included, would have had a hearty laugh, and then gone on with more practical school business.**

When Logos School first began in the early eighties, the idea of student uniforms was as remote from our considerations as the idea of e-mail. In fact, a number of very serious discussions were held at board-level to decide whether we would require the students to wear shoes in class, or if they could be "free" to go barefoot. Sanitation won out over individuality. Had uniforms even been mentioned, I am confident that all present, self included, would have had a hearty laugh, and then gone on with more practical school business.

But why would we have laughed? And why is it that today, when the idea of student uniforms in Logos is even mentioned, reactions from thinking adults are never in the ambivalent range? It seems people either love the idea and would embrace it immediately, or hate it, and see the wearing of uniforms as a step in the unraveling of civilization as we know it. Not long ago, in a meeting with the staff, I broached the idea of some selected school clothing, not uniforms per se, for the students. Shortly afterwards, I received a strident, three-page letter from one father. Among other objections to the idea, he equated the wearing of school uniforms with the advent of hippies, Nazis, and Chinese communists. In other words, he was against the proposal. Not wanting to risk a Logos version of the War Between the States over dress, I retreated.

But, I still love a student in uniform. Consider these points:
1. Uniforms would eliminate those wonderful morning madness times.
2. Uniforms would teach the students that school is indeed their place of work. This would not only prepare them for part-time jobs in "the real world," like the fast-food scenario above; they would understand why adults dress in their "uniforms" for work.
3. Uniforms, like other nice clothes, affect the attitude of the wearer. Both logic and experience have demonstrated that students will act differently, depending upon how they are attired. When our students dress up for our Protocol nights, they assume the sophistication their clothes require. Even public schools that have tried uniforms attest, often to the surprise of doubters, that much improved behavior among the students resulted (ask Salem, Oregon).
4. Uniforms can and have actually saved money for parents. Considering the normal life-span of styles and the cheaply-made clothes today, this point is very easy to substantiate.
5. Uniforms, whether in the military, on the sports field, or even in fast-food restaurants, often contribute strongly to a sense of pride in the institution. There is nothing wrong, and much right with students having a

sense of pride in the school their uniform and they represent, especially if that school is a worthy institution. That pride and bearing can also contribute to the community's awareness of the reputation of that school. To anticipate a common argument raised by that last point elitism is only an attitude. Uniforms don't produce arrogance, anymore than uniforms produce excellence in education. Humility comes from the heart and is seen on the outside, regardless of the apparel.

6. Uniforms eliminate clothing competition and its attendant feelings. No matter how little it may appear kids seem to care about clothes and style while at school, they still care. Why else would there be so much "uniformity" already among the appearance of our students?

But uniforms at Logos? "The kids wouldn't want to all look alike!" "The kids don't want to look dorky!" "They would lose their individuality!" Oh, well, maybe someday ... maybe ...

\* \* \*


SWEET DREAMS

He knew this place. Yes, of course, it was the church sanctuary and he was in his regular seat. Everything was as it always was each Sunday morning. The pianist was finishing the pre-sermon hymn with a flourish, and he knew it was time to approach the pulpit, Bible in hand. But he seemed strangely disturbed. His eyes felt very tired, and he seemed generally disheveled. Rather than the typical light joke or two to get things rolling, he plunged right in. His tone was low and somber....

"Good morning, my friends. I am sorry to appear before you in this state, but I had a rather sleepless night, pondering just how I was going to say to you what I must."

This caused the entire congregation to virtually jerk up to a much higher degree of attentiveness. Looks of confusion and concern flickered among the members like so much heat lightening. He paused, he had anticipated just this reaction. Then, taking a shaky breath, he continued...

"Today, I won't be continuing our series on "Helping Hurting Hearts Heal

With Heavenly Humor." In fact, I'm not sure I will be able to get back to that theme soon at all...." Another pause. Low murmurs were audible among the hard-of-hearing members. Great consternation was certainly setting in.

"Well, to come to the point, not long ago I was asked by a good friend of mine, who is also a pastor, to speak on Christian education at his church's annual Father-Daughter Banquet. I don't know why my friend asked me to do this; you all know I try to avoid applying Scripture to areas in which Christians may hold different opinions or may find upsetting. But he did, and I owed him a favor, so I did some research. For a change, I thought I would just try sticking to the Bible, rather than referring to our church's national newsletter."

A quiet gasp of amazement escaped from the pianist. The pastor turned his head. "I understand. And it only gets worse...." He shuddered and took a deep breath for the final plunge.

"My dear friends, for years I thought God had little to say about how we practically educate our children. I sincerely thought our Sunday School and other wonderful youth programs were enough. I was sincerely wrong. Not that our programs were all that bad; I was wrong about what God said. Last night I read and read, all night, and I discovered, among other things, that the Bible clearly says ... oh my ... that parents are commanded by God Himself to make sure their children are exposed to the Word of God, His creation, and His thoughts almost 24 hours a day. Do you realize what this means?!" His voice thundered up to the ceiling beams. Every eye and ear were open to their fullest...

## "It means that we, you and I, have been so wrong for so many years!"

"It means that we, you and I, have been so wrong for so many years! We have much to undo. Oh, my dear friends ... we haven't a day to lose. Our very children's education is at stake and God Himself holds us responsible!" He was gripping his Bible so hard, he was sure it would tear in two at any moment. Yet he had never felt so wonderful! He had privately prayed for this day for years. Unrestrained talk broke out among the congregation. Here a group began a discussion on starting a Christian school; over there others were talking of the ramifications of pulling their kids out of the local schools; others were just grinning from ear to ear. It was incredible, lively, chaos....

"Perhaps this is a beginning," he thought. "Perhaps this is happening in churches across the nation! Perhaps..."

Thunder and a slap of rain against the window glass awoke him with a start. It was still dark ... so very dark out. He lay back and sadly sighed. It was Sunday morning and his sermon was still unfinished. Perhaps he really should consider saying ... oh no, not yet. Besides, dreams don't come true today, do they?

\* \* \*

MOTHER BEARS

Let a man meet a bear robbed of her cubs, rather than a fool in his folly.
~Prov. 17:12

Scripture makes it clear that there are indeed worse things than coming face-to-teeth with a mama grizzly who thinks you've been messing with her kids. But it is a relative comparison, as you see in the above quote. In fact, the relative undesirability of being in company with a fool is quite heightened by the comparison, in my opinion. True, I have never actually had the occasion to be any closer to a bear than when he's been safely behind the bars of a zoo, but I have read too many of those Drama In Real Life Stories in Reader's Digest: "his teeth were as big as railroad spikes, crushing my head with the power of a hundred vises! I knew I was going to die!" Right. If I ever had had the desire to backpack in the wilds of Yellowstone Park, those stories would have cured that impulse very quickly. In fact, I take walks in the city parks only during the day.

Nevertheless, in my own little way, I believe I have had more than one encounter with "mother bears" right here in Logos School. My tangles have left only a few mental and emotional scars on my psyche, but they haven't been real pretty sights, either. Hackles raised, blazing eyes boring into mine, claws at the ready, growls barely restrained under the surface of her strained voice, mothers of not a few students have held me at bay. Under my calm demeanor, sweat glands and heart were at maximum pumping power, and I mentally thanked Providence that a rather hefty desk was between me and certain destruction. Lacking any real firepower at hand, I have had to rely only on my own wits and the power of calming rhetoric: "Now, Betty, I understand exactly how you feel, but you have to see it from my side, too. If you kill me now, my own four little ones will be really disappointed! You do see that, don't you?" I have also discovered that my rhetoric can also be enhanced by my kneeling behind my desk.

How do these situations come about? I frequently ask myself that same question. In fact it often comes to mind when I find myself kneeling behind my desk, pleading for my life. Actually, these situations, unlike a real bear hunting trip, often spring upon me without much warning at all. I mean, when one heads into the woods, with some anticipation, and better yet, some preparation for such an encounter, then the bear arriving on the scene should cause little more surprise than seeing another actor come on stage at his cue. "Oh, there you are!" the hunter might even say, "It's about time! I was beginning to wonder if I had the right forest!"

**Hackles raised, blazing eyes boring into mine, claws at the ready, growls barely restrained under the surface of her strained voice, mothers of not a few students have held me at bay.**

But no such deliberate anticipation or planning do I enjoy. No, usually the first I know of these life-threatening experiences is when my office door bursts open, and hovering over me is a seething mother, often with semi-crumbled school papers in her paw, er, her fist. Then, if I am lucky, instead of instantly shredding my sensitive emotions with her razor-sharp remarks and accusations, she holds herself in check and asks if I have a "few minutes" for her to ask me some questions. Often those situations can hold out the hope that life may go on and we can come to some reconciliation.

However, appearances can be deceiving and, though outwardly calm with me, she may have committed some bloodletting before she got to my door. I have had occasions when I thought we had separated with all my parts still functioning as they should, only to find, upon tracing the mother's tracks through the school building, a teacher bleeding profusely from multiple wounds. The teacher is not really close to death: she just has the look of a wife at the site of a mining accident, barely holding herself together, and obviously suffering from shock and disbelief. So we work through it: her telling me that after twelve years of teaching she now realizes that she is a total failure and should take up garbage-collecting; me telling her that she is not a failure and that Logos, yay verily, the entire Christian school movement in the United States of America needs her to stay in teaching.

Godly perspective, as always, is the key to these situations. The "mother bear" moms usually calm down and come to see that we are truly sorry for causing mental anguish for her cubs, er, kids. And we usually come to see that we may have been hasty in assigning blame, or too many homework pages, or whatever. Dads, like softening music when present, often play a key role in providing that calming effect on upset moms: "Martha, you heard Mr. Garfield say he will review the test with Mrs. Johanson. OK? Now, let's go home and maybe he'll come down off the roof."

* * *

REBEL WITHOUT A CLUE

There are virtually countless joys associated with this job. But one of my greatest heartaches has come from witnessing, from time to time, a teenager flounder in search of direction. This hapless young person is usually a young lady, but I've seen young men in similar quandaries. Frequently, from my experience, two major areas of decision-making are often laid on these young peoples' shoulders by their well-meaning parents. No doubt from the best of intentions, parents seem to often leave the following decisions to their high school-aged children:
- Whether or not to continue in and graduate from Logos.
- Issues related to getting to know (and care about) the opposite sex.

Regarding the first issue, going the distance at Logos, we have learned the hard way that retaining a student here who doesn't want to be here is a real drag for everyone concerned. So, as part of our application process for new secondary students, we ask the student to write a statement addressing why the student wants to come to Logos. These statements are often very revealing. If the student basically says, "I'm coming because my parents say I have to!", this trips off our mental warning lights, and chances are pretty good that student will not be part of the entering class in the fall.

> These students, for a number of reasons, often get to a point in their lives where they feel the "call of the wild," and begin considering a transfer to the public schools.

However, it is not among our newer secondary students that I usually see the anguished indecision mentioned above. It is more prevalent among the students we get to know the best: those that began with us in their kindergarten or first grade years. These students, for a number of reasons, often get to a point in their lives where they feel the "call of the wild," and begin considering a transfer to the public schools. This restlessness, and it really manifests itself as such in the kids, typically hits at around the ninth grade year. Like the man who has seen the "greener grass" in his neighbor's yard, these students no longer find satisfaction in their current conditions: Logos classes, teachers, even friends seem pretty lackluster compared to whatever lies beyond the rainbow. Enticements to these "richer" fields can come from the students' own ideas of what will bring them satisfaction, or can also come from church friends already in the government schools. The draw to be with "everybody else" can be a powerful impulse at this age.

There is little, if anything, we at the school can do to help these teens decide whether to exit or not. In most cases, we would dearly love to see them stay and finish the course here. Yet, while they are on the horns of this dilemma they are almost different people. Relationships can become strained, and even academic performance can fall off. It can get to the point where, even though no formal decision has been made on their part, we know that parting is just a matter of time.

On the other hand, I have seen another result in many of these instances. Parents have stepped in and given the teens the guidance that only loving parents can give. When that happens, the restlessness and indecisiveness vanishes overnight. Even when parents decide that the government schools are the place for the student, the student's mental burden is lifted and there is almost a visible relief in their demeanor. Though I strongly disagree with such a decision, I still am pleased to see the parents fill at least the decision-making role they should, if not the educational responsibility. Thankfully, the opposite decision is made more frequently. That is, the student is gently, but firmly informed that the parents have decided to have their child graduate from Logos. Since those same parents have elicited loving trust from their children since the crib, the young person willingly and cheerfully complies. Here again, we see the student walk with a lighter step, somewhat as Christian did upon leaving his burden at the cross.

A very similar kind of change can be observed in older students when they first become "twitter-pated." Only instead of a mental burden and restlessness, this sends their emotional state into orbit. In case you are unfamiliar with the above terminology, the state of being twitter-pated comes from the Disney movie, *Bambi*, and refers to the dizzy effects brought on by being "in love." I put that in quotes because, according to Scripture, real love has little if anything to do with the crazy emotional state of being infatuated. But better men and women have written volumes upon that very issue. Suffice it to say, being "twitter-pated" is no more an indication of the beginning of a godly relationship than feeling really hungry is an indication that a life of eating only nourishing meals is inevitable. It might lead to that, but a more substantive commitment is necessary.

These students are also confronting decisions regarding the opposite sex for which they frequently have few answers. Here, again, they can go for months at school in a state of semi-awareness of their surroundings as they are tossed about by every wind of feeling. While they may consider this a light weight burden, it is a burden nevertheless, and one that may indeed weigh more than they think. Our students here are hardly immune from the dangers and disasters accompanying a "romantic" relationship that goes out of control.

Once again, but not as often as necessary, sometimes parents do step in and help their "twitter-pated" child by making decisions that curb potential problems, and enforce godly guidelines. Frankly, though, for many Christian parents, trying to step in at this point can be a dicey proposition. If biblical patterns of relationships have been part of the child's training for years, then it is a relatively simple matter to gently enforce those. If biblical patterns are first discussed when the emotional tide is at its height ... all bets are off.

*(Note to self: This sounds more like an attempt at family-counseling. Drag it out and finish it only when you come up dry on other topics, or feel really brave!)*

\* \* \*

### TRIGGER-HAPPY OR JUST STRAIGHT SHOOTING?

Mr. Bliponship was not happy. I figured that out pretty fast. His call came late on a gray, wet Thursday afternoon. I was in the office unfortunately, 'cause that meant I had to take the call. But that's my job. I wear a tie and carry a Day-Timer; I'm a P.A., a private administrator. Taking nasty calls or just sweating out long board meetings it's what I get paid for.

My secretary, a sweet gal with lots of front office experience behind her, buzzed me and let me know I had a hot one on the line.

"Tom, hang on to your chair, Mr. Bliponship is on line one, and he doesn't sound happy."

I thanked her, and my facial muscles uncontrollably twitched as I punched the blinking red light...

"Well hi there, Bob!" I blurted cheerfully. "Getting kind of damp out there, isn't it? What can I do for you?" I really hoped I could do something for him, rather than have him do something to me.

"Garfield! Don't give me that happy-go-lucky, you-don't-suspect-anything's-wrong attitude! You know what I calling about ... you shot at my sister again last night. After all she puts up with each day in her job, and then you go and ... and ...." he couldn't continue and sputtered incoherently in his anger.

"...and told the newspaper reporter my opinions of government schools, right?", I finished helpfully, I hoped.

"Yeah! That's right! She read that article in the paper last night and called me in tears. What kind of P.A. are you? Didn't they teach you about shooting off your mouth at innocent bystanders in whatever bubblegum joint you got your license from?"

"Well, Bob, as a matter of fact, the 'bubblegum joint' I got most of my administrator training from was the state university here. You know, the university that teaches future 'public' school teachers? Anyhow, they didn't train us to watch where or how we expressed our opinions. I kind of think they didn't expect us to have any opinions worth expressing. But I am sorry your sister got hurt in the crossfire last night..."

"Oh, sure, that's easy for you to say! What in the world did you mean by that thing you said ... just a minute ... yeah, here it is: "government education in the United States is possibly that last, best holdout of socialistic training in the world. Attempts to "fix" this flawed-from-the-start system are as foolish as it would have been for the U.S. to send money and arms to the old guard Soviet Communists in 1989." What are you saying there? You calling my sister a commie, just 'cause she teaches in the public schools!?"

The phone was getting warmer in my hand, or maybe it was just the heat emanating from it. "Whoa, Bob. I certainly wasn't calling your sister a commie. I have relatives teaching in that system, too, and they aren't commies either. Tell you what, let's meet for lunch at Eric's grill tomorrow and we can discuss this more. My treat. What do you say?"

"Well, ok. I'll meet you there at noon. Don't bring any backup." Click.

As I hung up the receiver, I mentally wiped the brow, and heaved a sigh. But my relaxing was short-lived. My office door opened and a short, lovely brunette sauntered in. Without a word, she came and stood by my chair. Close. Too close for my comfort. Her hand touched my shoulder softly as she purred, "Mr. Garfield, I hear you're a very capable P.A. I need help with a very special problem. Do you think you could give me some of your time? Hmmmmm?"

Gathering my tumbled senses, I thought quickly. I instinctively knew what she wanted. And I didn't want any part of it, not now, not ever.

"Sorry, sweetheart. I, uh, have a pretty important case, er, course to work on just now. Why don't you ask some other stooge to help you out?"

"Oh come on, Tom. The other guys are busy, and besides, I know you are pretty adept at unjamming the copier. Please, honey?" Well, when she put it that way, I knew I had to help her. I mean, how do you say no to your wife, especially when she has a jammed photocopier slowing her down?

The next noon found me at Eric's grill, sitting on a stool, leaning on the counter and awaiting Bob's entrance. He finally came in. He looked like a week of bad weather stormy, you know. I waved him to the stool next to me, and after ordering two Mega-burger specials, we got down to business.

"Bob, I want you to know again that I meant no offense to your sister. She's got a tough job and is probably not very appreciated by her students or the parents."

"Boy, you got that right! The stories she tells me.... Look, I'm sorry I blew up at you yesterday. But I just don't understand why you feel you gotta take shots at the public schools. Wouldn't it be better to just brag up your school? I mean, our kids are doing really well there, and we tell folks how much we like it. Do you have to make the public schools sound so bad?"

I tried to choose my words carefully, especially as they came out around bites of Mega-burger. "If you only knew how many times I have wanted to pop off a few rounds in their direction, you'd realize that I am the soul of restraint. Do you read the papers? Do you see what they're doing to those kids? Believe me, I don't go looking for stories; they come to me with Technicolor detail from parents wanting to enroll their kids. No, I know there isn't much good in shooting at the government schools, with their deeply rooted religion of social Darwinistic engineering. Besides, nailing their problems is as tough as shooting at the Kibbie Dome: you can't miss, if you follow me. But sometimes I feel like I need to be the watcher on the wall in Ezekiel you know, giving the alarm so that at least the blood isn't on my hands."

We talked and ate for a bit longer. We found we agreed more than either of us had thought. Bob drove off and I walked back to school just as it started to rain again. As I sloshed through the puddles and the water dripped off my hat, I reflected upon Bob. He wasn't such a bad guy. Who knows? Maybe this could be the beginning of a beautiful friendship.

*(Note to self: Definitely save this one for a real slow day. Bogie I ain't.)*

# 8

## FRUIT OF THE LABOR

*For all sorts of reasons it is a good practice to remind everyone (including myself) what God has accomplished in the years Logos has existed. From a purely developmental view, it is a good idea to let our supporters know that their prayers and financial support have not been wasted. From an educational view, it is a good idea to let parents know that not only are their precious little ones getting a solid foundation, but that looking down the road, their young ones will follow the path of very successful graduates. Telling the stories of some of those graduates can be a real inspiration to many. But the fruit of the work of Logos School has gone beyond any conception I ever had. The very idea of our work in Moscow being noticed, much less being copied by hundreds, and now thousands of people around the United States still overloads this poor boy's mind. But our Father has seen fit to do this, and we pray that many unnumbered and unknown (to us) children will be blessed by what He is doing.*

### LOGOS COMES UNDER SCRUTINY FROM ACROSS THE NATION

Okay, okay; so once again my predictive abilities showed their lack of prophetic inspiration. I guess that's why I push papers and leave the vision-forming to those more adequately gifted in that ability.

Background time: About in 1991 Doug Wilson, one of the original founders and board members for Logos School, wrote a book entitled *Recovering the Lost Tools of Learning*. It was essentially a philosophical and practical discussion of how Logos School has, since its inception tried to flesh-out the model of education presented by Dorothy Sayers in her 1941 article, *The Lost Tools of Learning*. She reintroduced the model of classical learning based on the Trivium: Grammar, Logic, and Rhetoric, a form of teaching used successfully for centuries in European schools. Mrs. Sayers also matched the general stages of children's learning characteristics and growth to the three parts of the Trivium. Doug Wilson's book was the latest in a series of books by various authors addressing applied biblical principles. (The series was published by Crossway publishers.)

Well, as I told Doug later, I felt like the wife whose husband calls to say he's bringing home the boss for supper ... tonight! The book did an accurate job of describing the key founding philosophical themes and ideas Logos was founded on. It even accurately described some of the practical programs, policies, and curriculum goals we've developed. What it did not include was a strong statement saying that, while certainly beneficiaries of God's grace, we have still managed to pull some boners. We are still very much under construction. In other words, a Surgeon General's warning about mistaking Logos for the perfect school would not have been amiss, in my opinion.

Nevertheless, the book went out and struck an empathetic nerve in numerous homes and schools across the nation. Calls and letters starting pouring in to the Wilsons' home, Doug's office, and Logos. "How can we do what you're doing?" So many came in that the Association of Classical and Christian Schools was formed. The fledgling organization was designed to encourage and assist schools with beliefs and goals similar to Logos's regarding a uniquely classical approach to Christian education.

All along, Doug kept informing me that there was a "need" for a conference and a market for the written materials, such as the curriculum guides, that Logos School has produced. I did not out and out scoff, but I did have profound doubts (a true blue "Thomas").

The conference was put together for the summer of 1993, having as its theme "Repairing the Ruins," with loads of preparatory work done by Nancy Wilson and Doug, as well as Chris LaMoreaux and many others. It was announced through *Credenda Agenda* (another locally produced Christian newsletter) and people from around the nation signed up. The conference was held at Logos School over three days. Over seventy delegates from around the United States came for seminars and workshops. Representatives came from schools and homeschools as far away as Florida, Texas, New York, Wisconsin, Minnesota, and Ohio. California, Washington, and southern Idaho were also represented. Seminars included topics addressing: "What is a Christian Worldview?"; "Biblical Discipline in the Christian School"; "What is Classical Education?"; "Assessing Student Progress and Learning"; as well as seminars in teaching Bible, Latin, Rhetoric, and Formal Logic in a Christian school. Seminar and workshop leaders were all staff members of Logos School—secondary teachers and school administrators: Doug Wilson, Tom Spencer, Wes Callihan, Jim Nance, Chris Schlect, and me. Book tables and Logos School publications were extremely popular with the delegates.

The reviews of the conference were very encouraging:

"Thank you all so very much for the hard work and generous spirit that went into making such a rich, meaningful (conference) available to us at such a modest price. My husband strongly encouraged me to go ... and I admit I was very hesitant. But now I am so thankful for the affirmation of our vision of what education can be, for the challenge to press on in biblical thinking, and for the great quantity and quality of practical assistance." ~An Ohio delegate.

Ok, so I was wrong. I was concentrating on what we still need to do, not on what God has done already in this small Christian school in Moscow, Idaho, of all places. We are humbled by the overwhelming positive responses and praise and can only ask our Father to keep helping us all in accomplishing His goals for this and similar family-assisting works.

*　*　*

*The beginning conference by ACCS was just that, a beginning that initiated growth only our Father can foresee in its entirety. But one of the blessings I have already seen and pray we will see in increasing amounts is the tangible benefits Logos School derives from having sister classical schools out there "pushing the envelope," too. The sharing of new, yet old, discoveries of what works well in classically educating children is happening literally around the United States, with Logos being one of the receivers. We are already benefit ing from the seeds laid just over a few years.*

## GENERATIONAL BUILDING: AT HOME AND AROUND THE NATION

Dad was far more confident than I was... and, once again, he was proven right. As he and I pounded the last roof shingles into place on our final day of working together on my house's addition, he said, "I was trusting we could get the roof on in the time I was here." He and Mom had come up from Portland to spend a week with us, turning our foundation (or "the pit," as our kids called it) into a new bedroom and bathroom, and making our lives a lot easier. Dad, Seth, and I were able to spend seven full, work-filled days building together. My dad turned seventy last winter, after almost single-handedly (Mom helped with the tough spots) finishing his own two-car garage addition. (That should tell you who led the pace in hammering, even though thirty years the senior!)

Three generations working together was not all that unique in America's farming days a hundred years ago. Today, though, I know it is somewhat unusual. In any case, it was an extremely special time for all of us. To be able to work side-by-side with my father and my son, literally building a home, was, as C.S. Lewis describes times like these, a "glimpse of heaven." I believe there will be good work to do in heaven; imagine doing it alongside generations from previous centuries!

The week before I took the time off to work with my dad, Logos School hosted the second annual Association of Classical and Christian Schools (A.C.C.S.) conference. In 1993, about seventy-five delegates attended the first conference; this year over one hundred and thirty came from over twenty states in the Union. In the year between the conferences, more than half-a-dozen new classical and Christian schools had sprung up. Two new schools shared their testimonies of how hard it was to get started, and the many rewards they are already seeing in the lives of their students. This year we had many more workshops to offer, with more emphasis on "nuts and bolts" ideas, as well as far more representation from the Logos elementary program. In addition, we introduced the elementary science program designed by Logos parents and staff. It was a big hit! Meetings were also held during the three days of the conference to lay the groundwork for the national board and bylaws of A.C.C.S. It is the hope of all connected with A.C.C.S. that regional conferences can begin to be held throughout the United States. This would allow even more people who are excited by the idea of this type of education to get together for planning and sharing ideas.

Throughout all three days, time and again, I was almost overwhelmed by the thought of so many people traveling thousands of miles, and spending thousands of dollars in the hope of building a better education for their children and others'. As was emphasized many times in the conference, Logos is not seeking to see franchises, "McLogos's" spring up all over the nation. Rather, we are praying and working through A.C.C.S. to assist more and more families who recognize their God-given mandate to educate their children and choose to do so by means of the classical vision. A biblically-grounded vision will enable families to build generationally; a copycat project will last for a very short time, and never succeed in its mission.

> **As was emphasized many times in the conference, Logos is not seeking to see franchises, "McLogos's" spring up all over the nation.**

The edifices—facilities, texts, rules, staffs, etc.—of these new schools already look very different from Logos. But, like the work with my dad, the visible structure is not the real blessing or even the real purpose of working together; it is the hope of building and training generation after generation of those who will love and honor God's Holy Name! What better work could we strive to do?

\* \* \*

*As exciting as it is to watch the growing numbers of ACCS schools around the nation, and as enjoyable as it is to share teaching insights with them, the greatest thrill I have each year is our high school graduation. It is truly a bittersweet occasion. Even though many graduating seniors promise to come back to say hi once in awhile, I know their lives are changing and they won't pass really pass this way again. Also, as the classes move up to their turn at the top, they have increasing numbers of students who have been with us since kindergarten or first grade—a long time to live with and love those students!*

179

## "THE GLADNESS OF HARVEST"

> So then neither the one who plants nor the one who waters is anything, but God who causes the growth.... For we are God's fellow workers; you are God's field, God's building.
> ~1 Corinthians 3:7, 9

Never did a graduating class look more lovely and elegant. The setting—the cathedral-like vaulted room, abundant with rich old wood trimming and suspended chandeliers—provided an appropriate framing to the engaging picture the nine young ladies made in their royal blue robes. As they made their way down the two aisles, solemnly (for the most part) walking to the stage, the organ throbbed out the timeless strains of "Pomp and Circumstance," adding just the right finishing touch to a classic scene.

As the ladies approached the stage, our secondary principal Tom Spencer, standing with me behind the podium, leaned over to me and said, "See what you've invested your life in?" It almost undid me to consider that thought as I watched with an already full heart.

Less than two weeks later, I was in another cathedral-like, high vaulted room (I notice these things). This time there was only one young woman coming down the aisle and she wore all white, instead of the Logos colors, blue and white. She had worn those colors only last spring. Although I was sitting with many others in a pew instead of officiating, and had nothing to do with this particular ceremony, Tom's words came back to me: "See what you've invested your life in?"

Recently, I was doing my semiannual cleaning out of the school's large storage room. It's sort of a therapeutic activity I always do at Christmas time and the beginning of summer. This time I came across a long-buried bunch of photos. Long past events, and much younger faces (including mine) from years ago easily recalled good memories. I think photographs are so interesting because they're the only way we are able to stop time. Again, though, it caused me to stop and think: these, too, represent the investment of many years of my life, as well as those of other people.

Logos School had completed its thirteenth year of helping students grow. Jeremiah talks about the "gladness of harvest" people experience when God blesses their work. In the passage quoted above, Paul affirms that universal, timeless truth;

it is "God who causes the growth." We have seen that growth in the individual lives of the students I referred to above: the girls who graduated in 1994 represented over seventy-five years of education and investment at Logos! Two of the girls, Jessica Lucas and Bekah Wilson, comprised part of our first kindergarten class. They had both been here all thirteen years. The young lady who was married a few weeks later, Jade Miller (Kohl), came as a sixth grader to Logos, and graduated in 1993. The following month one of the 1994 graduates, Heather Johnson (Casebolt), was married. This is common enough stuff to older institutions and individuals, but it is all new and significant to us because it's happening to our kids!

As we close the 1993-94 school year, I am pleased and honored, along with our staff and board, to have joined with you in the "planting and watering" of these young people. Let us corporately and individually praise our Lord for the very obvious growth He was pleased to bestow on our work. The time in those "fields" was a good investment, wasn't it!

\* \* \*

*I have mentioned above some of the fruit we as a school have seen from the years of labor. But individual students need to see fruit from their work, too. Hence the need to establish reasons and ways to honor and recognize student achievements. And, as with everything else we see working with children, there are bound to be parental questions and concerns regarding rewards. We better have the answers, and they better be consistent with Scripture....*

A BIBLICAL VIEW OF REWARDS:
NOT WHETHER, BUT WHY AND WHAT

As I read the long list of names, and the group of elementary kids up front grew to a fair sized crowd, I marveled, not for the first time, at the sheer number of students earning the year-end awards. The next day Tom Spencer went through the same routine: his lists were long, too, and many people attending the secondary awards assembly just shook their heads in wonder at the number of awards.

In this newsletter you will see some of the lists of awards we handed out on the last days of the school year. For a wider perspective, I can tell you that well over a third of the elementary students, and more than half of the secondary students placed on the respective honor rolls for the year. In addition to the honor rolls, many other rewards were distributed, recognizing various hard-earned achievements.

Why go through all this? Won't it make some students feel bad if they don't receive an award? Is it consistent with biblical standards and practice? Our culture's current educational establishment asks the first two questions and comes up with one of two answers, generally. (I'll get to the third, and most important question in a moment.) One answer educationists come up with in regard to rewards is to "lower the bar," so to speak, low enough that just about anyone breathing can "earn" a reward, and thereby, no one feels bad. Perhaps you've seen this at graduations where there are more valedictorians than there are people in the audience. The other response, or answer modern educationists come up with is to try to eliminate all competition en mass. Competition, they say, is bad since it necessitates that somebody is not going to do as well as the others, and ... you guessed it ... that somebody will feel bad. They even try to eliminate striving for a goal or standard that might earn a prize, since, again, everyone might not make it.

So, the popular philosophical options on rewards seem to be: give it to everybody (making the award meaningless), or give it to no one (making the effort meaningless).

Does scripture address this topic, and if so, what does it say? It does, and it says a lot! Just an abbreviated list of applicable scriptures and principles is noted below:

- Rewards are promised by our Lord to believers: Matthew 5:12, 10:42
- Rewards are related to the work of the competitor: Psalm 58:11, 2 John 8
- Rewards are not to be an end in themselves: Isaiah 1:23
- Rewards, when kept in a right perspective, initiate tangible consequences: Proverbs 22:4, 23:29

In our school context, then, we regard rewards highly. Yes, it is true that those students who do not earn any rewards, for whatever reason, will and do feel badly at times. We ache for them, too, and seek to find other ways to encourage those have truly put forth a good effort, with a good attitude. But we still believe that a brief taste of discouragement is better than lying to them about the nature of work and rewards. We also believe that what we award and why we esteem that work will teach all the students valuable lessons. For example, we don't award cash gifts to students for academic work, lest they be tempted to violate principle number three above. Also, among our various rewards we include the recognition of improvement, in light of principle number two. And, even in our current culture, good grades (representing real standards), and their recognition produce tangible benefits,

## Yes, it is true that those students who do not earn any rewards, for whatever reason, will and do feel badly at times.

In Philippians 3:23 Paul says, "I press on toward the goal for the prize of the upward call of God in Christ Jesus." Our most important principle regarding rewards is that good work brings glory to God and to the parents of the students. While they are students, they experience the joy of pleasing their parents whom they represent in their work. We pray that as adults, if they are Christians, they will experience the joy of pleasing their Lord Whom they will represent in their lives.

A special note of recognition to the families of the many students who received awards of any kind: We at Logos are just building upon the foundation you have laid. And while many students do well at Logos, we consistently see that students whose homes reflect the Savior's presence and authority set the pace, in many ways, for their peers. We praise God for you; our work is delightful because of your obedience to Him.

\* \* \*

*Dwelling on, or worse, resting upon ones laurels (a classical recognition of success) is still considered to be a foolish thing to do, even in our current culture. Not only is it prideful, it can, like the hare in the fable, allow the steadfast tortoise to pass you by toward higher goals. Logos cannot, in any sense, afford to become arrogant about the successes God has been good enough to bestow on us. Ever since we have had some rather tangible returns on our labors, I have become more and more concerned lest we succumb to the temptations, pitfalls, and internal decline that have destroyed or derailed many once-biblically centered schools. History has given us many examples of such schools. I pray Logos will not be added to the list someday...*

## BREE'S DILEMMA

> Humble yourselves in the presence of the Lord, and He will exalt you.
> ~James 4:10

It had been a close call, but thanks to Shasta's bravery, the lion had not killed either of the horses or the children as they raced toward sanctuary. One of the children, Shasta, a poor fisherman's boy, had leapt off of Bree's back and, with only a stick as a weapon, confronted the lion as the others galloped away. Miraculously, the lion seemed startled and fled. The next day Bree, a mighty war horse from Calormen (but born a talking horse in Narnia), felt ashamed for running when he too should have fought the lion. He was dejected and wouldn't eat when their host, the Hermit, brought him food. He was too lost in self-pity and hurt pride to want to continue their journey north to freedom in Narnia. The Hermit gave Bree some good counsel:

> If you are really so humbled as you sounded a minute ago, you must learn to listen to sense. You're not quite the great horse you had come to think, from living among poor dumb horses. Of course you were braver and cleverer than *them*. You could hardly help being that. It doesn't follow that you'll be anyone very special in Narnia. But as long as you know you're nobody very special, you'll be a very decent sort of Horse, on the whole, and taking one thing with another.
> ~From *A Horse and His Boy* by C.S. Lewis

In the early years of Logos School's existence, it wasn't very hard to be humble. Given a heavy responsibility (teaching impressionable, precious young minds) and equipped only with a profound knowledge of one's own ignorance, an inflated view of oneself is rarely the result. Fortunately, the first families to invest in Logos had greater confidence in the staff than the staff had in themselves. But it was still pretty iffy at times. Mistakes abounded, small and rather large, and it didn't help knowing that out there, somewhere, other families and educators were watching the first stumbling steps of this new school on the block.

It only made it easier to be humble, not harder, when we had enough students to warrant purchasing buses and picking up our students on routes in Moscow. When our bus would drive by the local junior high school, our kids slowly, but obviously, slid down in the seats, out of sight of the mocking catcalls. The name on the bus was enough to elicit such taunts, but the buses frequently breaking down in front of the world didn't help either. Sitting by the road, steam coming out from the hood and/or parts on the ground beneath, our name placarded on the side for all passing motorists to see—our buses were certainly not fodder for the cannons of pride.

But, as they say, times change. God was full of grace to the often humiliated little school. Years passed and more families came, staff members stayed longer, the curriculum and program improved, the vision became clearer, the board found more unity in purpose and direction, and we moved to our own, far more visible and school-like site. The morale of the student population rose, the secondary program flourished, building upon a solid foundation in the grammar years until today, scores of laudable graduates later, we have an increasing number of National Merit finalists, SAT and ACT scores continue to improve, families move to Moscow from around the country to put their children in Logos, and dozens of other sister classical schools look to us as an example. Pretty heady stuff.

Like Bree, we have, in educational terms, become kind of a war horse. It would be foolish and even ungrateful to deny the good gifts God has blessed us with as evidenced by the preceding list. But it would be even more foolish and far more destructive to allow the arrogance of the mind and pride of the flesh to be tolerated in this school. We don't want to forget the lesson of Nebuchadnezzar and think by our cleverness we have built Logos.

Humility begins and flows from a heart surrendered to the living God, not a mind full of even good knowledge. This is truly a difficult task: the more we teach these students, the more tempting it is for them to be arrogant toward our culture's "educational" system or instructors who continue to teach foolishness. We must teach what we know, and the world will continue to show its folly. The only variable in the equation above is our students' heart attitude. We can and do teach these students truly wonderful ideas, facts, and concepts that, when humbly used "in the presence of the Lord" can be great weapons that tear down worldly philosophies. We have had the joy of seeing our graduates discombobulate secular university professors. But by God's grace we can only model; we can't use a curriculum to instill true humility in those same students. Like all the most important teachings, only the home and the parents can impress on their children the vital need to walk humbly before their Creator.

DEAR PARENTS

# We don't want to forget the lesson of Nebuchadnezzar and think by our cleverness we have built Logos.

We thank God that He has blessed us with many blessings, including many students who are indeed humble in light of the many gifts they have received. Please continue to pray for us that the root of arrogance and pride will not find ready soil at Logos. As part of our Lord's advancing Kingdom, and taking one thing with another, we would like to continue to be a "very decent sort" of school.

> He has told you, O man, what is good; and what does the Lord requires of you, but to do justice, to love kindness, and to *walk humbly* with your God?
> ~Micah 6:8

\* \* \*

"HOW THE MIGHTY ARE FALLEN"

> Let every student be plainly instructed, and earnestly pressed to consider well, the main end of his life and studies is, to know God and Jesus Christ which is eternal life and therefore lay Christ at the bottom, as the only foundation of all sound knowledge and learning. And seeing the Lord only giveth wisdom, let every one seriously set himself by prayer in secret to seek it of Him.
> ~From Harvard College's "Rules and Precepts," 1646

> Every student shall consider the main end of his study to wit to know God in Jesus Christ and answerably to lead a Godly, sober life.
> ~From Yale College founding goals, 1701

> In all its levels, programs, and teachings, Logos School seeks to: teach all subjects as part of an integrated whole with the Scriptures at the center; provide a clear model of the biblical Christian life through our staff and board; encourage every child to begin and develop his relationship with God the Father through Jesus Christ.
> ~From Logos School Goals, 1981

Putting Logos in the "neighborhood" above is not intended to be presumptuous name-dropping or any warped delusions of grandeur. Au contraire. Considering the current moral (and arguably, the intellectual) condition of Harvard and Yale, some may wonder why I would want to place Logos in their company at all. Nevertheless, there was a time when these schools were the bastions of both moral and intellectual training. And not only these, but the list of famous higher education schools founded on God's Word includes: William and Mary, Princeton, Columbia (King's College), Brown, Rutgers, and Dartmouth. Yet, it is rather obvious to the casual observer of such things that none of these schools publicly profess and practice the Lordship of Jesus Christ on their campuses today.

What happened? Is it just a given that no institution over two hundred years old will retain its first love, no matter how godly its founding visionaries and purposes? Sadly it appears to be the case. In fact, Harvard was considered by Cotton Mather to be drifting into Unitarianism as early as 1700, less than seventy years after its inception. There is not space or time here to relate all the sad tales of moral and intellectual surrender. Suffice it to say, God is not mocked; as these schools lost their spiritual bearings, they also lost God's blessings, until they reached the moral and academic slough they wallow in today.

Logos School is currently only fifteen years old and we seem to be enjoying God's blessings as never before. Our enrollment increase this year has initiated several local newspaper and TV stories. Very often I am stopped in a store or restaurant and told by someone that they've seen the good reports about Logos. The Association of Classical and Christian Schools continues to grow, and barely a day goes by without several calls from inquiring people around the nation asking how they can emulate Logos. Our staff this year is the best I can remember; I sincerely marvel at the quality of people God has brought to us.

All these blessings and more thrill me, and scare me speechless at the same time! Our dear Lord said to "beware when all men speak well of you." The Scriptures are full of many similar warnings against thinking you stand tall, lest you quickly do a major face plant (a slight paraphrase). There is nothing inherently different about Logos; no inoculation or insulation we've received that the famous schools listed above did not have. God has not give us any guarantee or promise of an untainted future. Logos is made up of individuals: forgiven and unforgiven sinners all. Without God's sovereign protection, a "small" sin, unchecked, could become the match that kindled the forest fire. It would take relatively little sin to damage or destroy the school's reputation, and by association, bring disgrace on the name of Christ. And like many other formerly Christian institutions, the sin would likely originate from the school's staff, board, or families, as opposed to coming from "outside" elements.

> **Without God's sovereign protection, a "small" sin, unchecked, could become the match that kindled the forest fire.**

I urge you, in light of history and our current blessings, please continue to include Logos School, as it carries our Lord's name through its work, in your prayers. From day to day, and Lord willing, from generation to generation, may we collectively bring glory to His Name.

\* \* \*

ORATE, LABORATE, MENETE FIDELES:
(PRAY, WORK, STAY FAITHFUL)

It was in our third year, I believe. We had seen very positive responses to Logos from the local Christian community, so I was not real surprised, though very pleased, when one summer day a pastor I hadn't met came into my office to inquire about Logos. He had a fairly small congregation in a nearby town and wanted to "check us out" for the families of his church. We spent a good amount of time talking of various aspects about our program, and finally he said he was satisfied we were on the right track. Shortly after his visit, we received a flurry of new applications, all from that one small church. About six families altogether joined us, bringing in about nine new students.

The teachers and I were very happy to welcome such a relatively good-sized bunch of new kids, making up about ten percent of our enrollment that year. However, (ominous chord here to inform you that things were not real chipper) it wasn't long before one parent, and then another from that church, started complaining about various aspects of the school. Criticism is never easy to take, but I was determined from the start to listen well and without being defensive to parent concerns or even complaints. But the pattern of complaining quickly escalated to where I had several of my teachers visit me in tears, describing the harsh manner in which these parents had upbraided them.

It finally came to a head in November. I knew I couldn't let it go on the day my third grade teacher, a kind, soft-spoken, single lady, came into my office and burst into tears. She told me she had been invited to dinner at one family's home. Sounded ok. However, immediately after the meal, they had brusquely confronted her with the "unbiblical view of salvation" her own church held. They accused her, and Logos, of not being Christian because she came from a church that didn't teach eternal security. And, therefore, we had been in sin by hiring her. A rather nasty dessert.

## The threat of a lawsuit would become a reality if we did not fork over a refund of all the tuition fees paid to date by the families of the church.

I told my board about the ongoing problem at their next meeting. They wrote a gracious yet firm letter to the pastor, strongly encouraging him to have his families cease and desist their harsh criticism of the staff or look elsewhere for an education. Sad to say, they responded by removing all of their children within a few days. The saddest part was that several of the families had really sweet kids and had never harassed us at all. Yet, even these parents, with tears on both their and our side, came to say they were removing their kids. They didn't even try to give a legitimate reason ... we all knew why.

I thought that was that. But the pastor wasn't done with us yet. About a week after the kids had been removed, I received a registered letter in the mail with a return address of an area attorney's office. Puzzled, I opened it right away. I didn't understand much legal-eze in those days, but the import was clear even to me, especially the word "lawsuit" that leapt angrily off the page. The basic accusation was that we had violated the "promises" in our school handbook to provide a Christian education because we had hired "non-Christian teachers" and, therefore, to wit, had committed a breach of promise. The threat of a lawsuit would become a reality if we did not fork over a refund of all the tuition fees paid to date by the families of the church. I believe for the first, but not last, time in my life, I reeled upon reading a letter.

The board met several times over the next couple of weeks to pray and determine the best course of action. Meanwhile, I received registered letters from the families; some were vehement and vindictive in their language, others were almost apologetic, but all demanded their money back. Doug Wilson wrote a personal letter to the pastor asking him to take a more biblical approach to this disagreement. The pastor returned the letter to Doug with a four-letter epithet boldly stamped on it in red ink. To me the shock of such an action by a pastor was almost matched by the wonder of him owning such a crude stamp. Did he need to use that message so often he had a stamp made?!

Those were very hard weeks. Christmas was approaching, so it took all the meager acting ability I had to be cheerful around the kids at school. Frequently Julie and I would weep and pray at home, extremely discouraged by this attack and fearing the Lord would allow it to bring Logos to a swift end. Such was my weak view of the Lord's sovereign grace and care at the time.

In spite of my fears, our school board prayed for and acted with much wisdom. First they hired a Christian lawyer to check out our legal vulnerability. Secondly, in accordance with our Lord's command to give a coat in addition to the shirt someone demands, they let our constituency know they were not only going to return the tuition money, but they would double it! Praise be to God, our school families and friends rallied around, and, in addition to much prayer support, they contributed enough of their own monetary gifts to send the double fees without hurting the school's slim budget. Meanwhile our lawyer concluded that not only did the protesting families not have a legal leg to stand on, but in a letter he sent to their attorney, he stated how much fun it would be to eat his (the other attorney's) lunch in court (or legal terms to that same effect). The board sent a copy of that letter, a lovely fruit basket, the money, and a letter from the board wishing them a joyful Christmas to each of the disgruntled families.

To this day, I believe that was one of the most soundly scriptural acts by a group of God's people I have ever beheld. The board had been extremely wise and we received a very specific grace in time of need. We never heard directly from those families or their pastor again.

That was certainly one of the more dramatic "dark" times we have experienced as a school. Reflecting on it now, I believe the Father was teaching us a critical lesson early on in the school's life. That lesson was best expressed by the valuable counsel I received from the pastor of the church we were housed in during those early years. During the above crisis he told me, "Don't doubt in the dark what God has shown you in the light." I can't say I've unwaveringly held to that advise, but it has stuck with me.

In the *Screwtape Letters*, C.S. Lewis noted that it seems during a crisis Christians allow their faith to cave just before the relief or answer comes. Many years after the above trial, and after a number of other school and personal crises, I was telling Ed Van Nuland, our development officer that I wanted, both personally and corporately, to remain faithful all the way *through* each new challenge we face. And I am sure there will be more crises that Logos will face. We live and work in the real world, after all, with real children and adults who sin, get hurt, get sick, and face all the trials other humans do. The differences are not seen in *what* afflicts us, but to Whom we turn and how we deal with the trial. God has no crises. So, Ed came up with the above title as a motto we frequently toss at each other. (Try saying it in the Latin—it rolls off better than in English!) I pray it may come to characterize not only Logos School, but all the believers associated with this and other works of the Kingdom. God is faithful. Thank you for your prayers on our behalf. We must pray, and we desire to work, and stay faithful. Merry Christmas!

\* \* \*

## THE RIGHT STUFF

If asked to list what they would consider the top five toughest and most dangerous jobs, most folks would not include teaching in a classical, Christian school among those five. Granted, that could be because most folks haven't even HEARD of a "classical, Christian school," but that's beside my point. I believe I have an idea of what teaching in a classical, Christian school is like and, ok, I probably wouldn't rate the job among the top five toughest and most dangerous jobs either. It certainly isn't like being an F-18 pilot or being an honorable United States President or being a Christian police officer. But, by George, it's got to be in the top ten list!

Teaching children in any situation is tough enough, due to the nature of children and the nature of parents. When you teach children, you are touching the apple of someone's eye, biblically speaking. In fact, you are touching the apple of many people's eyes in most cases. For every child in any class, there are (or should be) dozens of loving aunts, uncles, grandparents, cousins, friends, etc., who care very much how that child is treated. So, when a teacher gazes out at a full class of children, she should consider that she is about to influence hundreds of people's lives by what she says and does that day. Then, as Christian teachers, there is the aspect of considering that you are teaching eternal beings who, as God directs, will grow and influence many, many others for good or evil, down through generations. Golly! When you stop to consider what these teachers are facing each day, you have to wonder that they even get out of bed!

> **When you stop to consider what these teachers are facing each day, you have to wonder that they even get out of bed!**

But, thank God, they do get up each day, some at very early hours, and make their way here. As the classical, Christian schooling reclamation has spread, many other people have had the chance to meet and even be instructed by our Logos teachers. A very frequently asked question I receive from these folks is, "Where do you find all those wonderful people?" Let me tell you—it wasn't easy. In the early years of Logos, it seemed we had a revolving front door for staff members. In retrospect, that's not too surprising. We were a young, untried, possibly short-lived, little school. So we had young, untried, mostly single people come to teach for us. (I was the only married person on staff for quite a number of years and, for the first two years, the only male!) But what they (we) lacked in knowledge and experience, they made up for in zeal and energy. They were, for all their faults and brief terms, the pioneers and trail-blazers of reviving a unique form of educating children, based on an antiquated system of teaching. For instance, I easily remember gathering in the early eighties with the teachers (all female) at Julie's and my apartment over a number of evenings to hash out our first Logos curriculum guide. (We had been more than a little disappointed with the Christian publisher's materials we had tried for our first few months.)

Those years contained lots of wonderful, as well as awkward, situations. Many of the ladies were sharp, superb teachers who contributed a great deal to our program's quality. Then, after a year or two, some young cad would snatch them away in matrimony. Or, if they were already married ... yes, you guessed it, they would get pregnant. It seemed to happen so often in those days, I would have sworn had Logos existed in Abraham's time, Sarah could have had Isaac a whole lot sooner if only she'd worked here! The men, particularly the single ones, were frequently the occasion for the "awkward" times. Put simply, we have yet to have a single man work for us more than two years. They have either gotten married and stayed, got a hankering to travel, or were fired.

The board (and I) learned a bit through some of the more "unique" situations, and now a teacher has to go through an intensive scrutiny prior to being hired. Also, as the years went by, I was thrilled to see a shift in who applied and how long they stayed. Among these new recruits were many parents—committed, intelligent, loving parents of students in Logos—who were seeking employment where their children were enrolled. They came with a strong desire to understand and apply the classical methodology, as well as having a profound understanding of children. What some "lacked" in college training or teaching certification was easily overshadowed by their and their children's characters. Through in-service training we could instruct these long-term teachers in the classical, Christian pedagogy; we can't train adults to selflessly love and understand children as God made them. This has to come from His hand.

But, as I mentioned earlier, this is still a very difficult, dangerous profession. These teachers live in a world that requires an unerring balance. It is absolutely critical they maintain a spiritual even keel in spite of the fact that demands placed on them are often from opposite extremes. They must consistently, overtly love the children, even when provoked by a rapscallion. They must insist on keeping the bar high, academically, all the while aching for and working with the "caboose" child. They must respond graciously to an irate parent (even a Christian one) who berates before listening to the other side of the story. They are not allowed the luxury of a "bad day," especially in front of the kids. That is, bad attitudes are sin, no matter what the provocation. As they are told each year in staff orientation, every staff member is to come to school each day walking in the joy of the Lord, or they are to stay at home until the sin is dealt with.

They must be lifelong learners themselves, loving to grow in their own knowledge. They must be creative, yet willing to submit to a firm, established philosophical structure. They must strive for improvement, all the while following a very similar schedule year after year. They must be willing and able to go long periods of time without receiving much personal recognition, yet pouring out regular praise to their students. The women must be biblically respectful of their husbands and good moms at home; the men must be godly, loving husbands at home, with a good reputation outside the school, as well.

Most of all, these Logos teachers cannot forget for a moment that they are walking, talking examples to these students of what adult Christians are be like. When their students see them at Safeway on Saturday, in their jeans and sweatshirts, sans make-up or tie (as the case may be), the students must see the very same saint they see each day in the classroom. Whew! And these kids do see just that, by God's grace.

But, you know, now that I think about it, those F-18 pilots have it easy!

\* \* \*

## SOAKED STONES

> And he said, "Do it a second time," and they did it a second time. And he said, "Do it a third time," and they did it a third time. And the water flowed around the altar, and he also filled the trench with water.
> ~1 Kings 18:34-35

To quote one of the wise guys of our age, Han Solo, "Never tell me the odds!" Though not intended to be, given the context and character, that could still be considered a biblical worldview remark. *If* events were indeed always in keeping with "the odds," i.e., the most likely prospect to happen based on the "norm," Elijah was certainly setting himself up for a huge embarrassment. Earthy wisdom would dictate that he at least make firing up his altar as easy for God as possible. Instead, he purposely made it as hard as he could.

Closer to home, given the normal odds, Logos School should not be here. The "odds" of a new small business making it past five years are about one in five, or so I've been informed. And that's with most business startups having some up-front capital to get going on the right foot. We didn't have any. The altar was rather wet. Through God's provisions, we began anyway.

In 1986, we were informed that the "odds" were against us getting a facility of our own, after renting a church basement for six years. We were told that just to house the number of students we had at that point, about 130, it would take one to one and a half million dollars to build a suitable school building. Our entire annual budget was about $300,000 at that time. Annual giving totaled around $25,000, on a good year. Bad odds. The stones were soaked. Through God's provision, we found and remodeled a roller rink for about a quarter of those projected costs.

In 1998, we were told that we would have to come up with $250,000 in cash in order help fund the possible purchase of additional land and the materials to build a gym. The board set a goal of raising that amount in about a month. If it was not provided, we would assume the Lord didn't want us to build a gym in the coming school year. At that time gift revenue for an entire year was about $70,000. The largest gift in cash we had ever received to that point was $10,000. Raise $250,000 in about thirty days? Bad odds. Even our "fund-raising" letter was not a professional, well-designed presentation. It was low-key and simply informative. Talk about a drenched set of rocks! (Personally, I was thinking we'd walk away empty-handed, leaving the damp altar to drip-dry.) But God's provision of all we needed lit us up and we built a gym!

God's Word commands us to be wise in our planning (Christ's analogy of making sure you have enough bricks to build a tower), and yet He delights in defying the "odds," to His glory alone. Consider Gideon and his small band.

Logos exists and has grown because God wanted it to. Period. Many folks have labored and sacrificed to carry out His will to this point in our history. We planned and worked, but there has never been a point where we *knew* for sure what the outcome would be. That would have been presumptuous, at best. Instead, we labored with His strength and prayed for His will.

For quite some time we, the board and administration, have been praying about where we are to go from here, facility-wise. During the last few years, we have very seriously considered and researched the possibility of moving the whole school to another site and start over. Nothing has come of this idea. Instead, last fall we were greatly encouraged to pursue another option for growth and improvement. Mark Wintz, a school dad and a developer, presented us with a vision, a visual concept, of putting a second story on this building. The elementary would have their first-floor rooms expanded and the secondary would move upstairs. Further, he advocated that we seek to beautify our school with a brick facade, new roof, and a central grand entrance. Logos School would have the American classical architecture lookan attractive, serious aspect.

After months of more research, consideration and prayer, on April 21 the school board approved a three priority, overall capital campaign plan. We will seek to concurrently retire our current mortgage, buy some more property south of us, and remodel the entire current building. We estimate the entire project would cost about two million dollars.

## First, there really never will be a "good" time, if we look to circumstancesfor guidance.

It hardly needs to be said that, considering the times and economy we live in, not to mention our school's tight finances, once again the odds are stacked very much against us. Talk a soaked altar! "Why seek this now?" is a legitimate question. First, there really never will be a "good" time, if we look to circumstances for guidance. Secondly, Scripture says without a vision, people perish. We are avidly seeking God's direction in our vision, through His provision. The amount we need is so immense, there is absolutely no way we, on our own, could bring the fire from heaven, as it were.

So, we are letting you know, as a first step in this campaign, what our goals are. Ed Van Nuland and I will be making other practical plans to inform and seek supporters in the coming year, at least. It'll take a good bit of work to do that well. But simply put, if this is of God, the odds really don't matter and the water we see everywhere will disappear. If it's not of Him, (and we are fully willing for that possibility) then even Bill Gates couldn't ignite our altar.

Please pray for God's direction and provision—obviously we'd love to see the fire come down. Soli Deo Gloria!

# 9

## PERSONAL THOUGHTS

*Every once in awhile "great thoughts" are hard to come by, and I just like to shoot from the hip, so to speak, in my columns. Personal experiences, friends, family, and random thoughts comprise the fodder for these relatively rare tangents. Nevertheless, I find that when I choose to take one of these mental jaunts, the writing flows pretty easily.*

*I was raised in a Christian home in Ann Arbor, Michigan. My parents have been the best models of the fleshed-out Christian life I have met yet, and I have met many godly men and women whom I admire. The impressions, memories, and loving support I have had from my home form my thinking and goals to this day, and I trust, will until I'm called to my real home. When I left my Michigan home to join the Navy at eighteen, although I didn't know it then, I was leaving for good. My four years in the service left me, as with all vets, with indelible memories, for good or ill...*

### A (NAVY) BLUE CHRISTMAS

It was a dark and stormy night. But that was normal. What was unusual was that it was cold and very stormy. I mean, you expect to rock and roll a bit, even in a 650' long ship when you're in the middle of the ocean, but not when you are anchored in the Naples, Italy harbor.

Unlike other U.S. Navy ships, as a fleet oiler we could not tie up to the piers.

Wherever we went we were, in a nautical sort of way, persona non grata. This had nothing to do with the manners of our crew; we were carrying the liquid equivalent of a small nuclear warhead. Our gymnasium-sized tanks held highly combustible fuel for ships and planes. Hence I suppose it was understandable that highly populated cities were a bit nervous about our cozying up to one of their docks. (No one seemed to care about our self-esteem!)

That night, Christmas eve, 1973, Naples harbor was doing its best to send us back out to sea. The worst watch of the night is the midnight to four slot. Yours truly was the junior member of the watch team of three. In unadulterated wording that meant I got to do whatever the others didn't want to do. In this case it meant frequently braving the elements to check on the ship's anchorage movement, if any. "If any!?" At about two o'clock in the morning the anchor chain was stretched out like a fishing line with a twelve pound bass on the other end! Not a good sign.

"Check the utility boats," the officer of the watch responded, after I informed him that I believed the anchor was virtually trolling the bottom. I checked the utility boats. Actually one was a 20' utility boat, the other was the Captain's gig. The two boats were normally lashed to a boom, or long beam, that extended out perpendicularly from the deck of the ship. By the madly swinging boom light I looked down into the water and counted all the way up to one boat. Unless the captain was on a lonely night cruise by himself, his gig had gone AWOL. And, from all appearances, the other boat was contemplating the same action. It had the same demeanor as a bronco waiting for the gate to open at a rodeo. On the way back to the quarterdeck I also noticed that the gangway (the stairway leading down to the water) was unattached at the bottom and doing its best to bash a hole in the side of the ship with each wave. I reported the absence of the gig to the officer and passed along my conviction that we were little better off than the Lusitania. At least, I didn't think I had seen any stray torpedoes headed our way.

As it was now three o'clock am and the three of us on watch couldn't correct all the ship's ills, we set about awakening the rest of the crew to a dark Christmas morning. The captain seemed particularly anxious to recover his gig, as well as to move the ship to a less exciting spot. The looks on the crew members faces bore little similarity to exuberant children's visages upon rising on a Christmas morn. There was a profound absence of squeals of joy and anticipation. In fact, no amount of cajoling could turn the mutterings to carols. Anyway, the singing would have been overwhelmed by the clanking of the raised anchor chain, the slap of large waves, and all manner of machinery and shouted orders.

Finally we were resettled: the ship had been moved and re-anchored securely, the truant gig was retethered to the boom, the ladder was hoisted and awaiting repairs, and the crew was staggering back to their bunks. The dawn was cautiously introducing itself as I heeded my bunk's call. Before turning in, though, I reflected on this most unique of Christmas mornings in my experience. It couldn't have been more dissimilar to the years of precious Christ and family-centered holiday mornings I'd grown up with. Nevertheless, those memories, the knowledge that my family was still following those intimate traditions back home, and the profound sense of my Lord's presence made it still Christmas. I didn't even miss the presents. Besides, a love and Christmas gift-filled box did make its way to me ... in March. Ah, the Navy!

* * *

THE PROVERBS

*(As Compiled From Logos School)*

CHAPTER 1
1. Some proverbs of an administrator, the son of an administrator:
2. To know a few good ideas, but mostly to understand various accumulated opinions and experiences of dubious worth, gathered over time by the son of an administrator,
3. And maybe to gain some sympathy, if not agreement in passing them along to others.
4. As rain comes in the spring, so snow will come immediately after paying for a new load of gravel for the driveway.
5. Like vinegar to the back teeth is a copier that breaks down as soon as it is desperately needed to run off a last-minute paper.
6. He who once gives a foot ride to a first grader will find he must do so daily.

7. As pearls carried in a paper sack is a lovely girl in a t-shirt and old jeans.
8. The fool says in his heart, "I don't need to study tonight; the test isn't until two days from now."
9. Grass will be able to grow where there are no children playing, but much joy comes from watching children play.
10. Like discovering you have lost five pounds is the gladness that comes from a student's sincere compliment.
11. Expediency is a tyrannical master, listen not to him when hiring a teacher or other staff members
12. Many are the ideas education colleges give new teachers, but few are of value to the biblically-minded teacher.
13. The righteous father does not hold back spanking from his son, nor does the righteous mother withhold chocolate-chip cookies from the administrator.

## CHAPTER 2

1. D.A.R.E. is a mocker and provides no limits to a student's evil desires for blowing his mind.
2. The sluggard student leaves his jacket on the floor and remembers not where he put it.
3. Four things an administrator hates; five incur his displeasure: a lying tongue, a hand that is quick to strike others, a bus that will not start on a winter morning, anything coming from the N.E.A., and yet another jacket lying on the floor.
4. The Lord blesses even little schools in Moscow, Idaho; who can understand His ways?
5. A capable, friendly secretary is a gift from the Lord, as our competent teachers.
6. Look to the kindergarten teacher, O you teacher of higher learning, and see how productive she is and the work her students produce. Be like her in your energies.
7. "Remain in school!" cries the fool, yet he looks not at why his schools continue to empty.
8. He who greets a staff meeting with a loud voice early in the morning,

it will be counted to him as a curse, though none would actually say so.
9. Where there are many formers of a new school, sin and disorganization will be present shortly. Good leadership lies with the few of one mind.
10. A foolish student seeks for a lost paper in a trashed locker and finds it not; a wise student finds his paper in an organized notebook.
11. The fool thinks education is like computer technology; only the newest innovation will do. Look back, O man, to how the fathers taught for generations; there lies education.
12. Three things are wondrous to behold, yea four are the delight of the administrator: A student who loves school, a father who leads his home, a staff working well and harmoniously toward a goal, and a person who prays for Logos School.

\* \* \*

*As I mentioned above, my parents and first home not only profoundly shaped my early years, they still exercise a fair amount of influence over my thought life. This influence took a huge leap in 1988 when, for the first time in about twenty years by my reckoning, the Garfield clan actually got together for a reunion. It was held in Breckenridge, Colorado for about a week. This was immediately followed by a special trip, with my wife Julie, our four children, my two unmarried sisters (at that time), and my parents to Michigan and back. If you counted ten people, you would be correct. And we all rode in the same large van for about two weeks of traveling. Despite the potential for homicides in such situations, we all thoroughly enjoyed our time together, as well as enjoying visiting the old stomping grounds.*

## SNEAK PREVIEWS OF HEAVEN

It started with a funeral. My dad's father, the spiritual patriarch of the Garfield clan, went to glory in 1987. And, although he was 96 when he died, 'his eye was not dim, nor his vigor abated.' His funeral in Florida was the gathering point for many of our relatives who had not had such a compelling reason to see each other for many years. The Garfield heirs are literally at all points of the compass. It took this godly man's passing to bring so many so far. But they came. Because they came, not only was there great rejoicing in knowing our precious grandfather was now seeing the One he lived for, but the idea of a too-long delayed, all-inclusive Garfield family reunion was born at that time.

The first such reunion was held in 1988 in the Rocky Mountains of Colorado. The brief week was filled, from my perception, mostly with rekindling old, but close, relationships. In a way it was like making lots of new friends, but they were instantly old friends, too. Also, since the third generation had now grown to adulthood and had gone forth and multiplied, there were spouses and fourth generation-ers to get to know. Out of a possible sixty-two people who could have come, sixty-one made it! Another amazing fact soon emerged from all the hubbub ... from all appearances, the vast majority of those present shared not only similar DNA, but more importantly, the cleansing blood of the Savior!

Time passed; another reunion was planned. Hey, if Hollywood can do a sequel of a smash hit, why can't a family? July, 1992, same time (four years later), same place. Once again they came. This time there were even more spouses and offspring to meet and hug. The mountains were just as magnificent and the views were just as breathtaking this time, but something else was different. Instead of a kaleidoscope of names and faces to sort out and assimilate, there was a common sense of family; we were able to build on what had gone before. Even more, we were able, during the course of the week, to have several rich evenings together, sharing testimonies of God's enduring faithfulness to us as individuals and families.

Those times together were sort of like wonderful, small-town church worship services, where all the congregation is related. They were also sort of like good parties, except the focus was on the faith and Lord we shared, not on the jokes and food that accompanied all we did. Tears flowed, but it was not from sorrow; the goodness of our Father was the cause for both the joy and the tears. The last night we had together was spent mostly singing the great hymns that had meant so much to us through the many years and the generations we represented. It struck me at that time that this was not only what an extended family in the Lord should be like, but maybe a bit like what Heaven will be—the reuniting and corporate worship of those we have loved and known for years.

I come from a rich, spiritual background, through no work or credit of mine. As David said, "The lines have fallen to me in pleasant places; indeed, my heritage is beautiful to me" (Ps. 16:6). Many of the students here at Logos, if not now, one day will also realize the profoundly rich spiritual gift they too have been given by their parents—an inheritance of family built on the solid foundation of God's Word and love. Day after day, we seek to build on that foundation in all the work of Logos School, looking toward that Greatest Family Reunion.

\* \* \*

*When Logos School opened, Carolyn, our oldest child, was two-and-a half years old. Seth, our next youngest (really "youngest", as a three-month premature baby), was still in the hospital, trying to gain weight so he could come home. So, in the very earliest days of the school, I not only had very little experience with children, I had none of my own in the school who would undergo this brand new education. Looking back, I have to say I didn't and couldn't appreciate what kind of feelings, decisions, sacrifices, and doubts the parents of our first students had to confront. However, because of the willingness of those first families to put up with all our blunders and amateurish mistakes, my own four children have benefited from all the school has learned in the intervening years. As of this writing, we have four children; the three oldest (with addition of daughter #2—Kajsa) in the secondary, and Kathryn (daughter #3) in the elementary.*

*I can now say I do understand and appreciate what all our families go through to have their children in Logos. And, I trust also like them, I can say it is worth every sacrifice and more.*

TRUE CONFESSIONS: I ENVY MY KIDS!

> The heavens are telling of the glory of God; and their expanse is declaring the work of His hands.
> Day to day pours forth speech, and night to night reveals knowledge.
> ~Ps. 19:1-2

Quite a few years ago I was asked to be a guest on a local television program that, I gather, was supposed to be a scaled-down version of Firing Line. I was to take on some local public school educators in a debate over the issue of private vs. public education. At one point after I had been saying less than complimentary things about government education, the moderator turned to me and said, "Well, you attended public schools and you seem to have turned out OK." While many might debate the accuracy of the latter part of his statement, I would merely submit that the moderator was talking through his hat, i.e. he was drawing an incredibly poor deduction. If I have turned out "OK," it is not due to the state education I received; rather it is in spite of the education I received and due greatly to the godliness of my parents and the unmitigated grace of God.

Further, what the moderator based his assessment of my OK-ness on was slim to say the least. He had known me for all of thirty minutes and I don't think we have met since. Being able to speak in more than monosyllabic terms and not be a social embarrassment while on camera are not necessarily the litmus tests for measuring a person's education.

> **Then, as now, many Christian parents did not actually know what their children were being taught, day after day.**

No, my parents didn't send me or my sisters to Christian schools. (I did attend a private Lutheran kindergarten—maybe that subliminally shaped the rest of my life.) Knowing my parents, had there been a Christian school in Ann Arbor and had they known just how public education was radically changing for the worse, I have little doubt they would have sought to give us the best, biblical education available. However, like most Christian parents then and, sadly, like many Christian parents even today, they assumed that their children were getting the best education available. Then, as now, many Christian parents did not actually know what their children were being taught, day after day.

The education I received, to put it in the best light, was largely made up of earnest and kind teachers, telling me falsehoods (albeit unintentionally) about God and His world. Much of what I learned I have had to unlearn in the years since graduating. For example, for twelve years I had no idea that the very heavens themselves constantly tell us of God's marvelous handiwork and faithful, daily care for a rebellious creation. Instead, I was told, day after day, year after year, that God, if He existed, had nothing to do with what I was learning. Even as a

Christian child coming from a solid Christian home, I bought the whole lie. What I heard in church one day a week regarding God and His world had no bearing on what I heard in school five days a week. Since I was not encouraged or taught to think from a biblical worldview, I was able to compartmentalize the material I was taught into Christian and secular realms. And there was an impermeable wall between those compartments.

My children, and many others, are receiving an education I desperately wish I had received. Not only are they daily being loved and disciplined by men and women who are my sisters and brothers in Christ, my kids are being told the truth about God and His world. In every class, from preschool through the senior year, I can count on my four children being exposed to God's Word and how every discipline they study finds its basis in the Word. They are being taught to think "Christianly," viewing all things in light of the Word, as opposed to my own file-drawer thought patterns.

I know they may not get all the frills and goodies I had in Ann Arbor's well-financed school system; for instance, Logos will probably never have an Olympic-size pool or a planetarium on campus. Nevertheless, I truly envy the experiences and training my kids will have. There are certainly ways that the teaching they get could be better and, thankfully, because it's grounded on God's Word, we know where to look to learn how to improve. In addition to all this, my kids have friends here, some of whom they have known for years, who also come from homes founded on Christ's love. That certainly will have a profound affect on the memories they are accumulating from their school years.

Yes, I do have twinges of envy, but they're nothing to the immense sense of gratitude I have to God for how He is blessing my children's education. Thank you for your prayer support that makes this education possible for all the kids here.

\* \* \*

*Working with children is the closest thing to regularly dipping in the proverbial fountain of youth that I can see. Day after day they remind me of what it means to be a child, and yet, because we have grades through high school, these same little ones grow to young adulthood right under my eyes. But, even as I ache to see a class full of dearly-loved seniors graduate, there is a new, wonder-filled, wide-eyed group of kindergartners who are*

DEAR PARENTS

*just starting. These young ones remind me, day after day, through their excited voices and wonderful handiworks just how the world looks from their level and experience. That's probably why it is so easy for me to slip back in time to my own childhood memories. Maybe I'll just never grow up...*

## 'TWAS THE KNIGHT BEFORE CHRISTMAS...

My wife Julie says one of the best things about Christmas is the anticipation. And, as with most things she says, she's right. Quick fade to a Christmas many years ago....

As tradition demanded, my three sisters and I had decorated the tree in what we (especially they) thought an incredibly tasteful manner. What my parents thought is anyone's guess. The glittering, fragile spheres hung alongside the pink, three-pound, clay ornament constructed with great care by my youngest sister. She and I had also spent numerous hours designing a snow scene (with glued-on cotton balls) on the bulletin board in my bedroom. It even had a workable sled that would slide down the cotton slopes. Along one edge of the bulletin board was a daily countdown, which we watched with no less intensity than a NASA engineer prior to a shuttle liftoff.

Now it was the morning! The evening before my sisters and I had gone into executive session to determine whose bedroom we would open our stocking gifts in, and the all-important question—when to get up. Looking back, it seems that Jill, the eldest, always got the most votes on her motion. Or maybe she just issued the edict. Either way somehow we frequently ended up in her room. Darkness still reigned when I heard the reveille whisper. Then came the tiptoeing into the living room to behold where last night only our few, misshapen bundles of wrapping paper had lain scattered under the tree. Now, like Jack's beans, overnight they had magically turned into a mountain of presents in all sizes, colors, and shapes! Ever conscious of the need for silence (really more because noise would somehow break the spell, than out of consideration for our parents who had tumbled into bed scarcely a few hours before), we would search the pile for gift identification.

"This huge one is for Tom! Sheesh, he always gets the big ones!" "Yeah, well, it's probably all full of socks!"

"SSHHHHHH!"

For some unstated reason, we had to replace the gifts in exactly the same position they were in prior to our pawing. Maybe we thought a siren would go off if one gift was put back the "wrong" way.

Then, like Aladdin clutching only the lamp retrieved from the cave of treasures, we grabbed just our stockings and dashed to Jill's room, of course. There we would open the two or three small gifts we each had, eat the oranges found in the toes of the stockings, and all read my new *Mad* magazine.

You can figure out how it went from there. First, the descending upon the exhausted parents (who always received God's gift of grace not to curse us for 'greeting them with a loud voice early in the morning'). Then the seeming four-and-a-half hour breakfast before the main event. Finally, after prayer, the grand (but still slightly anticlimactic) revealing of secrets.

Fade to 1994 ... You may have noticed that not once in that whole recollection did the word "school" enter in. That's not only because school was a low priority in my life in those early years, but rather more that school and Christmas, while not antithetical, had little to do with each other in my experience.

I praise God each Christmas for the fact that my children experience the truth and purpose of the Incarnation literally year-round. Their teachers, and many of their friends and classmates live lives honoring the One born as a Man in Bethlehem. At Christmas, my children experience at school, as well as at home, the joyful anticipation of this timeless event! Their Christmas memories will be even richer and deeper than mine.

For all the staff, board members, and students of Logos School, I wish you and your family a Christmas celebration as full of Christ's joy and presence as is earthly possible!

God grant us all a better understanding of His gift of salvation.

*　*　*

*In writing personal thoughts for my columns, I have had to be mindful not to write too much, or too often about my wonderful parents. The fact that many of you may feel that way about your parents attests to God's goodness in blessing so many with such good parents. But, sadly, that sentiment is becoming less and less of a general part of our culture's population. It seems that families, if you believe the news, are becoming more fragmented, to the point where there aren't many that seek to mirror God's plan for families.*

DEAR PARENTS

*But I have been blessed with uniquely special parents, as have many of the children here at Logos. Even now in my middle-age (yikes!), barely a day goes by that I don't think of them with tremendous fondness and thankfulness. They have come to visit me and my family in Moscow countless times, including a surprise visit on my 40th birthday. But that is typical for them; they met my ship every time it came in from a long cruise, even though it meant two days of driving each time. To say they have always been there for me, and my sisters, would sound trite and cliche, but would be the absolute, rock-solid truth.*

*So, with those credentials, it shouldn't be surprising that I have to include at least one column on my best mentor, my father...*

IT'S MY DAD'S FAULT

At some point in almost every school year, some little person will ask me, "Do you like being a principal?" or "How did you get to be a principal?"

The answer to the first question is easy. I cannot imagine doing anything else that would bring me greater joy and satisfaction! True, it also brings real sorrow and frustrations at times. The answer to the second question is more complicated and the little person usually doesn't want to hear the real explanation. So I've given the explanation I saw in a cartoon several years ago: two little boys were standing outside the principal's office, and one asked the other how he thought someone becomes a principal. The other little boy replied "I think you have to be bitten by one."

## How did I come to walk precisely in my father's footsteps, when I had had no such intention?

Actually, as late in life as ninth grade I was so intent on not being an administrator "like my father," that I distinctly stated so in a vocational research paper at the time. My career options, as I saw them from that height of maturity, were to be a veterinarian or an FBI agent. My father was an administrator of student finances at a nearby university. I couldn't imagine too many jobs more boring than "shuffling papers" at a desk all day. I wanted to do something exciting! (My wife,

Julie, often says that my life reminds her of the classic movie, *It's A Wonderful Life*. George Bailey didn't want to be like his dad, either, at first.)

After that adamant denial of such a pursuing such a dismal future career, imagine the shock I had when halfway through my master's degree work, I discovered that not only was I doing a very similar job to my father's, he had exactly the *same* master's degree! I never knew what he had done in college, such was my lack of consideration of his past. What happened? How did I come to walk precisely in my father's footsteps, when I had had no such intention? He had never even put his arm around my shoulders in his office and, while choking back a tear of joy, told me that someday all this would be mine, file cabinets and all!

The serious conclusion I have come to is that because my father is the kind of man he is, and because my heavenly Father is the kind of God He is, I didn't stand a chance. You see, my dad is the only man on earth I would love to be exactly like—as a father, as a husband, as a godly man, and yes, even as an effective administrator. My heavenly Father is the only One who really knows me and how I can best serve Him. I know it was the combination of my desire to emulate my dad (primarily because of his life, not because he in anyway pushed me), and the Lord's consistent love and guidance, that placed me in this position and I love it. Now, Lord willing, I hope I can help foster future "surprises" for these children at Logos School. They, too, make "wake up" someday and find that, to their great surprise and joy, they are indeed like their parents, thank God!

\* \* \*

JOY TO THE WORLD

The snowflakes mesmerized him. They were coming down rapidly, millions of them, yet because of their crystalline thickness, if he tried, he could follow an individual flake as it tilted and swirled past the window. For a few moments they distracted him from his heartsick, depressed mood. Then his focus returned to the restaurant table-top before him and the now cold bowl of chicken noodle soup in his hands. He pushed the bowl aside and slowly leaned his weary, aching back against the chair. "I've lived too long," he thought. "God help me, but I wish I had died years ago, remembering it as it was. What a fool I was to think it would be the same. If only I had not gone back to see...." He shook his head several times, slowly, repeating to himself, "I never should have gone back ... never should have gone back...."

Earlier that afternoon he had visited the Christian school he had last seen twenty-nine years before. Of course the office personnel treated him with some courtesy, after all, even though no one knew him personally, his name and photograph were still in the foyer. He had been the school's first principal so the library was named after him, but everyone just called it the library. He could tell the very young principal was surprised and not a little bothered to have to deal with this fragile old man, but the principal forced a smile and said, why of course, he would be happy to show the special visitor around.

As they walked slowly down the halls, passing obviously new, handsome classrooms, the principal chattered rapidly about the state-of-art this and the technically advanced that, but the old man quickly tuned him out. It wasn't hard; there was too much else to be distracted by. Students rushed by, nearly knocking him over several times. He finally asked to stop and rest on a bench in the student commons before they passed it. Something was wrong, dreadfully, inescapably wrong; the old man knew it. The principal, impatient, rose and excused himself to some business, but not before inviting the old man to make himself "at home." He looked around. The walls told a story; they were covered, but in an orderly fashion, with plaques and posters. He rose to read them. They were full of praise, congratulations, awards to the school, to various named students, to faculty. He didn't recognize the names of the awardees, which didn't surprise him, but he didn't know the companies or groups doing the awarding either. Wait. There's an acronym he knew ... ACLU. No, that couldn't be right. A "A Multi-Species Toleration Award?" How strange....

## What was missing, what was so wrong that he felt almost in a daze?

He wandered off to other parts of the school. Most adults he saw made a point of ignoring his presence; the younger children just stared as they walked purposefully past, grim little mouths in straight lines. What was missing, what was so wrong that he felt almost in a daze? Certainly hard work was being done; he could see that as he peered in through several classroom door windows. The building was far bigger than he ever imagined it would be, especially when he recalled the church basement in which the school had begun. And everything was well-built and attractive. Wasn't that fine? Shouldn't that delight him, he asked himself. The school was obviously doing well financially and had more students than he could have dreamed of in his day. What was bothering him so? The building was far bigger than he ever imagined it would be, especially when he recalled the church basement in which the school had begun. And everything was well-built and attractive. Wasn't that fine? Shouldn't that delight him, he asked himself. The school was obviously doing well financially and had more students than he could have dreamed of in his day. What was bothering him so?

Finally, after seeking directions, he was told how to get back to the main offices. His feet and back were hurting a great deal now, as they did more each day, it seemed. But he wanted to thank the young principal before he left. As he waited in an office chair for the principal to return, he saw a literature rack on the wall. He pulled out the attractive brochure, obviously the school's latest promotional piece. He looked for the old, familiar motto on the cover, but it wasn't there. Instead, it said something about preparing market managers, CEOs, and statesmen of tomorrow. His eyes were tired and the print was so small inside, he couldn't make it out at all. Suddenly a cold thought formed in his mind. He had to ask someone. He stood just as the principal came bustling into the office.

"Excuse me, but I just have to ask. The students seem a bit somber. Has there been a recent tragedy or accident that affected them?"

The principal looked puzzled and glanced at the secretaries, now all looking at him.

"The students are just fine. We don't expect or allow them to be silly, not with the prices we are charging and the education they are getting."

"No, no," the old man persisted. "I don't mean that either. But they just don't seem very ... joyful. And, frankly, neither do the teachers I saw." He paused. "You do still require the staff members to be Christians, don't you?" It was an impertinent question, but it just came out.

The principal's puzzlement vanished. Both he and the secretaries burst into relieved laughter. "Oh, I see what you mean now. I forgot how long you've been away. No, no, of course we don't require that! In fact, it would be against the school's by-laws. No, you see, it must be at least, oh, fourteen years ago or so that our board voted to remove all references to Christianity from the school's program. So, of course, out-dated hiring requirements like that went, too. We are now one of the leading private academies in the state…" and he droned on, listing other ways the school was lauded regionally and nationally.

The old man had left in a mental fog, his hands full of brochures and pamphlets about the school. His school.

No, not his school, what had been God's school. Had been a place of joy … had been….

He jerked and sat up. The snowflakes had mesmerized him. Weird dream…. But now he remembered. Christmas was coming and he had been mentally stalled at his waiting computer, trying to think of a unique column to write. How about something on joy being the hallmark of a Christian? … and therefore a Christian school? …What if even Logos lost that joy? Hmmm … might work.

\* \* \*

## BLESSED BY THE AFFLICTED

> Sing, O heavens, and be joyful, O earth; and break forth into singing,
> O mountains:
> for the LORD hath comforted his people, and will have mercy upon
> His afflicted.
> ~Isaiah 49:13

If you have followed our news in recent months you know we have had quite a year, especially in terms of honors and recognitions earned by our students, not to mention the finishing of the Knights' Court facility. You would also rightly guess that for every story we share with you, there are many others that we would love to tell we, but we can't for space or time limitations. Some stories would also take a fair bit of explanation to "bring you up to speed" and help you appreciate why they mean so much to us. This may be one of those, but I believe it's worth a try due to its unique nature. We would like to share the blessing.

Nathan Hatcher is a bright, strong lad of ten. His family moved here from Maryland in 1997. They had been active in another classical, Christian school there. Nathan's folks wanted him to attend Logos in second grade, but they were unable to find an aide to be with him while at school, so he was home that year. You see, while Nathan's mind is alert and sharp, for some reason known to God, his muscles do not always do what he wants them to do. That includes the muscles and connections that regulate speech. Nathan, therefore, needs physical assistance constantly. He communicates in writing through a special computer board which he types on. He can walk and even run a bit, but he must be closely monitored lest he stumble into someone or something. Sometimes his head needs to be pointed at whatever he is to pay attention to. His excitement and frustrations frequently come out in either happy squeals or deep moans.

## Would he be too great a distraction to the other students in the class?

Two aides were found in preparation for Nathan entering Logos' third grade, but I confess I had a good deal of concern and hesitation as I considered accepting him for the few hours each day his folks requested. Would he be too great a distraction to the other students in the class? Would his needs, even with the aide present, draw too much attention from the tender-hearted teachers? And would his time in school really be of any benefit to Nathan himself? Finally, with the encouragement from one of his former teachers in Maryland, a good friend of mine, I accepted him. To be brief, it was one of the smartest decisions (by God's grace) I have ever made. His parents sent us the following letter after this last year was over and they were preparing for their planned move to Bellevue, Washington this summer:

> We would like to take this opportunity to express our deep gratitude to Logos School and to you, the Board of Directors, for allowing Nathan to attend your school this last academic year.

Through your generosity, the Lord saw fit to bless Nathan and us in many ways. Nathan had one of his best years in terms of academic improvements. He was able, with assistance, to complete the Third Grade math curriculum, and showed us that his ability to work with these concepts continues to improve. In addition, we saw a marked breakthrough in his ability to use his computer with greater independence. But this was even more pronounced in the reading curriculum, where Nathan began spelling words, one letter at a time, while totally independent of any assistance.

While this work was achieved through the services we provided with Oriel Gunn and additional work in the home, we believe that much of this would not have occurred without the help of Logos School. We saw Nathan's countenance and enjoyment of life increase this last year as he found friends who would reach out to him at school. Both in the classroom, as well as in the lunchroom and at recess, Nathan was rarely left alone. This simple integration motivated Nathan to strive to do what others around him were doing, whether that was playing freeze-tag or silently reading at one's own desk. In addition, church became a place of greater fellowship for Nate because so many kids (and adults) were used to seeing him everyday.

We are certainly aware that Logos has no intention of becoming a 'full-inclusion' school, and we do not buy the egalitarian nonsense either. However, this effort to reach out to our family and to Nathan, as well as to provide an opportunity to other kids to serve someone like Nathan, has produced blessings that will multiply for years to come in many lives. But it required a substantial risk on your part, and for that we are very grateful.

We have often heard many reports of what a blessing Nate was in the school. If, however, you did ever receive complaints or concerns, they were never passed on to us. If you have any concerns that would be of help to us in future settings, we would appreciate your comments.

Thank you for your patience with us and with Nathan. (Matthew 25:34-40).

To say we will miss Nathan (and his family) is probably obvious. He and his younger brother Tyler were two of the most well-liked students in the elementary. The Hatchers no-nonsense, biblical approach to their son's affliction was truly a lesson for all who saw them love and train their son at school. And all the elementary kids saw them at some time. Our prayers for Nathan's continued improvement go with the Hatchers, but the wonderful memories of times we had with them will stay with these children, Nathan's friends. God does indeed often choose to glorify Himself through those we deem humble and afflicted. But for those who love as He does, He blesses them *through* the humble and afflicted. Yes, we certainly had a blessed year!

\* \* \*

## STUDENTS ABOVE THEIR TEACHERS?

> A disciple (pupil) is not above his teacher, nor a slave above his master. It is enough for the disciple that he become as his teacher....
> ~Matt. 10:24-25

> A pupil is not above his teacher; but everyone, after he has been fully trained, will be like ( or reach the same level as) his teacher.
> ~John 6:40

The above words of our Master and Teacher, Jesus Christ, seem to underscore the apparent paradox of the modern teacher seeking to provide young minds with a classical, Christian education. The paradox goes something like this: From examining the offerings of modern education, both secular and Christian, a number of folks have desired to implement the successful teaching methods of the past—classical instruction and education. The need is desperate, yet how does one offer what one has not received? It is not as simple as restarting a long unused engine, where, with enough patience, oil, fuel, and a lot of tinkering, it should kick into life and away you go. Classical education has been unused for so long, we don't even know all the necessary parts, much less how it should look when it's up and running. Then on top of our own ignorance we have the burden of wanting and needing to give this potential, immense blessing to our descendants.

The final brick on the stack, as our Lord seems to be saying, is that our students will only rise to our level of understanding, just as water seeks its own level. So, are we classical neophytes then just a bunch of pathetic Don Quixotes, fighting reality? Or, is there hope after all because we are not just passing on a certain quantity of knowledge, but rather the *means* of seeking greater, and increasing knowledge?

A personal testimony may not be out of place here. Twelve years of government education (my kindergarten year was at a private, Lutheran school) left me largely stranded on a desert island of knowledge, with little hope for rescue, or even the knowledge that I was in bad shape. I knew about my little sand spit and one palm tree, and everything else was just a lot of water. What's the big deal? I was fairly content with my extremely limited understanding of the world, and blithely went into adult life. Courtesy of the U.S. Navy I was able to visit Rome and Athens. While in Rome, I did as the Romans did, or at least Roman tourists and saw most of what was there. In Athens, I rode my bike to the base of the Acropolis and then climbed the stone road and steps to the Parthenon. I hugged a pillar to fulfill a request from my sister. I took lots of pictures because I knew, vaguely, that these were really old, famous places; kind of like Disneyland, but a whole lot older, even if not as colorful.

Pompeii was also a site I visited, with the ever present Mount Vesuvius looming over it. It had very cool fossilized people and dogs. The guide told us something about the culture but I can't recall much of what he said. I remember the stone bodies though.

It was to be years later that I would finally gain an appreciation for the Sistine Chapel ceiling, the Colosseum, the Golden Age of Greece, the final, horrific days of Pompeii, and read hitherto unheard of stories called *The Iliad* and *The Odyssey*. Not to mention reading good quantities of the fascinating history of the United States, which I was called upon to teach at Logos School. Why wasn't I told about the vast world and its history during the twelve years of my life supposedly given to that purpose? Why did it take until I was in my forties to discover the wonderful works of Homer or Jane Austen, or read about the great man that Theodore Roosevelt was?

# Ignorant as we are, we can still, through classical, time-tested means, point our students to where worthy knowledge still resides.

Rather than degenerate into worthless finger-pointing, suffice it to say that, along with numerous other Christian, classical teachers I wasn't given all the requisite knowledge I wished I'd had. But because God is good and He enjoys blessing His children, we can grow and continue to have our understanding enlarged even into middle age. Maybe not new tricks, but by God's grace old dogs can still learn and appreciate learning. And that is what we can pass along to our students. Ignorant as we are, we can still, through classical, time-tested means, point our students to where worthy knowledge still resides. And possibly, through study and application of these means and methods, we can help equip these younger, more supple minds to more quickly grasp the significance of truth, goodness, and beauty.

I thrill to see young students discussing and enjoying the critical battles of the Persian War or World War II. Even more I am immeasurably encouraged to hear from alums who are living godly lives, understanding much of the world, not just a little island.

Students cannot be greater than their teachers, by definition and God's Word, but like their teachers, they can grow in grace and truth, and *do* even greater things than their teachers. May God grant this for our descendants.

Find more books on education. Go to

**JOINCANONPLUS.COM**

SCAN TO
GET STARTED!

www.ingramcontent.com/pod-product-compliance
Lightning Source LLC
Chambersburg PA
CBHW022102090426
42743CB00008B/692